July 2018

Heaven All Around Us

Heaven All Around Us

DISCOVERING GOD IN EVERYDAY LIFE

Simon Carey Holt

CASCADE *Books* · Eugene, Oregon

HEAVEN ALL AROUND US
Discovering God in Everyday Life

Cascade Books
An Imprint of Wipf and Stock Publishers
199 W. 8th Ave., Suite 3
Eugene, OR 97401

www.wipfandstock.com

PAPERBACK ISBN: 978-1-4982-7885-0
HARDCOVER ISBN: 978-1-4982-7887-4
EBOOK ISBN: 978-1-4982-7886-7

Cataloguing-in-Publication data:

Names: Holt, Simon Carey.
Title: Heaven all around us : discovering God in everyday life / Simon Carey Holt.
Description: Eugene, OR: Cascade Books, 2018 | Includes bibliographical references.
Identifiers: ISBN 978-1-4982-7885-0 (paperback) | ISBN 978-1-4982-7887-4 (hardcover) | ISBN 978-1-4982-7886-7 (ebook)
Subjects: LCSH: Spirituality—Christian. | Spiritual life—Christianity. | Title.
Classification: BV4501.2 .H5235 2018 (print) | BV4501 (ebook)

Manufactured in the U.S.A.   FEBRUARY 5, 2018

To Robert J. Banks
Mentor, colleague, and friend

Table of Contents

Preface

My father was raised on a wheat farm in the Mallee of northern Victoria, Australia. It is vast and beautiful country, but flat, dry, and unforgiving to those who work its land. The closest town to the family farm is Quambatook, the archetypal Mallee town of grain silos and big skies, though as a place of life and community it has seen better days. In 2011 the population was 361. Now it is less.

If you walk the main street of Quambatook today you'll find most of the shops are empty and boarded up, but there is one window display that holds a constant tribute to one of Quambatook's famous sons, the singer and song writer John Williamson. It is nothing more than a framed picture really, with newspaper cuttings scattered around it that celebrate the performer's success. Regardless, the little town is proud.

Likely, Williamson will never know that it is the words to one of his songs that inspired the title of this book. The song is "Cootamundra Wattle." Cootamundra is another rural town about a five hour drive northeast. Wattle is a native plant that thrives in Cootamundra's climate and blossoms every spring with the most beautiful yellow flowers.

In the song, Williamson puts to music the bidding of a farmer to his elderly wife. As she sits inside mulling over picture albums and memories collected in her "old camphor box," her tears betray a longing for times past. Through the course of the song, her husband gently urges her to put old things and memories away, to come outside and enjoy the beauty of the day. He describes "the colours of the rainbow in the garden" and "the symphony of music in the skies" before concluding with his invitation: "Heaven's all around us if you're looking. How can you see it if you cry?"

I am a product of the Australian church and remain deeply committed to its life and mission. At the same time, I find my roots and identity within a wider culture that has never embraced or celebrated the presence of the church. From the beginning of white settlement, the church has been an alien presence in Australia, representative of historical ties to distant places. For so much of my life, the church I know struggled to identify God's presence as local. "God with us" was a doctrine we adhered to but rarely an experience we lived. In our passion to see God's church take root in this soil, we were preoccupied with importing God in from other places. We grasped at North American and European models of church growth, evangelism, and spirituality. We feted their gurus, sang their songs, and reproduced their programs. Our hope was that in importing spiritual success in from other places, we would begin to see evidence of God's presence here.

Though our importing hasn't stopped, thankfully we are more conscious today that God *is* with us. Indeed, we've discovered that God was here all along, as profoundly present on our shores as God is anywhere else. In many cases we've been humbled by the discovery, aware that God's presence in this land so far precedes our trifling efforts it renders our prior ignorance almost laughable. While the Australian church still struggles to find footholds for its ministry, there are numerous men and women of faith and countless Christian communities that have planted their roots deep in the soil of this land's cities, suburbs, and rural communities. What's more, they are discovering rich seams of the sacred running through their neighborhoods. "Heaven's all around us if you're looking," and we've finally opened our eyes to it.

This is not a book written only for the Australian church, nor is it focused on the challenges unique to this context. It is written for a much wider audience, people of faith in places near and far. It is for anyone who needs reminding that heaven *is* all around us, no matter where we are—that "God with us" is more than a doctrine; it is a reality that infuses all the nooks and crannies of our lives. The challenge to our seeing is a learned preoccupation with the pursuit of God in particular places and forms that leaves much of our lives untapped and devalued. So much so, we fail to notice what there is of God right under our noses. This book is an invitation to look again, to see the beauty and wonder of God afresh in the life that you live every day.

Acknowledgements

IN THE BIRTH OF this book, I am indebted to more people than I can name. Their stories, examples, and companionship have nurtured its evolution in my life.

For ten years my friend Ross Langmead and I had neighboring offices at Whitley College (University of Divinity). Ross was Professor of Mission Studies. Over numerous coffees and in hallway chats he prodded and nudged my vocation as a writer. Not only so, he embodied the content of this particular book in the gentlest and most prophetic ways. Ross's early death in 2013 left me and many others bereft. I still miss him.

For the last eight years I have been privileged to pastor the congregation of Collins Street Baptist Church. The generosity of this wonderful community in allowing time for writing has been a gift of great worth. My colleague in ministry Carolyn Francis has not only cheered me on in the process; she has inspired my thinking, laughed at my foibles, and carried the load when I've been missing in action.

My beloved in life, Brenda, features often in the text of this book. Indeed, the book and all that has inspired its writing would not exist without her. Her style, energy, and grace bring color and inspiration to my life every day.

Finally, the book is dedicated to Robert Banks. A fellow Australian, Robert was for a decade the foundation occupant of the Homer L. Goddard Chair of the Ministry of the Laity at Fuller Theological Seminary in Pasadena, California. I entered his life as a student and graduated to friend and colleague as the years progressed. It was when I was a postgraduate student at Fuller that Robert generously invited me into his class *Spirituality of Everyday Life* as a co-teacher. Really, there is nothing in this book that does not flow from my friendship with Robert and the extraordinary influence of his life and teaching. I am forever grateful.

PART 1

The Call of God to a Different Way

1

In Search of a Different Way

He was mad, an obsessive-compulsive given to freewheeling visions and the most bizarre behaviors of self-harm. Voices told him things; at one moment they inspired him and in the next condemned and ridiculed him. Today he would be diagnosed and medicated, with a mental health care plan to govern his days. But not then. For all his manic eccentricities, he was widely revered as a holy man. "That angel upon the earth," they called him, "that citizen in the flesh of the Heavenly Jerusalem."[1] Clearly, he was a man impossible to ignore. Even today he is venerated as one of the saints of the Christian church.

Symeon was his name, born in 388 in Sisan, a small town in the Roman province of Cilicia on the border of modern day Turkey and Syria. Even as a boy, the son of a shepherd, he was given to long periods of self-imposed fasting and the most troubling dreams. As he watched his brother's herds on the mountain slopes of Sis, he was moved by ancient stories of sacrifice and imagined his own—a boys-own-adventure with a religious twist. Not long after moving with his family to Antioch, by then a teenager, Symeon heard the Gospel passage from Matthew read aloud: "Blessed are they that mourn for they will be comforted; blessed are the pure in heart, for they will see God." Struck by the force of the words but mystified by their meaning, Symeon sought counsel from an old man in his village. The grey-headed sage explained to him that true devotion was only found through suffering, and that solitude was the most certain pathway to God. At just fourteen, captivated by this prospect, Symeon pledged to become an anchorite. He made plans to leave his family, his

---

1. Attributed to Evagrius, a theologian of the fourth century. Quoted by Gannon and Traub, *The Desert and the City*, 28.

home, and his shepherding for a life of solitude and separation; "a spiritual hunter" they would call him, roaming the mountains "to stalk his God."[2]

For the next twenty years, Symeon stalked the monasteries of northern Syria, but without finding the spiritual home he sought. In fact, he was routinely expelled because of his behavior. Apparently he slept so little and prayed so much, and so loudly, that the other monks could barely cope. At the same time his fasting practices became more extreme. Symeon developed the habit of standing upright for as long as his body would hold him, for days and even weeks on end. Finally, the monks judged him unfit for communal life and expelled him to an isolated hut in the mountains.

As a hermit, Symeon became known as a solitary miracle worker, and a good one at that. Such was his reputation that his beloved solitude evaporated. The endless stream of human need overwhelmed him. It was in 423 that Symeon, then aged thirty-five and desperate for relief, moved out to the desert of Telanissus, where he found a pillar among the ruins around nine feet high. He constructed a small platform on its top and made it his home. Small boys from the local village would climb up the pillar with parcels of flat bread and goat milk, but for the most part he was left alone.

Much to his dismay, Symeon's isolation was short lived. Soon he was overwhelmed again by need. Great crowds gathered with requests for mediation with God and each other. A man of compassion, Symeon could not refuse them, but clearly his pillar was too short. What's more, his personal thirst for God now consumed him. After six years on his pillar and with the aid of a small group of disciples, Symeon set about renovating his home. It was an extension he had in mind. The end result was a pillar some fifty feet high. An engineering feat, this was the deluxe version with a small platform at the top, a wooden enclosure to keep him from falling off in his sleep, and a very, very long ladder by which his disciples could bring him food and water and dispose of his waste. Once it was complete, Symeon moved in, or up as the case was, and there he sat, come wind, rain, and heat, for the next thirty years of his life. Tradition says he never came down once. His expired body was found stooped in the position of prayer. He was seventy-one.

2. Brown, "The Rise and Function of the Holy Man in Late Antiquity," 112.

I confess that I am quite taken by Symeon, or Saint Symeon the Stylite as he is better known—Simon of the Pillar. Since first reading his story thirty years ago, his portrait has hung in my mental gallery of saints. To be honest, they are all a bit odd, but that comes with the territory of sainthood. I have always wondered, what could possess a man to sit on a pole for thirty-six years? Was he just mad, or is there more to his story than that? Frankly, I am not averse to a bit of pole-sitting. To an introvert like me—though I have a terrible fear of heights—the thought of solitude is appealing. What's more, this drive to know God and to be with God resonates.

When I was twenty-seven years old, my brother gave me Psalm 27 for my birthday. Though at the time I judged it to be an especially cheap gift, it has been one of the most lasting of my life. It is a psalm attributed to David and one clearly composed in adversity. David describes God as his stronghold, his shelter, and his rock. Danger lurked in his life and enemies were numerous. He found in God the strength he needed to persevere. No matter how many times I read this psalm, I am stopped in my tracks by the fourth verse. "One thing I ask of the Lord," David says, "and this is what I seek; that I may dwell in the house of the Lord all the days of my life, to behold the beauty of the Lord, and to enquire in his temple." David's "one thing," his one desire that trumped all others, was to dwell in the presence of God each and every day, to gaze upon God's beauty forevermore.

As a person of faith—a person steeped in the Christian tradition—I have spent my life seeking to know God and to live in response to God's presence through Jesus Christ. As a pastor, I have given my professional life to leading others in the same pursuit. Further, through twenty-five years of research and teaching, I have wanted to understand the nature of the spiritual life, how it has been lived through history, and what it has meant to know God. Even more, if God is to be our "one thing" today, I want to know what that means and how we pursue it.

When I gaze up at Symeon sitting on his pillar in the Syrian desert, I may well shake my head in disbelief. At the same time, I cannot help but see in him the most tangible expression of David's prayer. Indeed, he might have been mad, but he was mad for God. David's "one thing" was Symeon's. They shared a spiritual longing as deep as longing can be. While I cannot fathom Symeon's choices in life, his resolve is extraordinary. Though I share his yearning, Symeon acted upon it in the most peculiar way. His "one thing" had him sitting on a pole for more than half his life.

Symeon is not alone in the history of the church. Indeed, countless women and men through history have gone to extraordinary lengths in pursuit of God. Symeon may have been the first pole-sitter, but so many others have sought the same goal through different means. There are those who have lived alone in caves; those who have chained themselves to crosses and circled the desert for years on end; others who have confined themselves to secluded monasteries, living by strict vows of silence and separation; and those who have passed their years isolated on rugged pinnacles of granite in the middle of the ocean. Whatever course they have chosen, these spiritual eccentrics have lived with a passion for the presence of God through Christ. In the grip of this desire, they have been compelled to relinquish all ambitions, possessions, and relationships judged peripheral to their pursuit: "One thing I ask of the Lord, and this is what I seek . . . ."

As much as I am enthralled by Symeon and captivated by these extraordinary men and women of faith, I am equally frustrated. The truth is, if people like these are the exemplars of real spirituality, then frankly, it's a journey from which I am excluded. It is not a pathway I can follow, not even in a moderate sense. Why? Because the spirituality of Symeon and his companions hinges almost entirely upon one thing: *withdrawal.* To pursue the presence of God, one must leave behind the pursuits of ordinary life. It is a spirituality of the desert, a journey to the margins. As a way of life, it centers upon practices of solitude, isolation, and retreat, and has almost nothing to do with the busy ebb and flow of my everyday life.

I am not an ascetic or desert recluse. What's more, as much as I long for a little solitude, I will never be solitary. The desert is not my home. The margins are not my neighborhood. I am a husband and a father. I have made certain life choices that mean acts of withdrawal will always be the exception and never the rule. I cannot run off to the desert or climb an isolated peak in the middle of the ocean. I certainly cannot live perched on a pole for the next thirty years. I have a marriage to nurture, a family to provide for, children who need my presence and support, and an aging father who needs a son. What's more, I have responsibilities in the workplace, friendships to maintain, neighbors to relate to, a mortgage to pay, groceries to buy, and lunches to make. Because of this, the spirituality of Symeon will always draw my attention as an admiring observer but never as a full participant. If I am to pray David's prayer with conviction—if I am to name my "one thing" as devotion to God and God's world—I need a different way.

Of course, I may be advised to simply brush this frustration aside, to honor the stories of these eccentric aunts and uncles of the faith, but then move on. The trouble is, if I have a heart for a deeper experience of God, moving on is a challenge. It's a challenge because the way the church understands the *spiritual* and our pursuit of it continues to be deeply tied to practices of separation. No matter how much has changed in our understandings of God, mission, and the sacredness of creation, once we shift the conversation to spirituality, we revert back to images of private prayer, mountaintops, and solitude.

In my Baptist tradition, the usual measure of one's piety is the daily "quiet time": a period of personal solitude for Bible reading, meditation, and prayer. It is a practice through which I have been deeply formed and continue to value in my daily routine. Across traditions, a practice like this might be broadened to include prayer books and the daily office, Eucharistic celebration, charismatic worship, or days of spiritual retreat. In every tradition, we have learned the value of setting aside regular time for focused prayer and meditation, whatever form they take. We do this with good reason. A spirituality disconnected from such practices is fool-ishness. You need only scan the Gospel accounts of Jesus or examine the rich traditions of spiritual practice through history to be reminded of the immeasurable worth of solitude and retreat for all people of faith. But is there not *more* to our pursuit than this?

David's "one thing" is a longing for depth with God. The spiritual shallows are no longer enough. He articulates it again in Psalm 42. "As a deer longs for flowing streams," he says, "so my soul longs for you, O God. My soul thirsts for God, for the living God" (42:1–2). It is this "deep calling to deep" (42:7) that compels him, a longing for life in its fullness all the way down. But if the only pathway to such a place with God is via practices of separation and relinquishment, then where does that leave those who will never live in the desert? By all means, let's nurture such practices where we can, but my contention is this: if the act of withdrawal defines our understanding of spirituality, then many of us are sold short when it comes to our experience of God. We who will only ever withdraw occasionally or momentarily end up feeling sidelined, having to content ourselves with being observers while others play center field with God.

I am a passionate cook and I love recipe books. My kitchen shelves are weighted down with a collection that far outstrips my need. I am not alone. In the world of publishing, food-related books outsell most other genres. What's more, the production values of these tomes are extraordinary. A recipe book today is a work of art. The sumptuous photography, the layout of text and image, the covers and binding all combine to make an object of pleasure and inspiration. However, research suggests the degree to which our fascination with such books increases corresponds with our declining presence in the kitchen. The truth is, these recipe books sit impressively on our coffee tables as we cradle our containers of take-out Thai. We know that we can never reproduce the stylized images contained in their pages, so we don't even try. Somehow the simple possession of such books enables us to live our culinary longings through someone else's expertise. It's coffee table gastronomy and has an interesting correlation with our current interests in the ancient arts of spirituality.

The classic stories of spirituality in the Christian tradition are a most precious resource. I have taught many classes in which students have been introduced to these texts and I've seen hearts opened in transformative ways: texts like *The Cloud of Unknowing*, Augustine's *Confessions*, and Teresa of Avila's *Interior Castle*. But all too often resources like these become nothing more than coffee table spirituality, reminders to us of a journey so different to our own, so removed from the daily realities of our world.

In his book *Journey to the Inner Mountain,* the Australian author James Cowan traces the life of Saint Antony, the third-century Egyptian ascetic known today as "the father of monks." Orphaned at eighteen, Antony was left with the care of his younger sister, a considerable fortune, and a large family estate. Having heard the words of Jesus read aloud in the town square, "If you want to be perfect, go, sell what you have and give to the poor . . . and come follow me," Antony was struck by a profound sense of God. His response was immediate: he gave away his estate, donated all his money to the poor, placed his sister in a "community of virgins," then moved out to the desert to live the life of a hermit. Indeed, Antony spent most of his life a cave dweller in complete isolation. His story inspired thousands to follow his lead.

At the very beginning of his book, Cowan entices the reader to believe that this model of spirituality is more than an interesting story from the distant past. "Few people inspire us more than those who take themselves off to the wilderness," he writes; "they awaken in us an urge to abandon the normal constraints of society so as to pursue a free and open life."[3] Indeed, but all too often we leave such encounters no more able to address that urge than when we began. The question persists: how does an ordinary person with a job, a spouse, dependents, a mortgage, and an overflowing diary give expression to this "free and open life"? The only hints that Antony and Cowan give us are that we must "dispense with diversion," and commit to the task of "renovating consciousness by a deliberate act of withdrawal."[4] Cowan's account of his own stay in an ancient monastery emphasizes the point:

> I am somehow content. In fact, I don't think I've known such contentment. In a place where there is nothing to do but read and think, gaze into the distance, eat a simple meal each day in the refectory, and sleep on a hard bed in a room that is bare of furniture save for a stool and a desk, there's something to be said for solitude.[5]

As a teacher of spirituality, I have deep respect for the contemplative disciplines and for the rich heritage of the monastic tradition upon which Cowan's book is a fine reflection, but I confess to scrawling in the margin, "So who does the school run?" I do not mean to be flippant, but I tire of feeling as though I, and many people like me, are left standing on the spiritual sidelines when it comes to the real treasures of the spiritual life. Honestly, accounts like this leave me feeling like an amateur in the professional world of spirituality. Like a lavishly presented recipe book, the story sits on my coffee table alongside the story of Symeon, testaments to my spiritual interest and corresponding poverty. Yes, I am inspired but not invited, intrigued but not empowered. At the end of the day, the spirituality of such stories is one to observe, but not one that invites my participation. Truthfully, I struggle to find entry points, handles on which to grab hold as a citizen of an entirely different time and place, and so I return to my everyday life enlightened but really none the wiser. It's back to the washing up.

Sharing my frustration with this desert-obsessed spirituality and its grip upon our understanding of devotion, the writer Ernest Boyer Jr. asks a simple but revealing question: "Is there childcare in the desert?"[6]

---

3. Cowan, *Journey to the Inner Mountain*, ix.

4. Ibid., 6.

5. Ibid., 33.

6. Boyer, *Finding God at Home*, xiii.

The answer is obvious. The simple fact is, desert spirituality requires a set of life circumstances foreign to the vast majority of ordinary Christians, and not just those with children. While we may be disciplined in our daily prayers and Bible reading, routine in our church attendance, even committed to periodic practices of meditation and retreat, the lion's share of our lives is taken up with other things. We can no more climb a pole than we can fly to the moon. Nor, frankly, do we wish to. The desert is not our home. Our lives are consumed with being sensitive partners and devoted parents, good neighbors and reliable friends, engaged workers and just employers, active citizens and carers for the environment. The fact is, our primary responsibilities are not to the desert but to the routines of domestic and community life. Because of this, we need models of spirituality that lead us to embrace these elements of our lives, not minimize them. We need daily practices of spirituality that press into the stuff of everyday life with intention and purpose, not require that we walk away from it. We need a different way.

In addressing this need, Boyer draws a contrast between two contexts for spirituality, two pathways to a life of devotion. The first, the spirituality of the desert, he calls "life at the edge" and the second, a spirituality for those who remain in the routines of everyday life he calls "life at the center."[7] Key to this is that the worth of the desert calling is not minimized. Indeed, it is honored as a valid and rich pathway in the expression of faith. The consequence, however, is that life at the center is lifted to a place of equal worth and opportunity.

Life at the Edge

The "edge" is the place of withdrawal. It's at the edge that numerous men and women of faith pursue that "one thing." This edge spirituality is a rich vein within the story of Christianity, easily caricatured but complex in its diversity and depth. The historian of spirituality Philip Sheldrake describes the earliest expressions of Christian monasticism as essentially "a movement to the margins."[8] From its beginning, it demanded of its participants the most decisive act of separation from the traditional centers of life. And this for good reason.

7. Ibid., chapters 1– 2.
8. Sheldrake, *Spirituality*, 50.

The early practices of Christian asceticism flourished in direct correlation with Christianity's movement from edge to cultural center, from
fringe and persecuted minority to sanctioned religion of the empire. It
was in the fourth century, in fact, that church and empire began to merge.
The call to follow the way of Jesus was no longer a call to physical mar-
tyrdom at the hands of the state, but to a spiritualized death to self and
"the world." Faced with the possibility of a new laxity in the expression of
discipleship, the desert hermits stood apart from the world in the most
tangible way. Indeed, this was and remains their genius.

For four years I lived with my family in the northern suburbs of
Los Angeles. Next door to our apartment complex in a quiet suburban
street was a small Carmelite monastery, home to a handful of nuns who
lived according to strict vows of silence and an unchanging cycle of
daily prayers. Occasionally we would see the nuns walking their dogs
around the neighborhood, though the rate at which the large animals
moved, pulling the stumbling nuns behind them, it was more likely the
dogs were in charge. These women would always smile warmly but never
stop to chat. The only public entrance into the cloistered community was
through the doors of its chapel. At particular times I could go and sit in
this space to pray. In the small narthex were some words of explanation
about the Carmelite order. According to the leaflet, the nuns' primary
vocation was "to pray for the city of Los Angeles." And this they did with
rigorous discipline day after day, month after month, year after year.

What's important to note is that the edge is never entirely separate
from the center. Lest we imagine the earliest ascetics hold away in some
vast and distant desert, an arduous journey from the edges of civilization, a little geography is revealing. According to the historian of Late
Antiquity, Peter Brown, the deserts of Egypt and Syria were not as we
imagine. To enter the desert was to wander into the "ever-present fringe"
of the village, not to disappear into another world. The desert was right
there, a "standing challenge" at the immediate edges of daily life.[9] At its
best, this withdrawal to the edge was not a hiding from the world but a
vantage point from which to see it more clearly and speak into it with a
particular authority.

The truth is, that small community of Carmelite nuns in suburban
Los Angeles was never meant to be cut off from its center, and neither
was Symeon centuries before. From the top of his pole he could see the

9. Brown, "The Rise and Function of the Holy Man in Late Antiquity," 111.

daily happenings in the village below and watch the farmers working on the nearby hills. From this vantage point and at his best, Symeon understood his vocation not as antithetical to society but marginal to it, and with purpose. History tells us that a steady trickle of delegations from the surrounding villages made their way to the base of Symeon's pole, seeking arbitration on matters as domestic as water rationing, crop harvesting, financial loans, and neighborhood disputes. Symeon's responses were often extraordinarily detailed and betrayed a man not of another world, but uniquely present to the one around him. According to Brown, it is only when we see beyond the bizarre feats of self-mortification in those like Symeon that we begin to understand the social significance of their role. Theirs was "a solemn ritual of disassociation, of becoming the total stranger,"[10] standing apart from the institutions and obligations of family, village and church so as to mediate the grace and calling of God back into them.

This calling to the edge has been part of the Christian church since its beginning. One of its more recent proponents was Thomas Merton (1915–1968), who lived his calling as a Trappist monk at the Abbey of Gethsemane in rural Kentucky. In the year of his death, he gave a lecture in which he described the essence of his own vocation, and that of all monastics, as a call to the edge. It is through this "marginality," as Merton called it, that the edge dweller seeks not only personal transformation but the transformation of society.[11] Indeed, as Bernard McGinn observes, this call to the edge is not, at its heart, a self-centered, other-worldly expression of faith. Rather, it remains a noble calling to a very different presence in the world.[12]

Life at the Center

In contrast to the edge, the "center" describes the contexts where most of us live the majority of our days. While the edge dwellers are called to a very different presence in the world, those at the center are called to a comparatively ordinary one. The center is the place of our homes, neighborhoods, and workplaces. It's where we buy and sell, cook and eat, work and play. It's the context of family and friends, neighborliness and

10. Ibid., 131.

11. Quoted by McGinn, "Withdrawal and Return," 149.

12. Ibid., 153.

citizenship. It's the place that hosts all the daily transactions, conflicts, and intimacies of life. While the edge is never far away—we may see it from the center and go out to it from time to time—the edge is not where we live and never will be. Our more pressing need is to know God at the center of our lives, to hear God's call with the same clarity with which Symeon heard it at the edge.

The language of the center necessarily differs to that of the edge. At the edge, it's the *language of withdrawal*: renunciation, relinquishment, surrender, leaving, and denying. Though this language is not exclusive to the edge, it is not as immediately helpful to those of us who inhabit the center. Life at the center has more to do with the equally risky *language of engagement*: embracing, enfolding, choosing, cleaving, and nurturing. The Catholic writer David Knight reflects on this difference in language and its importance for those who live in the world.[13] It's a spirituality of involvement, not withdrawal; a spirituality of risk, not renunciation; a spirituality of commitment that flows from our baptism, not from a particular order or rule of life; and a spirituality attained not through successive stages of prayer or purity but through successive choices made each day amidst the chaos of life. It's a spirituality that presses into the tasks, places, and encounters of the everyday, believing that God is as present there as God is anywhere else.

Despite its ordinariness, life at the center is as much a response to divine call as life at the edge. Typically, edge dwellers have embraced the notion of calling with a good deal of conviction. It's why they are there. Deserts and monasteries have always been full of people for whom moments of epiphany and life-changing redirection are standard. Frankly, life at the center seems too ordinary in comparison. Dazzled by Moses and his burning bush or Paul and his divine encounter on the road to Damascus, we've come to understand a good calling story to be as rare as it is mystical. Epiphanies aside, the truly biblical notion of calling is much less extraordinary. Importantly, it's as real at the center of life as it is at the edges. According to the Bible, the call of God is part and parcel of our identity as the body of Christ and the household of faith. It is not mine, nor is it yours. It is ours. It does not separate us into different strata of spirituality but unites us as one. *Together* we are called to be the people of God, to live in holiness and to serve the purposes of God in the world.

13. Knight, "A Practical Plan for Lay Spiritual Formation," 7–16.

The challenge for each of us, at the edge and the center, is to work out that calling in our particular circumstance.

Despite misgivings about Cowan's portrayal of St Antony, the gift of his book is the author's own immersion in the monk's story. Cowan retraces Antony's steps. He travels to the Egyptian desert where the ascetic lived in isolation as a cave dweller on the side of a mountain. When Cowan arrives at of the edge of this desert 1,700 years later, he is told there is now someone else living on Antony's mountain: "the last anchorite," they call him. Curious, Cowan seeks permission to visit him.

With the recluse's approval, a week's supply of bread and a clear set of instructions, Cowan makes the trek up the mountain to the foot of a terrace carved out of its slope. Following directions, he waits awkwardly at a distance. In time, a man emerges in a black habit and a hood that covers his head and casts a shadow across his bearded face. After a long pause, the man lifts his weathered hand in the air, bidding Cowan forward. Taking the final steps toward the terrace and with his heart still pumping from the journey, Cowan introduces himself, expecting from the aged man a strong Egyptian accent and broken English. Instead the man responds warmly and in a distinctive Australian drawl. "Lazarus is my name, because I am reborn," he says as he invites Cowan to sit down. Over two mugs of tea, a loaf of bread, and some honey for dipping, the two men talk. With some prodding, Lazarus tells his story.

It turns out Lazarus was a teacher of literature in an Australian university and happily ensconced in the suburbs when his mother was diagnosed with incurable cancer. Moving in with her for her last months of life, Lazarus was deeply affected and felt a growing sense of dissatisfaction with his own life. Upon her death, he found himself wandering the streets of Melbourne in deep distress. Overwhelmed with despair and a rising sense of meaninglessness, he walked in through the open doors of a church. Amidst the filtered light of the stained glass and the burning candles, he watched an elderly woman lie prostrate before an icon of the Virgin Mary. In that moment, Lazarus said, he heard a voice. He understood it as the voice of the Holy Mother calling to him. He fell on his knees and called out, "I have nowhere to go. Please help me!" The voice replied, "Poor man, place yourself in my care, just as this woman has done." As Lazarus exited the church into the stark light of the afternoon, he knew his life would never be the same. What followed for Lazarus were years of pilgrimage through the rituals and monasteries of the Orthodox Church, culminating decades later in his retirement to this desert home in pursuit of the same spiritual "exile" that Antony had sought.

In the weeks that follow this first encounter, Cowan makes a number of return visits to the mountain and each time the conversation with Lazarus is challenging. Eventually, though, Cowan has to say goodbye as he begins his journey home. His final question to Lazarus relates to the application of this anchorite way of life beyond the mountain. Lazarus is clear: the spirituality of the future will not be a spirituality of the edge. "I can't imagine," he says, "nor would I like to see it happen, that the desert becomes once more populated by thousands of hermits living in caves. This would be to repeat history rather than to honour its gift."[14]

According to Lazarus, our task is to cherish the stories of those who have preceded us while discerning new ways forward in the spiritual journey, ways that reflect the realities of today and for those who will never inhabit deserts or mount fifty-foot poles. The Catholic scholar in spirituality Elizabeth Dryer says it well. "Not only must we know, critique, and make use of the past," she writes, "but we must also envision and create new words and new categories that will reflect the experience of more black and yellow and female and married saints; plumber saints and teacher saints, secretary saints and mother and father saints."[15] As one such ordinary saint, I couldn't agree more. My hope is that this book can make a small contribution to that important task.

---

14. Cowan, *Journey to the Inner Mountain*, 171.
15. Dreyer, "Traditions of Lay Spirituality," 210.

2

Biblical Perspectives for a Different Way

MOMENTS OF EPIPHANY ARE rare for me. Mostly I notice the profound only in retrospect. That said, there have been encounters with truth stark enough to feel like a thump in the chest. One of those thumps came twenty years ago. I sat alone in a café in Pasadena, California, having recently enrolled in a doctoral program in theology. I had just come off a decade of pastoral ministry. It was not an easy ride and I was bone weary. By way of introduction, my supervisor recommended I read Dale Allison's book *The Silence of Angels*. I approached it with only mild enthusiasm, glad for the refuge of words but more committed to my coffee. Just pages in, the thump took my breath away.

Truth be told, this thud to my spirit was not the consequence of a direct hit from author to reader. It came in from the side. Allison's book is a fine read and his central thesis a good one. But his book managed to prod at an intuitive sense of something already festering within—a truth I had struggled to find words for. In fact, it was that unnamed intuition that led me across the Pacific.

I came to California to study spirituality, to better understand the experience of God and the ways that experience is impacted by culture and environment. As a pastor, I felt as though I had been a witness to and participant in a church in spiritual retreat. Perhaps we were overwhelmed by the relentless progress of scientific discovery and science's propensity to explain everything in non-religious terms. Our territory of confidence was diminished. At the same time we were increasingly enamored by mystical, out-of-body, and private expressions of spirituality. It seemed to me we Christians had so narrowed our concerns, we had released a large part of life to the *secular* realm while retreating into our *sacred* spaces and experiences. In so doing we narrowed our horizon and averted our eyes from the chaotic and compromised world under our noses. In my view, talk of spirituality had become insipid and self-obsessed.

Though I felt all of these things, and often deeply, I was unable to name them coherently. Allison helped push them to the surface. In words better than my own, he grieved our loss of wonder in a world shot through with a holiness so confronting and demanding there was nothing outside of its impact. The long-standing chasm between the *sacred* and the *secular* was deepening by the hour, or so it seemed, and had a lot to answer for. The need to address this divide was urgent.

Today the dysfunction of this sacred/secular chasm is old news. Indeed, it was probably old news twenty years ago; it just took me a while to catch on. Today we are certainly on to it and the church has done much to address it. Though we still value our sacred sites and rituals, we've long buried the notion that the presence of God is contained by them. No matter what our tradition, we affirm today a more porous boundary between heaven and earth and celebrate the presence of God in all of life. Our theology has shifted. It's our spiritual practice that has struggled to keep up.

Language is a powerful thing. How we use it changes over time, and our evolving use of terminology can generate change as much as respond to it. This is certainly the case with the language of spirituality.

On one hand, our use of it has broadened. On the back page of the mid-week real estate supplement of our local newspaper, there is a weekly interview with a local identity, a well-known resident questioned about his or her home and neighbourhood. One of the frequently asked questions is "How does your home reflect your spirituality?" Not long ago, a question like this would have been met with raised eyebrows, especially in the real estate pages. Today interviewees respond with ease. Spirituality has found a comfortable home in popular conversation.

There was a time, of course, when the language of spirituality was anything but popular. Even in the church it was a term specific to particular traditions, most often Roman Catholic or Eastern Orthodox. We Protestants steered clear of it. We preferred our only terminology of piety, devotion or, among evangelicals, "personal relationship" with God. This has changed. The idea of spirituality is now embraced widely among Christians of all stripes to describe the experience of God, but its use has not stopped there. Spirituality has become the preferred rhetoric for religious experience beyond the Christian fold, from Judaism to Islam, Taoism to Hinduism. It's not that experience was previously absent from these traditions, but the words used to describe it were distinctive. Thanks to the conversations of ecumenism and interreligious dialogue we have sought a common language to describe the deeper aspirations we share. Spirituality has provided it.

Beyond the realms of traditional religion of all brands, spirituality's creep has continued even further. Today you can find reference to it in secular discussions of literature, education, business, and politics. As an aspect of human experience it has caught the attention of psychologists, social workers, and medical practitioners. There are now feminist, Marxist, even secular spiritualities that have no connection at all with formal religious practice. Even more, spirituality has become the catch-all term of an eclectic mix of self-help strategies. A steady stream of best sellers draws loosely on the insights of psychology, folklore, Eastern mysticism, and mainstream religious language. Browse a local bookstore and you can scan the section titled *Spirituality* alongside *Cooking* and *Home Improvements*. Somewhere along the way spirituality morphed into a popular consumer item packaged for broad appeal.

In response to this amorphous and sometimes confusing conversation, Christians have scrambled to respond. Some have done so defensively. Concerned about compromise and the dilution of our convictions, they have wanted to jettison the Christian use of the word altogether and retreat to a purer alternative. Several years ago I had the privilege of teaching a unit on spirituality as part of the curriculum at a major state university in Sydney. To my surprise, I learned that a conservative Christian group on campus was actively dissuading its students from enrolling. Apparently such a unit was a dangerous dalliance with heresy and the term *spirituality* code for religious liberalism. Thankfully, most Christians have been more generous. We have wanted to affirm the multiple ways people seek, understand and live their spirituality, to learn from these perspectives and to be enriched by them. At the same time, we have been inspired to understand more clearly what we mean by the term and what distinctions we bring to it.

One of the foremost scholars in Christian spirituality, the Catholic theologian Sandra Schneiders, provides a helpful starting point.[1] She identifies two general approaches in definition. The first she calls a *dogmatic* approach in which spirituality is defined as movement toward God, however God is understood. The second is an *anthropological* approach

---

1. Schneiders, "Spirituality in the Academy."

in which spirituality is movement toward authentic human existence. The first revolves around God as revealer and the second around the human person as self-discoverer. While this certainly doesn't stitch things up, it does remind us how telling our starting point can be.

I write as a Christian. According to Schneider's division, I take a dogmatic approach, understanding spirituality as the movement toward God. While I don't care much for the tag *dogmatic*, in this instance it names my belief in a reality beyond myself. More particularly, my Christian faith finds its center in the self-revelation of God through Jesus Christ. Beyond that starting point, of course, Christians move in multiple directions as we seek to understand this encounter with God and how it works. What this encounter looks like, what aspects of life are impacted, and how it is played out in relationship to the world, have all been key points of difference.

Despite its broad use, the origin of the term *spirituality* is distinctively Christian. It comes from the Latin noun *spiritualitas,* a word coined in the fifth century to translate the Apostle Paul's use of the words *spirit* and *spiritual* in the New Testament.

What is striking is just how inclusive these terms are for Paul. Frankly, there's not much that sits outside their scope. He uses the adjective *spiritual* to describe things as diverse as gifts (Rom 1:11), law (Rom 7:14), worship (Rom 12:1), zeal (Rom 12:11), and truth (1 Cor 2:13). He describes the physical body as spiritual (1 Cor 15:44) along with blessings (Eph 1:3), songs (Eph 5:19), and wisdom (Col 1:9). What Paul does not do is use the concept of the spiritual to contrast with the physical or material aspects of our lives. There are no two tiers of reality for Paul. It's all one piece.

Of course, Paul does talk about "the flesh" in ways that make us wary of our own bodies. Who can forget the angst of Christian adolescence when the body and its cravings made it feel like the enemy had moved in and unpacked? However, when Paul compares *life in the flesh* with *life in the spirit* (Rom 8:5–13), he is not describing the human body as some sort of spiritual roadblock. He certainly doesn't isolate the body or other material aspects of life as sub-spiritual. Instead, Paul is describing two ways of living. A life lived in the Spirit is one lived in its fullness according to the purposes of God. It includes the body, the mind, the soul, and the spirit. A life in the flesh is that same life—all of it—lived in opposition to God (Gal 5:17), corrupt and shallow (Gal 6:8; Rom 7:5; 13:14). The theologian Jürgen Moltmann describes life in the flesh as a life that has "miscarried" and lurks in the shadow of death. Life in the Spirit, on the other hand, is "completely and wholly living . . . life which has found the broad space in the marvellous nearness of God."[2]

The notion that spirituality concerns a narrow religious sphere of life set apart from the rest is simply not present. What Paul has in mind is a life fully integrated, one that includes every task, every circumstance, every relationship and every place through which we celebrate and respond to this divine nearness. As Moltmann concludes, "True spirituality is the rebirth of the full and undivided *love of life; the total Yes to life* and the unhindered love of everything living."[3] When it comes to our spirituality, there is simply no part of life excluded.

Tragically, in the development of the church's theology, this broad understanding of spirituality did not last. To the contrary, it was relentlessly narrowed. In the early centuries of Christian faith this had much to do with the heady mix of philosophical ideas that permeated culture. The church's fledgling theology had to find its way amidst a veritable melting pot of ideas, mostly at full boil. There was the Hellenistic Judaism of Philo, Stoicism, Manichaeism, Gnosticism, and Neoplatonism, to name a few. Common to all of these was the powerful idea that life consisted of two distinct and antagonistic orders, the *spiritual* and the *material*. The transcendence of the body and the material world was universally understood as the path to enlightenment. The truth is, early Christian thinkers drank deeply at this well.

The narrowing of spirituality took on a new force in the twelfth century. Theology's adaptation to the rising influence of philosophy and its incessant pursuit of categories saw spirituality take another hit. The categories of *spirit* and *matter* and their separation in theological thought played a crucial role in corralling spirituality even further at the edges. This was followed closely in the thirteenth century by a territorial distinction in the church between the *sacred* (church-related) and the *secular* (world-related) realms of life. The boundaries were clear: what was in the territory of the institutional church was spiritual and what was out was not. Consequently, spirituality was increasingly defined as non-physical and non-secular.

2. Moltmann, *The Source of Life*, 72.

3. Ibid.

In the centuries to follow, spirituality was cornered even more. Increasingly it came to describe, in a very personal way, the *interior* experience of faith in contrast to our *exterior* preoccupations in daily life. One's inner life was spiritual while one's outer life was not. Furthermore, with the burgeoning popularity of mysticism in the nineteenth century, spirituality referred not just to the inner life of faith but a particular experience of God open only to those who could free themselves from all other concerns. In other words, the ability and time to surrender to this mystical encounter with the heavenly depended almost entirely on having someone else to do the laundry. And so, in all of this, we have gone from Paul's all-inclusive, world-embracing sense of the spiritual to a veritable pinhole of personal and mystical experience attainable only by an elite few.

The dysfunction of spirituality's narrowing has been named many times. We have well and truly outed the opposing notions of the *sacred* and the *secular*, the *spiritual* and the *physical,* and the serious disservice they have done to our faith. We know, too, that we are still living with the effects. The Orthodox theologian Alexander Schmemann argues that the church's embracing of these divides has led to a "desacralized world" in which God and the church are viewed as peripheral and irrelevant. The real fall of humanity, he contends, is in living a "non-eucharistic life in a non-eucharistic world."[4] It's not that we have preferred the world to God. Instead, we have dismissed the world as material and irrelevant to the pursuit of God. The truth is, when the church surrenders the physical world to science, retreats into its "sacred places" and talks of nothing but "the soul," it unwittingly contributes to an utterly demystified world and the reduction of Christian faith to a bland hope in life beyond.

Name it we may, but the reality is we are left with deep and lasting impacts upon our spiritual practice. If we are to rediscover spirituality as the movement toward God through Christ at life's center and make our devotion to God our "one thing," then our challenge is firstly theological. That is, it has to do with God and how we understand God in relationship to the world. After all, this world-embracing and life-affirming spirituality finds its genesis in the character and work of God. If we are in pursuit of this God, then the question is this: where do we look?

---

4. Schmemann, *For the Life of the World,* 18.

I suggest that the answer lies in what we call the trinitarian nature of God: God as Father, Son, and Holy Spirit. Each of these expressions of God's being has a profound connection with our own lives. God the Father is the origin of life, the creator and sustainer of life in its fullness. God the Son is the redeemer of life, God enfleshed in the most physical, human form. And God the Spirit is the great transformer of life, moving through all creation in the hope of eternity.

God the Creator: immersed in the world

We begin in the beginning. The very first words of the Genesis story establish God as the origin of all there is. "In the beginning when God created the heavens and the earth . . ." (Gen 1:1). As the story continues, it is God who separates the light from the darkness, God who creates the earth and the sky, the rivers and the oceans, the dry land and the vegetation that covers it. It is God who makes the sun and the moon and the stars above, the seasons that govern our days and set the rhythms of time, the life that teems in the deeps of the sea and fills the skies above. It is God who forms the creatures that roam the earth from end to end, the cattle and the wild beasts, the slugs and things that slither along the ground as well as those that glide through the trees above. And it is God who makes humankind in God's image to steward and govern it all. Frankly, there is nothing in this world that sits outside the realm of God's good work.

As I sit here writing, I'm in a lovely bed-and-breakfast in a small town in central Victoria. I look through the wooden slat blinds to the garden just beyond. It's an overcast spring day. I see the soft pink of the little trumpet flowers that hang just beyond the windowpane and a blue-faced honeyeater dancing from garden pot to branch. The familiar song of the magpies sounds in the distance as a breeze rustles through the greenery in front of me. Farther out are the garden's old trees: two elms, a fir, and an old eucalyptus this side of the garden fence. Beyond it, standing on the sidewalk, is an elderly man with a peak hat and black Labrador chatting with a middle-aged woman in blue, a newspaper under her arm. On the other side of the road a mother with a stroller walks her two young children to the school. It's just around the corner and if I listen carefully I can hear the sound of the school bell ringing. It's muffled, though, by the more persistent sound of the goods train making its way on the railroad that winds through the town. I can't see it but the sound is distinctive.

What I can see is a glimpse of the main road that runs north-south from here. It's always busy. A steady stream of cars, cattle trucks, and utilities go by almost constantly. It's a hum that blends into the background but is always there. And if I crane my head in the other direction and look above the tree line, I see a linesman crouched precariously in a bucket lift attending to the overhead power lines that run the length of the street.

In all of this is God. This world we inhabit in its ordinariness and its wonder comes to us from the hand of God. Each and every day we are immersed in it; from our morning bowl of cornflakes to the stars that hang above us at night, we are enveloped by the reality of God; and it is good. Yes, it's chaotic, painful, conflicted, and often terribly mundane. Our world is even scarred. The earth groans under the stress of its own decay just as our own bodies long for redemption and renewal, but it remains fundamentally good because it is of God. If we are in pursuit of God, it is ludicrous to think that we can bypass this world as irrelevant. Any expression of spiritualty that minimizes the glorious creativity of God that's right in front of our eyes is tragically wanting.

The Jewish philosopher Martin Buber made a confession that he lacked what he called "the mystic negation." In Buber's view, the religious mystic began by negating the entire world "in order, with new disembodied senses . . . to press forward to his God." This "annihilation" of the worldly was something Buber could not comprehend. "I am enormously concerned with just this world," he said, "this painful and precious fullness of all that I see, hear, taste. I cannot wish away any part of its reality. I can only wish that I might heighten this reality."[5]

As children of the Creator, we are obliged to live with our feet on the ground in order that the reality of God's world is heightened for us, not wished away. What Buber reaches for is an earthed spirituality, one that he can feel, taste, hear, and see in the now of life. So, too, our faith in the God of creation presuppose a spirituality grounded where we are. Our experience of God cannot float in midair, disconnected from our physical and social environment. When so much contemporary spirituality bears no social conscience, no accountability to the wretched pain and longing of this earth, we Christians are called to press in to it and discern within it the goodness and beauty of life as God made it.

The philosopher and psychologist John Dewey, one of America's most notable public intellectuals of the twentieth century, is best known

---

5. Buber, *Between Man and Man*, 28.

as a voice for education and social reform. He also wrote about art. As a lover of art, Dewey was mystified by the disjuncture he saw between the enjoyment of great art and the concerns of everyday life. In particular, he could not understand the antagonism among the intelligentsia toward connecting the two. Dewey believed that to put a work of fine art on a pedestal was to lessen its worth as that which helped us to name beauty in everyday life. According to Dewey, the task is to enrich the relationship between art and the everyday, not diminish it. While art may express an intensified form of human experience, it is still experience rooted in the ordinary. "Mountain peaks do not float unsupported," he writes; "they do not even just rest upon the earth. They are the earth in one of its manifest operations."[6]

It is the same with our spirituality. Indeed, there may be moments of revelation and epiphany, mountaintop experiences of transcendence. But mountains don't float unsupported. Edge and center are one. Life in this created world is of a piece; everything is connected and everything belongs. Whatever we conclude about differences between *matter* and *spirit* or *body* and *soul*, creation is first and foremost an integrated whole that God confidently affirms as "very good" (Gen 1:31). Our Christian faith implies a bold embracing of life as one full and complete response to God the Creator.

God as Redeemer: "in the flesh"

The Harvard philosopher Sam Keen once wrote, "When a wedge is driven between the holy and the quotidian, the concept of God becomes either insignificant or positively repressive." Keen's word *quotidian* refers to the ordinary and everyday. His point is that a God removed from our mundane world is a redundant God, and belief in his existence "a luxury of no positive consequence."[7]

I pastor a city church. We meet in a nineteenth-century building on a grand tree-lined boulevard that stretches between City Hall and State Parliament. The church is surrounded by glass towers of commerce, theaters of culture, and centers of learning. At our front door are the emporiums of privilege, Gucci and Prada, and the private clubs of the city's elite. At our back door are the laneways home to the city's mentally ill

6. Dewey, *Art as Experience*, 3.

7. Keen, *Apology for Wonder*, 90.

and drug addicted. Routinely I take groups of students to the rooftop garden of the building attached to our sanctuary. From there we have a commanding view of the city laid out below and we reflect together on our sense of things from here. High above its streets, the life of the city appears ordered but distant. It's the view of transcendence. Certainly we see things from here in ways that are unique, even necessary, but we are removed. The real life of the city is down there and its only as we dismount our pinnacle and walk the city's streets and laneways that we know the city in ways that make a difference. The Australian novelist Tim Winton describes his emergence from the rugged coastal country of Western Australia—a remote and unforgiving terrain for those who are brave enough to traverse it on foot—to board a helicopter that lifts him high above the very same land. "Within seconds you've gone from earthbound defeat to celestial transcendence," he writes, "and the higher you fly the less human your view."[8]

In the birth of Jesus, we encounter a God very much alive and employed. If ever there was a wedge between heaven and earth, between God and the quotidian, it has been dislodged in the birth of Jesus. God is with us. In Jesus, God became "flesh" (John 1:14) and moved in among us. This act is central to the redeeming work of God and its impact is extraordinary. Immersed in the most bodily form, Jesus has cemented the eternal fullness of God in the here and now. The incarnation challenges the form and practice of our spirituality in the most liberating ways.

First, it challenges *disembodied* expressions of the spiritual life, those that call us to leave behind our physical selves in pursuit of higher things. In fact, it is the body, the essential humanity of Jesus, that mediates God to us. The body is not that thing to overcome but is itself a celebration of the immanence of God. It's why Paul so confidently affirms our bodies as "members of Christ" and "temples of the Holy Spirit" (1 Cor 6:15–19) and calls us to present them as "living sacrifices" to God (Rom 12:1). Consequently, the Jesuit philosopher Pierre Teilhard de Chardin urges us to find in our bodies "footholds, intermediaries to be made use of, nourishment to be taken, sap to be purified and elements to be borne along with us."[9]

Second, the incarnation challenges *displaced* spiritualities that ignore the physical contexts of life—the homes, sidewalks, offices, and

8. Winton, *Island Home*, 164.

9. Teilhard de Chardin, *Le Milieu Divin*, 92.

shopping malls of our daily rounds. Frankly, a placeless spirituality is an unlikely path for followers of Jesus. Not only did God take bodily form, but in Jesus God chose to enter the places of human life. In homes, neighborhoods and marketplaces he proclaimed the mysteries of the kingdom of God as present among us, capable of transforming the most everyday contexts into sacred places rich with spiritual meaning. It is incredible that we would feel pressured to withdraw from these in order to know God.

The incarnation is a compelling affirmation that the divine and the earthly meet in God. God is not in the business of overcoming the material to lead us into this place of meeting. Rather, our encounter with God is rooted in *this* place and *this* time through Jesus Christ. Our belief in the incarnation demands of us a spirituality engaged fully with this life as one redeemed and sanctified by God. It will not allow us to be disengaged from the world around us. According to Anglican theologian Rowan Williams, Christian spirituality is a "demanding and far reaching matter" that is so much more than the interpretation of private inner experience. It touches every aspect of earthly existence, for "if the heart of meaning is a human story, a story of growth, conflict and death, then every human story, with all its oddity and ambivalence, becomes open to interpretation in terms of God's saving work."[10]

God as Transformer: the all-present force

As a seminarian in the United States in the 1990s, I was aware of a particular movement of the Holy Spirit that stirred interest and controversy among students. As a phenomenon, it found its origin in the Canadian city of Toronto. It was commonly dubbed a "blessing" and was being played out locally, night after night, in a gathering just north of our Pasadena campus. I went along to one of these meetings and, honestly, came away more perplexed than touched. There were so-called "manifestations" of the Spirit's presence that "visited" certain people in the congregation and caused them to do the most bizarre things. I was not easily critical of what I saw. I had been reading about some of the great figures of spirituality in history and, frankly, the bizarre was standard. I was, more simply, mystified, and just a little envious.

10. Williams, *The Wound of Knowledge*, 2.

I have never had what others define as an "experience" of the Spirit. Friends can point with confidence to a moment of fullness or renewal. Through particular rituals of prayer they have been "touched," "healed," or "baptized" by the Spirit's presence in an instance of great impact. My old friend Symeon certainly had them, many times over. I have no doubt that such experiences happen. I have even sought them, but with little to show for it. Certainly, I've been bowled over by grace, overwhelmed by beauty, convicted by failure, but generally speaking, my spiritual life has a much more ordinary feel to it. A significant part of the controversy that surrounded the events in Pasadena was around the language of those who were "in" and those who were not; those who had received the "blessing" and those who hadn't. It's as though there was an elite group privy to a higher experience of the Spirit that set them apart. What's always overwhelmed me about the presence and work of God's Spirit in the world, though, is just how all-pervasive it is. Containing, apportioning, or defining it is like trying to bottle the ocean.

In my late teens, I was an avid reader of missionary biographies. One of my heroes was Hudson Taylor, a medical doctor and one of the great Protestant missionaries of the nineteenth century. He certainly had his experiences of the Spirit. Following one such experience he recalled feeling like a small boy playing in the sand at the edge of the sea. Having dug a hole in the sand, he takes a little bucket and fills it with water from the ocean to pour in his hole. Deed done, he turns to look back at the ocean and notices that no matter how many buckets he fills, there's not even a dent in the endless volume of water before him. For Taylor, so it was with God; and so it is with the Spirit. The Spirit is God's all-pervasive presence in the world, a presence to which there is no end or limit. Not a crevice of life is hidden from God, nor can a crevice contain God. Certainly, we have our experiences but no experience can define or mete out the Spirit. Through it we are gathered up into something so much bigger than we are or will ever be.

The mission of the Spirit in the world is nothing less than the completion of God's saving work in Christ. That saving work involves the whole earth and all of life. The scope of the Holy Spirit's ministry is more than your personal sanctification or mine. It involves all of time, all of history, all of nature. Wherever in life there is corruption or decay, the Spirit is there to transform and renew.

As we appreciate the broadness of the Holy Spirit's presence and task, we understand afresh that the Spirit can never be the sole possession of individuals and certainly not of the church. Yes, the Spirit is uniquely present in the church and within those who are embraced by the grace of God, but this is not a restricted presence. As the theologian John Taylor says, the Spirit of God is present "through the whole fabric of the world."[11] Indeed, the Spirit is the "go-between," existing most profoundly between realities: between Christ and culture; between the church and the world; between the Christian and her neighborhood. To live in the fullness of the Spirit is to live in the fullness of these encounters. If our spirituality is of the Spirit, it will be genuinely worldly, leading us more authentically into the world as we move more deeply into God.

It is inconceivable to me that God would create this world as the revelation of God's being and bring redemption to it through the radical means of incarnation, only for the Holy Spirit to pluck us out of this world into some alternate realm of experience. Through the all-pervasive presence of the Spirit, God remains fully and completely committed to *this* world and to *this* life, the one we inhabit every day.

I have heard the Australian theologian Frank Rees define spirituality as "learning to be with God in all of life's experiences." There is something about this that resonates. Perhaps it's the lack of striving, the gentleness and humility of the endeavor. The North American writer Eugene Peterson says something similar. Those who live in the "mature wholeness of the gospel," he writes, are those able to take all of life's elements—marriage, children, work, possessions, relationships—and experience them as an "act of faith."[12] Both definitions remind me that spirituality is a very ordinary endeavor. There is nothing here of spiritual pinholes or mountaintops. Rather, it's the stuff of life. Certainly, that God would come to us in Jesus Christ and bid us to follow him—this is one of the great mysteries of eternity—but the living of it is not mystical. It is ordinary and within reach. I am convinced that once we begin to discern the depth and breadth of spirituality in the Christian faith and get just an inkling of the nature of this God we experience through Christ, we will be enticed with a sense of our humble lives shot through with sacred possibility.

My personal definition of spirituality, and one that guides my exploration from this point on, is this:

11. Taylor, *The Go-between God*, 180.

12. Peterson, *The Contemplative Pastor*, 4.

> Spirituality had to do with discerning and responding to the presence and purposes of God through Christ in every place, every task, and every encounter of every day.

There are several elements to this. *Firstly,* the seeking of God and living of faith are bound together; discerning and responding to God are one. Contemplation and action are never entirely separate activities in the spiritual life; they go hand in hand. *Secondly,* the same can be said of the God we seek. God's being and doing in the world—God's presence and purposes—are vitally connected. When we live according to God's purposes, we know God. In the musical version of Victor Hugo's story *Les Misérables,* Jean Valjean utters those moving words as he transitions from death into new life, "to love another person is to see the face of God." He knew it to be true just as we do: when we truly love in word and deed and in the most immediate experiences of life, we touch the eternal. *Thirdly,* we are called upon to seek God and live faith in the daily-ness of life. This is not a spirituality for there and later but for here and now.

For me, this spirituality of discernment and response is best pursued in company and at the very center of life. It's a journey that we share in community. We are the people of God, the body of Christ, the household of faith. The disciplines of isolation and solitude have their place, but if we are about pursuing the presence and purposes of God in the world, then we need to do it arm-in-arm with those around us. Frankly, it is too important to be otherwise.

3

Spiritual Practices for a Different Way

BEFORE MY DAYS IN church and seminary, my professional life was in the kitchen. Though it was a brief and inauspicious career, my ice sculpting skills were well honed. In preparation for banquets, my task was to turn a large unwieldy block of ice into something shapely and beautiful. Swans and dolphins were popular. These translucent creatures, sitting under colored lights and slowly melting into water trays hidden below, provided the wow factor for the assembling guests.

The creation of an ice sculpture usually involves a walk-in refrigerator, an oversized block of ice, and a sculptor with very cold hands. While I knew of others with handheld power saws, I never ventured beyond the simple tools of hammer and chisel. Frankly, a block of ice is a thing of transparent neutrality; to transform it into something visually arresting is a challenge. Before the ballroom doors opened, I would stand back to view my creation rising up at the center of the feast. It was a moment of pride.

Decades later, I sit in an office preparing lectures for a class in narrative theology. So much in my life has changed. As my tools of trade, knives, whisks, and chopping boards have given way to words, white boards, and computer screens. But the changes are deeper than that. Spurred on by the subject at hand, I reflect on my adolescent images of God, those understandings that morph and change through time. It occurs to me just how much my early view of God and of the nature of spirituality was aligned with those sculpting tools. As I labored in the kitchen, I understood God as the great ice sculptor wielding his divine chisel to bring my shapeless self into conformity with his purposes. Mine was the discipline of surrender while God chipped away at my angled corners and sharp edges. It was my daily choice to remain a compliant block of ice in the hands of the master.

The choice to surrender to the presence of God has long been ours to make. From the earliest days of Christian faith, people of devotion have sought ways to make it real. The invitation of Jesus to discipleship is compelling: "If any want to become my followers, let them deny themselves and take up their cross daily and follow me" (Luke 9:23). The advent of the *spiritual disciplines* arose out of a desire for practices to facilitate this following in daily life. Those disciplines most common through Christian history include things like solitude, silence, Bible reading, prayer, fasting, confession, meditation, worship, chastity, and simplicity. And these are just the beginning.

In truth, the word *discipline* is fraught, loaded with associations and images of God that warrant critique. My God the Heavenly Ice Sculptor is one of those. When the spiritual disciplines are associated primarily with sin, denial, penance, and punishment, there are theological yellow lights that flash caution. The fact is, I am not a shapeless and worthless block of ice. I am made in the image of God. While I certainly have rough edges and struggle with my frailty every day, the work of God's Spirit is to renew and revitalize the God-given beauty within. We are being transformed, slowly, from one degree of glory to another (2 Cor 3:18). Rather than a chisel-wielding sculptor, God is our loving parent and gracious host who, through the redemptive work of Jesus, invites us to sit at his table as beloved children.

That said, there is much more to the spiritual disciplines than hammers and chisels. To toss the category out is foolish, but to understand the nature of such practices and how we apply them today is a hefty task. Frankly, there is no nicely packaged set of disciplines in the New Testament. Jesus says much about the character of those who seek the kingdom of God and the values that shape their lives. Paul provides a compelling list of "fruit" borne in the lives of those who "live by the Spirit:" love, joy, peace, patience, kindness, generosity, faithfulness, gentleness, and self-control (Gal 5:22–23). But these are more outcomes than practices. Certainly, there are practices of faith all over the New Testament: "welcome the stranger"; "pray without ceasing"; "confess your sins to one another"; "forgive your enemies." The exhortations are many, but still no authorized list. Indeed, if we are looking for a nicely potted, ten-step program for a budding disciple, we'll not find it in the Bible. The terminology of spiritual disciplines comes much later.

Perhaps the closest we come in the New Testament is Paul's language of "exercises unto godliness" (1 Tim 4:7–8). He borrows it from the gymnasium. To "exercise" or "train" physically is to discipline the body for action. Paul was addressing his protégé Timothy, a young leader of the early church for whom the gymnasium was part of life. Paul is prompting him to the disciplines of spiritual exercise to match the physical workouts of the aspiring athlete. Elsewhere Paul urges the imitation of Jesus: "Imitate me as I imitate Christ" (1 Cor 11:1). As our model for living, Jesus certainly set a standard. Importantly, he undertook regular practices to nurture his spirit. His habits of solitude, fasting, and prayer, alongside apparent choices for homelessness, poverty, and chastity are evident in the Gospel stories. But Jesus' understanding of the most transformative spiritual practice was much broader than these particular actions convey.

Preceding Jesus' groundbreaking story of the Good Samaritan (Luke 10:25–37), he is asked by an expert in Jewish law how one guarantees entrance into eternal life. In the conversation that follows, it is the commandments to love God and neighbor that are identified as the summary of the entire law. "Do this and you will live," Jesus said. In other words, it is love that is the essence of the spiritual life; and it is love that is at the kernel of all spiritual practice. It is this same love that Jesus lived in his earthly life from beginning to end. Though it was a difficult love to sustain and one that required daily choice, this love of God and humankind was the deepest expression of his being. Ultimately, it cost him his life. Even more, it is this same love with which you and I are embraced. Paul's exhortation to the early Christians is to work out that experience of love in their daily lives. "Work out your salvation," he says (Phil 2:12). As those being conformed to the image of God's son (Rom 8:29), we are called to give daily expression to our experience of love and thus be continually transformed by it. In other words, we are called to *practice our faith*.

As a specific set of practices, the spiritual disciplines began taking a particular shape from the early decades of the fourth century. It was around the time that Symeon began sitting on his pole. Symeon and others were propelled in their practice by at least two factors, the first political and the second theological.

Politically, as we've noted already, there was the seismic change to the relationship between the Christian church and the empire of Rome

following the Emperor Constantine's conversion. Previously, devout followers of Christ were persecuted, tortured, even fed to lions. The cost of
following Jesus was never more literal. However, as the church and its
hierarchy edged into the center of political power, the integrity of true
discipleship was on the line. The flight to the desert by Symeon and thousands of other devoted lay people was, as much as anything, a rejection
of the church compromised by its own success. In the words of historian
Herbert Workman, these passionate believers fled not so much from the
world as from the world in the church, "from court bishops who fought
for richer sees, from people who bore the name of Christ but who were
still pagans at heart, from men who as soon as they were made clerics,
enlarged the fringes of their garments, rode on foaming steeds, and
dwelt in houses with many rooms, with sculptured doors and painted
wardrobes."[1] How quickly things can change. Spurred on by Jesus' call
to renunciation (deny yourself) and imitation (take up your cross and
follow me), those with a passionate commitment to Christian practice
felt compelled to leave the world and church behind and walk a more
rigorous path.

Theologically, this flight was intensified by the heady mix of philosophical ideas that permeated early Christian belief. We've referred to
them already in chapter 2. What these philosophies had in common was a
clear separation between the spiritual and material concerns of life. Transcendence of the body and renunciation of the world were considered
the most certain path to enlightenment. For Christians, it was repack-
aged as the way to salvation. One of the most influential theologians of
early spirituality was the Grecian Evagrius the Solitary (346–399). It was
Evagrius who first divided the spiritual life into two phases, the "active"
and the "contemplative." It was a distinction he borrowed from Aristotle
through Origen. But where Origen understood the two as complementary, Evagrius treated them as mutually exclusive stages on the way to
God, the second superior to the first. All of this underlines the fertile if
theologically tainted soil in which the early spiritual disciplines took root.

Certainly, Symeon was a man of his time. He was known then as
a model of austerity. Prior to mounting his pillar, Symeon dedicated an
entire summer to the daily task of digging a trench in which he buried
himself up to his neck for the daylight hours. Others of this era were
similarly resolute. We read stories of those who restrained their limbs

1. Workman, *The Evolution of the Monastic Ideal,* 10.

with iron braces and chains; exposed their naked bodies to poisonous flies while sleeping in marshes; ate uncooked food for seven years; carried heavy weights as they trudged an unchanging circuit in the desert; kept meticulous records of how long it had been since they set eyes upon a person of a different gender. All of these betrayed an understanding of the body as an evil to overcome. Inspired by Paul's anguished words in Romans 7, "For I know that nothing good dwells within me," the battle against the body was a spiritual fight to the death. The call of Christ was not only to renunciation and cross bearing, but a call to spiritual combat with one's own flesh.

These acts of extreme asceticism and personal warfare coupled with the more general practices of withdrawal set a rigorous scene for the development of the disciplines in the centuries to come. We know that by the twelfth century they had expanded dramatically and taken a much more legalistic tone, their application often prescribed in exhaustive detail. What's more, the severity of their enforcement upon the broader Christian population took the rigor of the disciplines to a whole new level. Rather than practices of choice for those especially devoted, particular disciplines were enforced upon all believers as mandatory signs of salvation. Association with the regimes of punishment and spiritual merit were never more blatant. Incited by local priests, entire communities across thirteenth- and fourteenth-century Europe were gripped by epidemics of self-flagellation, involuntary dancing, and stigmatization. The "mortification of the flesh" was pursued with gusto. The popular implements of self-discipline included whips, thorn branches, iron chains, and leather straps embedded with bone. In essence, the spiritual disciplines became a crushing burden to the masses, and all this mediated by the church.

The advent of Protestantism, set aflame in the early sixteenth century, was in no small part a response to the theological bankruptcy of the church and its practices. The great catalyst for reform, the German friar Martin Luther (1483–1546), was himself propelled in his youth by the most rigorous disciplines. His biographer Roland Bainton paints a telling picture:

> He fasted, sometimes three days on end without a crumb. The seasons of fasting were more consoling to him than those of feasting. Lent was more comforting than Easter. He laid upon himself vigils and prayers in excess of those stipulated by the rule. He cast off the blankets permitted him and well-nigh froze

himself to death. At times he was proud of his sanctity and would say, "I have done nothing wrong today." Then misgiving would arise. "Have you fasted enough? Are you poor enough?" He would then strip himself of all save that which decency required.[2]

With retrospect, Luther was scathing of the culture fostered by the church, one that left him and all Christendom with such an onerous view of religious life. In his view, the spiritual disciplines had become nothing more than a means of spiritual control—one through which the ecclesial gatekeepers meted out judgment and forgiveness according to their ledgers of spiritual merit. Luther's commitment was to strip away all forms of works-based salvation and nurture a more minimalist understanding of faithful Christian living. In Luther's view, the disciplines muddied the waters.

While Protestantism in its myriad forms followed Luther in dismissing the disciplines as bankrupt, they soon understood that the people of God needed practices through which to express their faith. For Luther and his fellow Reformers, however, these practices had to be for the living of salvation, not for earning it. Luther held to just two practices of the church, baptism and the Eucharist, believing that these provided all that was needed for the faithful. The Reformed branch of Protestantism added to these a strict rule of life for its adherents and a corresponding order of discipline for the wayward, believing that the law provided necessary instruction and correction for people of faith. The Methodists developed a structured method of "godly exercise," incorporating a handful of the traditional disciplines as "means of grace." The Anabaptists wanted to return to the practices of the New Testament church, including baptism for believers and a common life of prayer, learning, and service. The Puritans developed a rhythm of private and family prayers that mirrored the daily prayer cycles of the monastery. All this illustrates that while Protestants of all stripes vigorously distanced themselves from the language of spiritual disciplines, they still promoted practices to nurture faith.

It is interesting to note the disciplines that have lasted. In Catholicism, Orthodoxy, and the various Protestant traditions, certain spiritual practices persist. The disciplines that have stayed the course have done so for good reason: they have passed the test of time. While burying oneself up to the neckline in a self-dug ditch may have ceased, the value of

2. Bainton, *Here I Stand,* 34.

solitude is sustained. While exposing the naked body to nasty flies may have gone the way of bone-studded leather straps, the practices of prayer and meditation continue.

It is only in recent times that the language of spiritual disciplines has become more widely accepted across the Christian church. As conversations between traditions have flourished, the terminology of the disciplines has helped name our common practices just as the language of spirituality has named the deeper longings that bind us. It also has to do with the growing thirst for a deeper experience of faith that shaped the latter decades of the twentieth century. The Quaker Parker Palmer called it a "spiritual renaissance," one enabled by a greater openness across denominational lines and significantly shaped by "monastic metaphors and practices."[3] In my own corner of the church, it was writers like theologian Richard Foster and philosopher Dallas Willard who, in the 1980s, helped put the spiritual disciplines on the evangelical agenda. Foster's *Celebration of Discipline*, first published in 1978, argued that in the rediscovery of the spiritual disciplines we could find the depth essential to the transformative character of our faith. A decade later, Willard's *The Spirit of the Disciplines* challenged the spiritual flabbiness of American Christianity and argued that the traditional disciplines of the church added essential rigor to the practice of discipleship. In essence, the *spiritual disciplines* were resurrected across traditions, not as a path to salvation but as a tangible means of spiritual growth.

We return to the fact that the list of spiritual disciplines is not a closed one, and certainly not set in stone. It is a list informed by history, yet open. Willard suggests that the most sustained and time-honored disciplines include, firstly, *disciplines of abstinence:* solitude, silence, fasting, frugality, chastity, and secrecy. And secondly, *disciplines of engagement:* study, worship, celebration, service, prayer, fellowship, confession, and submission. This separation of practices under the categories of abstinence and engagement is helpful. It responds to the two aspects of Jesus' call to discipleship. First, we are called to deny ourselves: to give up, relinquish, let go. We agree to abstain from such things as speech, food, material possessions, sexual intimacy, and recognition. Second, we are called to carry our cross: to take up, embrace, and follow. We agree to

---

3. Palmer, *The Active Life*, 1.

live proactively as disciples of Jesus through practices of learning, prayer, worship, confession, service, and community.

This idea that spiritual practices can be found in the rhythm between abstinence and engagement, between relinquishment and embrace, is a good one. The trouble is, even some of the practices of engagement don't feel very engaged. As we continue in our pursuit of God at the center of life, we are looking for spiritual practices that see us rooted more deeply in the daily-ness of what we do. We are looking for practices that help us press into the contexts of daily life rather than pull away from them. To help us along, we need a broader understanding of what constitutes a spiritual practice. What's more, we need to be open to new avenues for God's transforming work in our lives. It does take some reimagining. It calls for a different way of looking at our lives and the things we do each day. The point is not to draw up a new list of practices but to nurture new ways of seeing. If we really believe that God is as richly present in the routine and ordinary as God is in the desert or cathedral, what we need are practices that make this sing.

The word *discipline* finds its root in the same word as *disciple.* In the Greek of the New Testament, the noun *disciple* (*mathétes*) comes from the root *math.* This refers to the "mental effort" needed to think something through to its application. In the broadest sense, I define a spiritual discipline in the following way:

> A spiritual discipline is any activity undertaken with intention, effort, and regularity that disciples us into the likeness of Christ.

This helps us to cast the net more broadly. It invites us to think inclusively about all aspects of our lives as potential avenues for growth. Of course, a spiritual discipline is never random in character, no matter how broad our net. The ones I describe have some elements in common.

Firstly, they are *intentional disciplines*, routine and repetitive in their practice. There is nothing off-the-cuff or sporadic about them. We choose them. Secondly, they are *disciplines of presence*, practices that take us more deeply into the here and now. As such, they require attention and focus. Thirdly, they are *communal disciplines*; for the most part we pursue these practices best in company not isolation. Fourthly, they are *contemplative disciplines* in the most inclusive sense of the term. That is, they are primarily disciplines of action through which we discover the gifts of contemplation.

Disciplines of Intention

There is no getting around it. A spiritual discipline requires discipline. Both intention and effort are non-negotiable, especially in its beginnings. We are not transformed through one-offs but in repetitive practice.

My own physical exercise includes swimming laps of an indoor pool. I am not naturally given to exercise. I have always been poor in the sports department of life. I have zero coordination and the most loathsome memories of inadequacy in the schoolyard; but I know, too, that at my stage of life, regular physical activity is essential. For me, swimming is the least offensive of the options. I have learned, too, that swimming sporadically does me little good. It is in the routine and regular discipline of swimming that my body reaps the benefits. I am transformed through time.

By its nature, a spiritual discipline is a practice we embrace with the specific and long-term intention of surrendering more fully to God's purposes. Certainly, we often have experiences of the most transformative growth without the slightest planning. God has a habit of deepening our spirits in unexpected ways. A spiritual discipline is different. It is a practice we embrace with intention and forethought. It is something we choose to do, regularly, with the express purpose of deepening our awareness of God.

The Catholic writer Thomas Ryan describes a spiritual discipline as a "method."[4] In the development of any practice one must first learn the time-honored methods of that practice before graduating to its natural pleasures. It requires persistence and discipline. Though a true method will eventually lead us beyond itself to a greater and more beautiful end, it is with the method that we begin.

Robert Redford's award-winning film *The River Runs Through It* is based on Norman McLaren's book by the same name. It's a moving story of a father and his two sons. The father's intentional mentoring of his boys happens through the art and practices of fly-fishing. Through years of patient practice, the boys eventually graduate from backyard to river, slowly mastering the practices as they progress from adolescence into manhood. There is a poignant scene in the film when Norman, the older brother, watches as his younger brother Paul wades further out into the stream and begins casting. Norman narrates: "And then an amazing thing

---

4. Ryan, "Discipline and the Spiritual Life," 162.

happened. Paul left his father's instructions behind and started casting to a unique and marvelous rhythm of his own."

There is something about the discipline involved in spiritual practices, traditional or otherwise, that is its own reward. As with learning to fish, to cook, or to speak a new language, discipline and attention mark our earliest efforts and the rewards seem far away. In time, though, we move beyond the methods, the practices, or the grammar to the real joy of what we pursue; so, too, with the spiritual disciplines. Long-term intentionality leads to a deeper reward.

Disciplines of Presence

In her book *Wisdom Distilled From the Daily*, the Benedictine nun Joan Chittister tells a wonderful story:

> A young monastic came upon an elder one day sitting among a group of praying, working, meditating people. "I have the capacity to walk on water," the young disciple said. "So, let's you and I go onto that small lake over there and sit down and carry on a spiritual discussion." But the teacher answered, "If what you are trying to do is to get away from all of these people, why do you not come with me and fly into the air and drift along in the quiet, open sky and talk there." And the young seeker replied, "I can't do that because the power you mention is not one that I possess." And the teacher explained, "Just so. Your power of remaining still on top of the water is one that is possessed by fish. And my capacity of floating through air can be done by any fly. These abilities have nothing to do with real truth and, in fact, may simply become the basis for arrogance and competition, not spirituality. If we're going to talk about spiritual things, we should really be talking here."[5]

There is something about *here* and God that are deeply connected. The presence of God is not something we conjure up through certain rituals, in particular places, or through altered states of mind. A good spiritual practice names the presence of God already with us. In whatever form a spiritual discipline takes, it proceeds on the assumption that the possibility of God is as real where we are as anywhere. An effective discipline is an act of presence, the choice to be fully in the moment and

---

5. Chittister, *Wisdom Distilled from the Daily*, 1–2.

its tasks, no matter how ordinary they seem, for in them we can know the divine.

An act of presence is an act of sacrament. The language of sacraments is more familiar to some than others. In theological terms, a sacrament is a tangible sign of God's grace. It's an object, ritual, or experience that embodies a deeper spiritual truth. When it comes to an official list of sacraments, Baptists like me have just two: baptism and the Lord's supper. In these, the everyday elements of water, bread, and wine are tangible signs of God's grace in our lives. Other traditions cast the net more broadly. The list might include the sacraments of reconciliation, marriage, ordination to priesthood, and more. However long or short the list, these sacraments are understood to be the rites of the church. It is the church that mediates them. But the very nature of a sacrament means it cannot be held under lock and key, not even by the church.

The Catholic theologian Leonardo Boff urges us to see the sacramental in all of life. Indeed, he says, it is in the "archaeology" of everyday life that the sacraments thrive. Rather than being the property of the church hierarchy, visible signs of grace are within reach every day. "A sacrament does not tear human beings away from this world," Boff writes, "it addresses an appeal to them, asking them to look more closely and deeply into the very heart of the world."[6] As a practice of presence, a good spiritual discipline nurtures our ability to do just that.

Disciplines of Community

The Lutheran theologian of the early twentieth century, Dietrich Bonhoeffer, once said that genuine Christian spirituality is only possible in "sociality."[7] In other words, it's all about relationships. He was right. Expressions of spiritualty that do nothing but lead us more deeply into ourselves to the exclusion of the world around us miss the mark by a mile. "There is no self-consciousness without community," Bonhoeffer asserts.[8] The Christian story is a constant reminder that abundant life is not about me. It's about us. Indeed, by faith we are gathered up in something much greater than ourselves. When we embrace Christ, we make the choice to leap into a river of faith—a great tradition, story, and community that

6. Boff, *Sacraments of Life*, 32.

7. Bonhoeffer, *Sanctorum Communio*, 44.

8. Ibid., 46

carries us along in its flow. A spirituality like this can never be reduced to the personalized business of self-realization. It certainly can't be an escape from the world or a sedative that dulls us to the pain of our neighbors. Ultimately, it should lead us more deeply into these relationships. You have only to look at the life and ministry of Jesus. His spirituality compels us into the streets, neighborhoods, and marketplaces of our lives.

Bonhoeffer was one of those Christian thinkers with his theological feet very much on the ground. Born in 1906, he was at the height of his influence during the Nazi regime of World War II. In fact, he was a vocal opponent of Hitler and his plans for world domination, and especially of his genocidal persecution of the Jews. Such was the strength of Bonhoeffer's opposition, he was arrested in 1943, imprisoned in a concentration camp, then eighteen months later executed for treason. During his relatively brief career as a theologian, Bonhoeffer wrote a small book called *Life Together*. In it he reflected on the nature of Christian community and the centrality of what he called a "community of love" to the mission of the church. He was not concerned by ideal or romantic images of Christian community, but the practical outworking of God's love and grace among his people. In this, Bonhoeffer struggled to understand how the spirituality of many pastors in the German Lutheran church could flourish alongside a complacency toward the Nazis' treatment of Jews. It was a disconnect he could neither fathom nor ignore.

The more recent theologian Sallie McFague describes the invitation that lies at the heart of our Christian faith: "an invitation to a marvelous, messy, muddle where we must live in and with and off of one another—if we are to live at all."[9] The truth is, a good spiritual discipline should be one that pulls us out of ourselves and presses us more deeply into the muddle of mutuality and accountability that marks genuine community. If it doesn't, then from an explicitly Christian perspective it serves no commendable purpose.

Disciplines of Contemplation

My beloved and I are very different people. As the introvert, I long for solitude and relish moments of retreat. I'm given naturally to poetry and quiet corners. Occasionally, I imagine the life of a monk as a good possibility. She is horrified, not only at losing her partner to the monastery

9. McFague, *Blessed are the Consumers*, 20.

but at the thought of such prolonged introspection. To her, the thought of a silent retreat brings panic; to sit alone with her thoughts for too long would be to shut down any sense of self or God that she knows. In fact, it would starve the daily connections to life and beauty that sustain and energize her days. For her, God is found in conversation, action, and the color of life at its most fecund and chaotic.

In traditional terms, my beloved is an activist while I am a contemplative. In reality, this simplistic division divides life in ways that are biblically suspect. What's more, they do my beloved a great disservice. Given all the most revered models of spirituality preference personality types like mine, those like my partner are left feeling spiritually second rate. It implies that the true contemplative is one set apart from the world that she inhabits every day. This is plainly wrong.

To contemplate is to look deeply into something in order to discern its truth. That something is life itself, its objects, contexts, routines, and encounters. The true contemplative is not a person of a particular personality but one who chooses to approach life assuming its sacredness and truth. In other words, the contemplative is one who sees. "A prayerful Christian person is one who has come to attention," writes Michael Frost, ". . . one who has their eyes wide open and their spiritual antennae up."[10] The fact is, my beloved has an antennae for things I do not see and likely never will. Together we long for truth and its transformation. While we may live it differently, contemplation is a posture we share. Spiritual practices for everyday life are practices of contemplation in its most life-connected form. They take us more deeply into the world for they help us to see the world through God's eyes.

In the chapters to follow, we will explore some of the most routine contexts of life as those imbued with the presence of God: contexts like the home, the neighborhood, the workplace, the sports field, and the supermarket. At the conclusion of each of these chapters we will explore a practice particular to them. These practices are ones that don't normally feature in our lists of spiritual disciplines: things like cooking, walking, sleeping, working, shopping, and conversation. In exploring these, it is not my intention to devalue the more traditional spiritual practices. On the contrary, I want to do two things: (i) to make more explicit connections between traditional practices and the tasks of daily life; and (ii) to

10. Frost, *Eyes Wide Open*, 43.

challenge our spiritual imagination as to how we can nurture Christlike-ness in ourselves and each other at the centers of life.

PART 2

Looking for God in Different Places

4

God at Home

IN ONE OF THE most memorable, even magical moments in film, a young Judy Garland stands at a farm gate on a Kansas prairie looking wistfully to the sky. As she does she imagines a place "beyond the moon, beyond the rain," a place "somewhere over the rainbow." As an eight-year-old sitting in front of the television, I was captivated. It may have been thirty years old at the time, but when the 1939 Hollywood version of *The Wizard of Oz* first featured as the Saturday night movie at our house, I grabbed a front-row seat. The reach of the film was extraordinary. Like so many other conversions from page to screen, the film's success eclipsed the novel on which it was based. Regardless, the story remains its genius.

L. Frank Baum's book, first published in 1900, tells the tale of a young Dorothy Gale, swept up in a cyclone from her family farm and transported to the fanciful land of Oz. Seeking return passage to her family, Dorothy makes the journey to the land's mythical Wizard with an unlikely group of fellow travelers, each one seeking something different from the great magician: a scarecrow in search of a brain; a tin woodman wanting a heart; and a cowardly lion craving courage. Early in their journey, while traveling the yellow-brick road to the magician's City of Emeralds, Dorothy and the straw-brained Scarecrow have a conversation over supper:

> "Tell me something about yourself, and the country you come from," said the Scarecrow, when she had finished her dinner. So she told him about Kansas, and how grey everything was there, and how the cyclone had carried her to this queer land of Oz. The Scarecrow listened carefully, and said, "I cannot understand why you should wish to leave this beautiful country and go back to the dry, grey place you call Kansas." "That is because you have

no brains," answered the girl. "No matter how dreary and grey our homes are, we people of flesh and blood would rather live there than in any other country, be it ever so beautiful. There is no place like home." The Scarecrow sighed. "Of course I cannot understand it," he said. "If your heads were stuffed with straw, like mine, you would probably all live in the beautiful places, and then Kansas would have no people at all. It is fortunate for Kansas that you have brains."[1]

There's no doubt, the word *home* is an evocative one. It speaks uniquely to the human heart. There is no place like it. As Dorothy observes, home's allure goes far beyond its physical attributes. It's where we belong. As a physical place, home can take many forms. It might be a room in a dormitory, a suburban house, a small city loft or rambling farmhouse, a caravan or rented room. Whatever shape home takes, the longing that undergirds it digs deep in the psyche.

In her acclaimed book *Dakota*, the poet Kathleen Norris tells the story of the move she made from her Manhattan apartment to her late grandmother's house in the small town of Lemmon on the plains of South Dakota. Though it began as an awkward transition, Norris remained, captivated by the vast, desolate, yet beautiful landscape of her ancestors. What she found was an unexpected sense of home. This change in perception took time. "My idea of what makes a place beautiful had to change,"[2] she writes, but change it did and her sense of self with it.

Celebrated novelist Tim Winton writes similarly of the profound sense of identity he knows in his homeland on the west coast of Australia, though for Winton its power was realized from a distance. Sheltering from a hailstorm in rural Ireland and sipping hot chocolate with his young son by an open fire, he gazes at family snaps pasted on the wall and reminders of the places that formed the backdrop to his life. "I am increasingly mindful," he reflects later, "of the degree to which geography, distance and weather have moulded my sensory palate, my imagination and expectations. The island continent has not been mere background. Landscape has exerted a kind of force upon me that is every bit as geological as family." He concludes, "Like many Australians, I feel this tectonic grind—call it a familial ache—most keenly when abroad."[3]

1. Baum, *Wizard of Oz*, 27.
2. Norris, *Dakota*, 3.
3. Winton, *Island Home*, 10.

Whether our notion of home is that of a place we inhabit, one we remember from the past, or one we long for, the true beauty of home speaks to who we are when we are there; its absence can bring a grief all its own. "If home is place and ease," theologian Mark Vander Hart writes, "then being away from home is *dis-placement*, being *dis-eased*, *dis-oriented*, being almost lost."[4] The truth is, while the need for home is always connected to a physical form, home is far more than an address. It goes to the human experiences of identity, memory, security, and belonging. The old cliché "home is where the heart is" speaks a truth deeper than itself.

When I hear the word *home*, my mind goes to a small brick-veneered house in a mid-twentieth century housing estate on the suburban edge of Melbourne, one of Australia's largest cities. I was an infant when my parents sold the dairy farm in rural Victoria and moved into a burgeoning, working-class suburb on the city's southern edge. It was an ordinary little house, much like those around it. Though it's been half a lifetime since I set foot inside it, I can still walk through it from memory, from entrance hall to living room to kitchen; from its single bathroom and pokey laundry to its three small bedrooms. In my mind I can still run my hand over the faux-wood paneling that lined the feature wall in the living room; I can feel the thin grey carpet under my feet; I can reach into the glass-fronted cabinet that overhung the kitchen bench. The smells, textures, and sounds of this place are as tangible in my imagination today as they ever were in reality. A family of eight, we crowded in without ever feeling it to be as small as it was.

The recollections of that home are powerful, both those that warm the heart and those that don't. As a place to live, I left it behind more than three decades ago, but its association with my sense of home remains just as strong. So much so I remember the reaction I had when I heard the news my parents were selling. By then I was living in an apartment in suburban Los Angeles with a family of my own, sitting at my computer and reveling in the early convenience of email. The news that the family home was to be sold appeared in my inbox from Dad. The grief was immediate. I remember feeling almost betrayed, though in the same moment conscious of how ridiculous such a feeling was. Clearly with this news my sense of home was rattled and my sense of self with it.

---

4. Vander Hart, "Resurrecting the House," 88.

My children never got to see that house from the inside. They were born overseas and by the time we returned to Australia, my parents had well and truly moved on. A couple of years ago I took my son by the old home. We were on our way from one place to another and the idea of a sudden detour through the old neighborhood sounded like a good idea to me. My son was less convinced. I'll never forget turning off the suburb's main thoroughfare into the street of my childhood and being overwhelmed with a flood of feelings, from being affronted by the claustrophobic smallness of it all and repelled by the rundown nature of the houses, to the waves of memory in every vista. We pulled up outside the house and I could barely look. Trees were gone, my mother's garden ravaged, the brick fence replaced, the front facade covered with a tacky rendered veneer. I tried to explain to my son ways the house used to be. "It was not like that," I kept saying, "not at all." But it was all too hard. We drove off in silence. Sometimes our sense of home is a complicated thing.

From a theological perspective, this primal connection to home is God-given. Our longing for it is illustrated in the Christian story and nests deeply in what it means to be made in the image of God. We are created for home. In the creation story, God provides a garden in which the man and woman belong in complete harmony with their surroundings, a home in which God's purposes for their lives are fulfilled. Upon the breakdown of relationship, the eviction from the garden is an expulsion from this place of belonging. The profound sense of disorientation that follows is a reminder of the violation of homelessness to the human story.

Much of the subsequent drama of the Hebrew Bible is centered around the people of God in search of home. God's promise to the people of Israel of "a land flowing with milk and honey" is one of belonging and identity in place (Exod 3:8). Home and human flourishing go hand in hand. The episodic story of wandering, settlement, exile, and homecoming that follows speaks to the lifelong yearning for home common to all people. As we move into the New Testament this longing is answered again in the promise of Jesus to his disciples, "I go to prepare a place for you," a home of ultimate belonging (John 14:2–3). It is a promise that reaches its culmination in the prophecies of Revelation, words that anticipate an eternal home in the city of God. This grand salvation narrative is nowhere more profoundly encapsulated than in the story of a prodigal son returning home to his waiting father (Luke 15:11–32).

The risk of theological language is that we separate the spiritual longing from the bricks and mortar of our lives. Indeed, we shy away from equating the spiritual yearning for home with the ordinary places we inhabit. We imagine that Jesus' words, "Foxes have holes, and birds of the air have nests, but the Son of Man has nowhere to lay his head" (Matt 8:20) point to the insignificance of earthly homes and the need to lift our vision beyond them. Speaking theologically, that is not a step easily made. Salvation is as much for today as it is for tomorrow, as much for here as for some other place. It is rooted deeply where we are. The call to follow Jesus is never a call to homelessness but to be present in the here and now, our roots deep in the soil of the earth and our feet planted firmly on the pavements of our neighborhoods. If we learn anything from Jesus, it is that our discipleship must be lived, walked, and talked in the concrete challenges of life. For seekers of God and of a way of life that honors God's presence, there is no better place to begin than in our homes.

As I write this chapter I am in the far north of England, just outside the village of Felton in Northumberland. From where I sit, I can see the eastern coastline in the distance and the cold North Sea stretching out beyond. I am staying with members of a religious community in their "motherhouse" of prayer and hospitality.

It is a beautiful part of the world, rich in religious history. The community draws on the Celtic traditions of spirituality that are rooted here and provides a place and a daily rhythm of prayer for those who come. Yesterday, after morning prayers, I sat at the breakfast table with fellow guests Nancy and Ken, an elderly couple from Minnesota. Their enthusiasm for conversation was infectious and I was soon hearing stories of their long association with this place and the transformation it has bought to their faith. Not long into the conversation, as we sipped tea and buttered our toast, Nancy was offering to take me to the site of an ancient church close by. Keen on the prospect, Ken added with the certainty of a well-informed tour guide that this was a "thin place." I did know the term—a place where the divide between earth and heaven is paper-thin—though I had never heard it assigned with such authority, as though it might be a category designated by the AA travel guide: cathedrals, bathroom stops, and thin places. Regardless, I understood his intent and accepted the invitation.

As we made our journey, Nancy spoke animatedly of her previous visits to the church known today as Holy Trinity of Old Bewick. This was a significant place for her as it has been for countless others. Dating back to the twelfth century, the little church has survived various restorations through its nine centuries and holds a unique place of pride in the region. After some wrong turns and awkward interactions between driver and navigator, we found our way. Turning in at an intersection with only the smallest of signs, we followed a winding lane with nothing but black-faced sheep to witness our progress. As we came to the lane's end, the sight of the ancient church tucked into the natural crevice of a hill was beautiful. Surrounded by a grove of mature trees, the circumference of its holiness was marked by a low stone wall. The churchyard was filled with weathered gravestones spaced respectfully apart and a little wooden seat that welcomed rest.

As we pulled in to park we were not alone. Just outside the stone-wall was a tradesman's van with its side door left open. I could sense Nancy's discomfort. Regardless, we wandered down the pathway to the chapel's entrance. As we poked our heads in the door, I noticed a ladder in the building's center reaching into the space above and the stocky legs of the tradesman perched up high. "Morning!" he called down in his northern brogue. He was there, apparently, to do electrical work near the roofline. Stepping in to the edge of the small narthex, we blinked at a bright fluorescent floodlight pointing upward and, looking down, saw a paint-stained tarpaulin spread out over the stone floor. The pews had been pushed aside and loud music filled the space from a radio sitting in the middle of the tarp. Nancy's face dropped, horrified at this crass desecration of thinness. Trying hard as host to pull herself together, she began pointing out the beautiful painted inscription on the arched stonework that framed the altar, but it was all too much. Interrupted by yet another advertising jingle from the radio, she turned and walked away muttering words of disbelief.

Once outside we stayed a while, wandering the pathways that wind through the gravestones. We found the iconic Celtic cross, a masterpiece in ancient stonework standing sentry near the front of the yard. Personally, I was moved by the place, conscious of the history of prayer that filled it and glad to have been invited into its holiness. In contrast, my hosts' silence on the way home betrayed their disappointment. I felt their regret.

The designation *sacred* is a curious thing. To imagine a place of deep spirituality, a truly thin place, is commonly to imagine a place set apart from the distraction of radios, fluorescent lights, and stocky-legged

tradesmen. Certainly there is something about a place in which the accumulated confessions of God's people over centuries render it holy in a
particular way. Even as you approach it your spiritual antenna is attuned:
this place is different. The trouble is, even different places exist in the real
world. Like the cries of a fractious child that pierce the silence of a Sunday
worship service, the mundane life of that world presses in. The wonderful
truth about genuine thinness, however, is that it's not easily negated. The
intrusive sound of a radio jingle cannot render it void. The sacred is more
durable than that. In fact, true thinness is tied to the earthiness of the
place in which it thrives.

The home is a thin place, potentially one of the thinnest of all. Granted,
the average home is far from a great cathedral or an ancient place of holy
pilgrimage. Such places are unique. Neither is the home a place to be
romanticized, made to sound more like the palace of Oz than the grey
Kansas farmhouse it often is. Honestly, the domestic home is too real, too
fraught with human frailty to be spiritually airbrushed into something
ethereal. Regardless, what we can affirm about the home is this: in its
persistent ordinariness the home is sacred, for in it we find a place of such
earthiness and one in which souls are formed over a lifetime. Indeed,
when it comes to the pursuit of God, there is no place like it.

It is intriguing to notice the prominent role of the home in the
ministry of Jesus. The fact is, he spent an inordinate amount of his time
in homes and neighborhoods, much more so than in synagogues and
temples. There was nothing that Jesus did in the name of his Father that
he was not prepared to do in the home: healing, teaching, preaching,
forgiveness, worship, prayer, prophecy, fellowship, deliverance, commissioning, and proclamation. What's more, the home was the venue for major events in the gospel story and in the early life of the church: the birth
of Jesus; the last supper; the resurrection appearances; the commissioning of the disciples; the events of Pentecost; the growth of the churches
and their opening to the Gentiles. All these played out in the home. That
we would look to the home in search of a closer encounter with God is
unsurprising. What is it about the home, then, that renders it a natural
venue for the work of God?

A Place of Spiritual Formation

Our homes are places in which we are formed as human beings. Indeed, the degree to which they host our development is unparalleled. Over the course of a lifetime we are shaped by them and the relationships they embody. When you consider the remarkable level of investment we make—financial, physical, and emotional—in the establishing and maintaining of homes, it's clear we intuit this importance. That we are prepared to pay such a price illustrates that the need we are seeking to meet runs deep in the soul.

The late social historian Hugh Stretton put his discerning finger on the family home as the key to measuring society's pulse. He observed that in affluent cultures like ours more than half our waking hours are spent in the home while more than a third of our work is done there. Over a lifetime, the home requires the investment of no less than a third of our capital and will play host to three quarters of our subsistence, social life, leisure, and recreation. "Above all," he writes, "people are produced there, and endowed there with the values and capacities which will determine most of the quality of their social life and government away from home."[5] In all of this, it is foolish to diminish the home and its role. More than neutral containers to our lives, our homes are part of who we are. As architects, historians, and psychologists have long argued, as we make our homes so our homes make us.

This is equally true in a spiritual sense. We are formed spiritually by our living environments and the people who share them with us. Our theology—our understandings of God and the world, and of ourselves in relationship to them—is shaped by the spaces, the conversations, the conflict, the prejudices and biases, and the patterns of relationship in our homes. Indeed there are things we come to believe in our childhood homes that take a lifetime to unlearn. They are the places in which we are wired emotionally and spiritually, for good and ill. Where rewiring is necessary, it is a complex and painful task. Let's be honest: to label home as formative is not to render it eternally positive. Our spiritual formation in the home can be as wounding as it is affirming, as destructive as it is life giving. But formative it is.

As a husband and father, I am ever conscious of this fact. Before having children, I imagined the role I would have in their lives. My responsibility was to be an active agent in the shaping of their minds,

5. Stretton, *Capitalism, Socialism and the Environment*, 183.

character, and faith. For me this was a calling and one I approached with equal parts privilege and trepidation. The day I first held my daughter in my arms was the day of her birth. Indeed, it was the most magnificent and terrifying of days. As I looked down at her, her swathe of red hair still matted from birth, it was as though I understood my life's vocation afresh. Fathering was a sacred trust. I would be her dad, her guide and confidant, and the provider of a home in which she was formed, nurtured, and forever safe.

It's true of course. At our best, we parents are those things and more. Deliberate or not, we are formative agents. As a pastor, I see the consequences played out every day; the gulf is wide between those who have been parented well and those who have not. But what is equally true is that as we shape our children so they shape us. In reality, we make home together and we are all different for it.

I look back on two decades of sharing bathrooms and kitchen tables, arguing over chores and who gets the remote control for the TV, of doors slammed in anger and of lingering hugs, of making beds and folding laundry, of cooking and eating, washing dishes and managing disputes about homework, of post-dinner laughter and storytelling and tears. While churches and cathedrals will always be significant places, they are also places where much of our life is hidden from view. In the home there is no hiding. We are shaped by its daily encounters in ways unequalled elsewhere. It is often said that it's not in the romance of love that we are formed, but in its routines; so in our spirituality. The demand of real and lasting love is that we keep showing up, and it's in our homes that we do so.

A Place of Refuge and Healing

At its best, the home is a place of sanctuary and safe harbor. Like a pair of strong arms that enfold and protect, the home is designed as refuge for those within. As cultural anthropologists have long told us, the human need for personal territory—a sense of boundary and security—is universal. In his classic work *Signs of Our Time,* Jack Solomon defines this need as human rather than cultural. In societies across the world, he argues, the home's doorway constitutes an "absolute territorial marker" that should not be crossed without invitation.[6]

6. Solomon, *Signs of Our Time,* 100.

Solomon gives the example of a nomadic tribe in southwest Africa among whom personal shelter is shunned yet their private sleeping space is marked by two sticks in the ground; crossing the boundary of those sticks without permission is an act of disrespect, even violence. When this human need for personal space is denied or violated, the results are damaging for the individual and for society. The denial of refuge is what can happen in public housing estates and prisons, Solomon contends, where inhabitants "lose their desire or even ability to respect the behavioral codes that govern society at large."[7] The violation of refuge, however, happens more often within the home. As a pastor I have been witness to its tragic consequences more times than I can count. When the sacred trust of personal boundaries are shattered within families, most especially through sexual and physical violence, the scars can last a lifetime.

Once we understand that this need for refuge is hardwired into our spirits, we appreciate more deeply the role of the home to spiritual well-being. It is a need affirmed in the Gospels. In the stories surrounding Jesus' birth we read of Elizabeth, mother of John the Baptist, who, upon conceiving, "remained in seclusion" for five months (Luke 1:24). Once Mary and Elizabeth are united with the news that they are both bearing children of promise, they stayed together in Elizabeth's house for three months, caring for each other (Luke 1:56). On several occasions Jesus entered the private sleeping quarters of a home, intentionally closing out the crowds to bring healing to those within (Matt 8:14; Mark 5:38–43). Jesus' direction to those who pray was to go to their homes, close their doors, and pray in private (Matt 6:6). On many occasions Jesus used the home as a place to be alone with his disciples for the purposes of teaching and renewal (Matt 13:36–52; 17:25; 18:6–35; Mark 9:33–37; 10:10; Luke 10:38–42). What's more, Jesus comforted his disciples by describing a house with many rooms that he would prepare for them, a place of refuge and peace (John 14:1–3). Even as Jesus hung on the cross he expressed concern for his mother by directing John to take Mary home with him to protect and provide for her (John 19:25–27). It is interesting, too, to note the occasions in which Jesus told those he healed to "go home" (Mark 5:19; 8:22–26; Luke 5:25). Rather than commanding that they go and do, go and proclaim, or go into all the world, he simply tells them to return home.

---

7. Ibid., 97.

We people of faith are called to live differently in the world, to challenge boundaries that exclude the exile, distance the foreigner, and ignore the stranger. When others close doors, we are challenged to open them. That said, the need for refuge remains a God-given one. We may live life with open doors, but the doors remain as essential indicators of the place that defines us. If there are no moments in which those doors can be closed, our spirits will struggle to breathe and our households will suffer.

A Place of Community and Mission

Alongside need for personal territory, Solomon identifies the complementary need for shared space. Territorial well-being, he argues, requires a sense of the shared as well as the private, "a feeling of community in neighb0rhood in a space that is neither *mine* nor *yours* but *ours*."[8] Environmental psychologists agree. The home is at its human best, they say, when refuge and community lie together at its heart. Even more, where the home's communal role is ignored, the consequences are significant.

Left unchecked, the need for personal space can turn easily into obsessions with privacy and self-interest. One can see this writ large in my own country. The long-standing fixation we have with bricks and mortar—part of our national creed of home ownership—has developed into an obsession with house prices and property values, interest rates and home renovations. At the same time our fear of the outsider deepens. The cultural critic Fiona Allon argues that the narratives around the domestic home and the national home are connected. In each, we are enamored with our own security and safety, investing our primary energy into the guarding of prosperity and borders. All the while we become increasingly deaf to the needs of those beyond our doors. Allon concludes, "Our obsession with home not only transforms the houses we live in and the cities, places and communities around us, but has profound consequences for how we understand our sense of identity (who we are) and our place in the world (where we belong)."[9]

It was Jesus who persistently challenged the narratives of boundary and exclusion. Seated at dining room tables with the caretakers of these narratives, Jesus told stories of the household of God as an open and inclusive feast to which all are welcomed. Even in the practice of

8. Ibid., 100.

9. Allon, *Renovation Nation,* 3.

Jesus, the home was as much a place of mission as of refuge. There are many occasions when the house where Jesus ministered was so crowded there was barely room to move. We read that "the whole city gathered about the door" (Mark 1:33), and "so many gathered around that there was no longer room for them, not even in front of the door" (Mark 2:2). When meeting with his disciples "a crowd gathered so that he and his disciples were not even able to eat" (Mark 3:20) and when his family came to see him they had to wait outside the house because of the crowd (Matt 12:46–50). As we continue into the Acts of the Apostles the same pattern is evident as people crowded into houses to hear the good news (Acts 10:27; 20:7–12).

Perhaps the spirituality of the home is found in the movement between these two needs: the needs for refuge and community. Certainly the effectiveness of our mission is birthed in the tension between them. I have often said that for all the strategies and programs of mission available to the church, the most effective strategy of all is to set another place at the table. In doing so we acknowledge the home as a place of identity and family and yet one into which others are welcome. For the duration of the meal at least, the stranger is enfolded into our experience of home.

A Place of the Now and the Not Yet

As we explore the picture of home in the Gospels, there are two realities that sit side by side: what we have and what we hope for. In theological terms, it's the kingdom now and the kingdom yet to come. A spirituality of home must hold these two realities in tension. First, Jesus existed in the present. Indeed, he was the presence of God in the most immediate settings and the most human form. Even more, wherever he went Jesus embodied the immediate concerns of God's kingdom. Just as God in the flesh is no momentary convenience but a vital theological truth, so Jesus present in the home is not an aside of circumstance but a tangible demonstration of God's being. In this we are reminded that the concerns of the earthly home are not separate to the concerns of God's kingdom. Rather, they are central to it.

On the other hand, we have Jesus' promise that he goes to prepare a place for us, a house of many rooms. This is the kingdom yet to be, the fullness of heaven still to come. Our resurrection hope refuses to accept the limitations and fragility of our present home as the end of the story.

In Christ we look beyond present circumstances to the promises of God fulfilled beyond the grave and its shadows. The truth is, many of the most intractable human struggles play out in the home. They are struggles not easily fixed.

Not long before the birth of our first child, my beloved and I were in the market for a baby's crib. As students in Los Angeles we had little money and so we scoured the pages of the local paper for second-hand items listed for sale. Finding a crib we were keen to see, we called ahead and arranged a time to drop in. As agreed, we arrived at night to a run-down apartment complex that sat just meters from a feeder road onto a major freeway. Having parked, we made our way up a set of external stairs to an unlighted porch. I knocked several times. Just as we were about to leave, the door opened. A young woman with a little boy on her hip and with badly bruised arms invited us in. It was a small flat of just one room with a sullen young man, the father perhaps, glaring at us from his seat. It may have been resentment at our intrusion or embarrassment at the mess that filled the place. We did our best to communicate, though the young woman's English was limited. Through broken conversation, we learned that they had been evicted from their home a month before. The young man has lost his job, and so they moved into this complex. Struggling to survive, they were forced to sell off what little furniture they had. The distress on the face of the mother matched the tension that filled the space. We left without a crib, leaving what cash we had on the table. As we drove away in silence, I could not help but wonder what that little boy's experience of home would bear in years to come.

Reflecting on the spirituality of the home, the Catholic writer Wendy Wright describes the twin longings of the human journey: one for stability and caring—the longing for home—and another for meaning and ultimacy—the longing for homecoming.[10] Somewhere between these two longings we make our homes and discover the breadth of our calling. At one moment we are called to be fully present in the midst of the pain, the domesticity, the routine, and the joys of the homes we have. In the next we are called to anticipate and reach toward the new and as yet unrealized possibilities. We are always on a journey into the waiting arms of God.

Within this dual calling there is a tension, one in which we discover afresh the depth of our brokenness and the reach of grace. Nowhere is

10. Wright, *Sacred Dwelling*, 21.

this tension more tangible than in the home. For our homes are the places of intimate love alongside the most tortuous pain and failure. In the home we are at our best and worst, the place where we cannot hide from ourselves or the fallibility of those around us. Yet it's here we hear the persistent call of God to keep at it—to keep loving, to keep confessing, to keep forgiving and believing. It is our anticipation of the kingdom yet to come that infuses our present reality with purpose. It's in the integration of Oz and Kansas that we discover the powerful spiritual reality of our homes.

Laundry as a Spiritual Practice

The laundry is never done. A laundry basket never empties completely. No matter how many loads we do, *done* is not a laundry word. There are some things in life that are done. Mostly they are big, momentous things: my work here is done; my schooling is done; our relationship is done. While there are things less momentous—a book can be done; so can a jig-saw—when it comes to life at home, *done* is only ever a provisional word. Done things at home are never really done: taking out the trash, mopping the floor, doing the dishes, mowing the lawn, cleaning the toilet, watering the plants, feeding the fish, or shopping for groceries. Things like these are only ever done for now, until they need doing again.

There is something about a good spiritual practice that defies *done* with the same persistence. I pray today and I will pray tomorrow. Today I confess my sin; tomorrow I will need to confess again. Like the disciplines of frugality and chastity, there is no end to the obligations of laundry. The average household generates eight to ten loads every week. Laundry is not something we get to do once and then move on, as though graduating to a laundry-less existence. Clothes get dirty, socks get smelly, sheets need changing. Laundry is one of the certainties of life. As with all spiritual practices worth their salt, laundry is our work today as it will be tomorrow.

That said, embracing laundry as a practice of spirituality takes some work. Getting beyond the novelty of the idea can be the biggest hurdle. The laundry is simply not where the mind naturally goes in pursuit of God. After all, holy places gleam, like the front rooms of our homes made ready for guests. The laundry is kept behind closed doors. It's the place we hope they don't see. The most profitable spiritual practices, however, are those that throw open the closed doors of our lives and allow light to shine where it's most needed.

The laundry door is one that deserves to be opened, and the practice of washing taken more seriously. There are significant things going on in the laundry; it's a place charged with spiritual possibility. The opportunity to name those things, to bring them to the surface, and to embrace them with intention is ours for the taking. Here are some places to begin.

1. Laundry as a Formative Act

It is the routine of laundry that is likely its greatest gift. According to Kathleen Norris, worship and laundry are the work given for us to do by God.[11] Both are repetitive, she says, mundane, even menial. Lest you think worship is nothing of the sort, take note the next time you are in church. Think first of the great and eternal God to whom this worship is offered, and then of the stilting, off-key, and sometimes humorous forms in which it comes. You would think after centuries of rehearsal we would finally have it right. Not so, for it is a work never done. Yet through our regular investment in it, we are nurtured in God's image. Week by week, year after year, we are formed by it. So, too, with laundry.

As a truly *menial* task—a word derived from the Latin "manor" meaning "to dwell in a household"—laundry is a task of connections and household ties. It's an act of stability, a mark of loyalty, the most basic provision of kindness and service. I wash your feet; I wash your underwear. I serve you and honor you. I will do it today and again tomorrow, load after load. In the process I am formed. My servant spirit, however reluctantly and at times resentfully, is gradually deepened by the doing. I have often noticed that in meetings where refreshments are served, it is the same people over and over who instinctively move to the kitchen sink once the meeting is done. Equally, it is the same people who don't. Domestic acts of service shape our instincts. We are formed in the doing.

It is because we are human, Norris says, that we must find our way to God through the mundane and the daily acts of our lives. "In our life of faith as well as in our most intimate relationships with other people," she writes, "our task is to transform the high romance of conversion, the

---

11. Norris, *The Quotidian Mysteries*, 29.

fervor of religious call, into daily commitment."[12] In this, laundry and worship are one of a kind.

2. Laundry as a Sacramental Act

A sacrament is most broadly defined as an outward sign of an inward grace, like the elements of bread and wine on the church's communion table. Through the ordinariness of wheat and grape, we encounter love in its most extraordinary form. While the officially sanctioned sacraments of the church are a gift to the people of God, the possibility of the sacramental does not end at the church doors. The world is shot through with grace. In acts large and small, we have opportunity to *sign* that grace for others. Laundry can be one of those: a demonstration of unearned favor. We don't deserve to have our laundry done. There is no universal right to clean laundry enshrined in a code of what it means to be human. It is either done for us as an act of grace, or it's an act of grace we gift to others. Either way, Ernest Boyer calls it "a sacrament of care."[13]

When I stand behind the communion table in our sanctuary, I handle things that are, in and of themselves, unremarkable: a loaf of bread; a goblet of grape juice. When we gather as the people of God around that table, we name these elements together as the signs of God's redeeming presence with us. It is in the naming that the unremarkable becomes the ineffable and grace is enfleshed. As you stand over the washing—whether it's in a state-of-the-art machine with multiple cycle options or a plastic tub filled with hot water and soap—you stand before ordinary, soiled elements. Each one has its own story to tell, though perhaps most should be left untold. Each sock, each blouse or shirt is known and submerged. Sometimes there may be words you say:

> *Lord God,*
> *I offer to you the work of my hands,*
> *and the soiled garments of our lives.*
> *May those who receive them washed clean*
> *know the cleansing of your grace.*
> *Amen.*

Your congregation is made up of those who will take and wear them. Occasionally they do so with gratitude, an awareness of the gift that is theirs. Mostly they don't. It's a routine they take for granted as much as

---

12. Ibid., 78.

13. Boyer, *Finding God at Home,* chapter 6.

you do. It is mystery and it is laundry; not all that different to the communion table really.

3. Laundry as a Prayerful Act

"Sometimes when people ask me about my prayer life," says the writer Barbara Brown Taylor, "I describe hanging laundry on the line." For Taylor, each item of clothing she hangs in the sun is like a prayer flag pegged in the open breeze.

> Since I am a compulsive person, I go to some trouble to impose order on the lines of laundry: handkerchiefs first, then jockey shorts, then T-shirts, then jeans. If I sang these clothes, the musical notes they made would lead me in a staccato, downward scale. The socks go all in a row at the end like exclamation points. All day long, as I watch the breeze toss these clothes in the wind, I imagine my prayers spinning away over the tops of the trees. This is good work, this prayer. This is good prayer, this work.[14]

Taylor's practice has in mind the pictures we see from Nepal: small pieces of colored cloth strung in their hundreds along mountain ridges high in the Himalayas. Though the practice has its origins elsewhere, Tibetan Buddhists have made it their own in a particular way. The tradition is that these flags come in sets of five colors arranged from left to right: the blue of sky and space; the white of air and wind; the red of fire; the green of water; and the yellow of earth. Together they call for peace, compassion, strength, and wisdom through all creation. For those who hang them, there is not a strong sense that these prayers are carried to God but are blown by the wind, filling the air with all they hope for.

As Christians, our faith centers more deeply in a particular encounter with God through Jesus Christ, but the longings embodied by these flags resonate. It is an ancient practice of prayer that we name our longings before God, that in time those longings are shaped by God, and in turn, those longings shape our lives and relationships. If a practice like hanging laundry can give form and structure to such prayers, and our prayers be gathered up in our daily work, both are enriched.

14. Taylor, *An Altar in the World*, 46.

5

God at the Table

Like initials carved into an old-school desk, recollections of particular tables are engraved in the mind. One of those is recent. Technically it is of tables plural—three of them pushed together and draped with a sweep of white linen. The venue was a family living room with a vaulted ceiling. At the table's center sat a pedestaled candle surrounded by daphne fresh from the garden. Standing sentry and at discreet distance either side were two tall beeswax tapers earthed in matching candelabra and reaching into the space above. The glow of the candles was complemented by strings of sparkling lights draped from the walls and others cascading down over curtained windows. High-stemmed glassware glistened above silverware laid out around the table's edge, while beautifully folded napkins made flourishes of forest green at perfect intervals. Each place setting was like a personalized invitation to stay a while. It was beautiful.

There were thirteen of us. We gathered to celebrate the significant birthday of our friend Dianne. She is unique, one of a kind, and we had each been touched by her life. A gregarious, intelligent, and no-nonsense sort of person, Dianne has consistently embraced all manner of people. Her circle of friendship is wide, with an unending capacity for more. To be included in such a small group was a privilege and we felt it.

The night's menu was extraordinary. Di knows how to cook. What's more, she and her husband, Paul, are committed to sustainable, ethically and locally sourced produce. They share a farm in central Victoria with a small community of like-minded people. Their fruit comes from the farm's orchard, salad greens from the garden, their milk from Rhonda the cow, and meat from lambs raised on site or the acorn-fed pigs they've invested in down the road. The five-course menu was a mingling of locally sourced ingredients, each dish a story in relationships with the people and places of their lives.

We began with canapés of slow-cooked pulled pork brioche and caramelized onion tarts with feta made from Rhonda's milk supply. Next was a beetroot and goats cheese ravioli, the beetroot pulled out of the garden the day before, the goat cheese and butter sourced from local dairies. Main course featured the slow-cooked shoulder of one of the three lambs raised on the farm that year, along with radicchio and other lettuce greens from the garden. Dianne's husband, Paul, baked the accompanying bread, a sourdough made with grain from a neighbor's wheat crop. Dessert was a beautifully plated trio of rhubarb crumble, walnut tart, and a creamy yogurt panna cotta—rhubarb from the back garden, walnuts fresh from a neighbor's harvest, and homemade yogurt thanks again to Rhonda's generous udder.

To complete the meal we lingered over coffee made from beans supplied by a local café and in a batch roasted specially for the occasion. There were Argentinean shortbreads filled with Dianne's Peruvian cocoa butter, and a generous selection of local cheeses served with Paul's homemade water crackers and quince paste. The farm's bumper harvest of quinces provided an endless supply of pastes, jellies, and curds that filled all our pantries.

It was a most delightful meal and an evening to match. The hospitality of the space, the laughter and sharing of stories, the vigorous discussion of politics and religion, the care and attention to detail in every element of the meal, the embrace of good friends, and the honoring of this one in particular—all this made our makeshift table a remarkable one. As my beloved and I said our reluctant good-byes at the end of the night and made our way out into the darkness, we had a strong sense that the table we had just shared was a holy one. It is certainly hard to forget.

Tables are the furniture of our lives, the four-legged props that sit beneath our days. Not all are as memorable as Dianne's, yet in remarkable meals and ordinary ones, at significant moments and those more common, the table plays host to the rituals of life. Some are epoch-making while most are not, but the accumulated history of these rituals forms life's backdrop; the meals we share are like the compost that feeds the soil in which we're planted. They make us who we are.

As a piece of household furniture, the meal table is an object we share in common. Granted, tables can be as different as the homes we inhabit:

from a small square table constructed from an IKEA flatpak and tucked into a tiny kitchen alcove, to a long and stately family heirloom that sits in its own formal room; from a sturdy, no-fuss 1970s model covered with a faux-wood laminate, to the distressed French provincial picked up at a garage sale by a vigilant aunt. No matter what they look like, no matter how hidden they become under the debris of our lives, these tables are a constant reminder of our identity as families and households.

In the inspiring collection *Kitchen Table Memoirs*, contributors reflect on the tables of their childhood. Writer and comedienne Jean Kitson recalls hers as "the center of everything" and the place where the family stories accumulated, chapter by chapter. It was not just an open book with imprints from all who sat there, she writes, "it was a whole library, a leather-bound, hand-sewn, copperplate record with mug rings and ink stains and spit on the corners and all."[1] The food writer Gemima Cody remembers hers as a sanctuary, "two square metres of civilisation" in what was otherwise a chaotic and challenging world:

> That scored and battered stretch of wood was classroom, courtroom, parliament and temple. It was theatre and restaurant and sometimes zoo. A place where peace was found in the meditative cutting of carrots. Where we learnt the rewards of trusting the unknown by taking a chance on the liver. And where, over a thousand chicken pies, and many more teas, we'd argue the world down to a size and shape that made some sense.[2]

They are significant things, these tables. I suspect it's why we keep persisting with them, why they continue to take center stage in most homes today. Whether or not we sit at them as often as we once did, we still have a strong sense of their importance. Though butter knives and fancy candelabras may have gone the way of grandma's glass-fronted china cabinet, the dining table remains one of the last vestiges of household order and togetherness. When everything else is changing around us we can still set the table, knives to the right and forks to the left. The rituals and gatherings of the family table keep us rooted. We learn so much about life there, who we are and how we belong. The essayist Adam Gopnik describes it as "the one plausible hearth of family life, the raft to ride down the river of our existence, even in the hardest times."[3]

1. Kitson, "The Table," 133.
2. Cody, "Two Square Metres of Civilisation," 182.
3. Gopnik, *The Table Comes First*, 8.

Of course, while our table stories begin in the family home, our lives include multiple tables, each significant in their own right. There are dining room tables and kitchen benches, café tables and picnic rugs, the tables of staff canteens, everyday diners, or those under white linen in fine restaurants. There are the trestle tables of church potlucks and of somber wakes that follow a funeral. There are the lavish tables of wedding feasts and those set festively for the holiday seasons. It is at all these tables that we share life together; and we are different for it. Given its prevalence, the proposition that we might discern God's presence at the table seems almost passé. And yet it is not.

We Christians are people of the table. In almost every tradition a table sits at the center of our life together. Whatever tag we give to its rituals—the Eucharist, Mass, the Lord's Supper, Communion—the table's liturgy of bread and wine forms part of our identity. What we do there gets to the heart of our beliefs. There are few of us who front up to this table without at least a modicum of spiritual expectation. We come, after all, to receive forgiveness, to remember the cost of grace borne by God, to express our community as the body of Christ, and to hear again the call of Jesus, "Follow me!" A good dose of divine anticipation is understandable; as a pastor, I would long for more of it. Yet what expectation of God do we bring to the other tables of our lives? Once the church service is done and the holy bread devoured, what sense of Christ do we expect to know at the lunch table as we eat our chicken sandwiches?

Spiritual expectation is a complicated thing. While we have been schooled to anticipate God at table of the church, other tables seem less divine. In honoring the significance of Communion and investing the church's table with the respect it deserves, we have leaned more toward its role as an altar at which sacrifice is remembered than a table at which dinner is served. Even more, the idea of discerning things eternal at the same table at which we serve the mashed potatoes risks making trivial what we esteem as sacred. And then there are the table-related sins of gluttony, greed, exclusion, and more. Our tables are compromised by human failings that find a particular potency over dinner. Let's be honest; we are not always at our best where bodily appetites are concerned.

The Athenian philosopher Plato certainly viewed life at the table with suspicion and his thought continues to influence. One of the most pivotal figures in the development of Western philosophy, this giant of the third century BC argued that the stomach (appetite) was situated well below the head (reason) and even under the heart (emotion) for good reason. While food might be necessary to physical survival, he concluded, it is irrelevant to the higher concerns of the spirit. For this reason, the human appetite is, at best, to be tolerated and, at worst, wrestled against. Plato's mockery for those who thought otherwise was fierce. "They bend over their tables," he wrote, "like sheep with heads bent over their pasture and eyes over ground, they stuff themselves and copulate, and in their greed for more they kick and butt with hooves and horns of steel, and kill each other because they are not satisfied, as they cannot be while they fill with unrealities a part of themselves which is itself unreal and insatiable."[4] Clearly, eating is more base animal instinct than expression of human virtue. So much for dinner!

Despite this view circulating in his time, Jesus reveled in the table, so much so his critics dismissed him as a glutton and a drunk (Matt 11:19). That Jesus was neither of these underlines the fact that he gave time and energy to sharing meals with people as a matter of priority. To him it was a statement of conviction. Jesus understood that it's at the table that we give tangible expression to our deepest commitments. It is why his enemies judged the table habits of Jesus with such disdain, for in them he embodied values deeply confronting—namely, the radically inclusive grace of God's kingdom. He did this by sharing the table with sinners and outcasts alongside the religious elite. While he was there he told uncomfortable stories that challenged the accepted norms of the table—those that excluded on the basis of religious purity or social caste.

For Jesus, no matter how obsessive your obedience of the law or fastidious your keeping of religious ritual, the real test of relationship with God has to do with where, how, and with whom you eat dinner. So, too, for us. Once we believe that God is as present at the kitchen table as God is at the communion table, the questions of our table life—what we eat, where and how often we eat, how much we eat and, perhaps most importantly, who we eat with—take on a new urgency. When it comes to the pursuit of God, these are no longer interesting asides but key issues to the journey.

If this notion of God at the table is more than platitude, then what specifically do we encounter of God at the table? What of God's character and activity do we know as we sit down to dinner? There is not space here for

---

4. Quoted by Symons, *The Pudding That Took a Thousand Cooks*, 36.

an authoritative list. What I offer are some table-related images of God that help us flesh out this divine table presence.

God as Creator and Provedore

The early chapters of Genesis establish God's primary work as that of creation and providence. God brings life into being and then provides everything necessary for its sustenance (Gen 1:29–30). This is not just God's past work, but God's continuing work today. The petition included in the prayer Jesus taught his followers to pray, "Give us this day our daily bread" (Matt 6:11) is acknowledgement of this fact. As we break bread, be it part of a religious ritual or as we grab another slice for the toaster, we are gathered up in the wonder of God's continuing work. Our pause before eating to say thank you is a daily confession of dependence on a source of life outside of ourselves and work done on our behalf. That said, it is not just the work of God that we encounter at the table. Creating and providing are more than what God does. They are part of God's being: God the creator and God the provedore.

Every Friday morning I get up early for my weekly pilgrimage to the iconic Queen Victoria Market. Dating back to 1867, the "Queen Vic" is central Melbourne's last remaining fresh produce market and sits proudly on the site of the city's original cemetery. It includes sprawling tin sheds home to the retail fruit and vegetable sellers, alongside halls dedicated to an array of delicatessens and vendors of meat, poultry, and seafood. My market provedores are many. There's Bill with his cheeses, dolmades, and yogurts. There's Chung's rickety wooden benches weighed down with seasonal fruits and vegetables. There's Don Jago, a third-generation Queen Vic butcher, with his ordered display of meats that never varies; Judy and her fresh eggs; Joe's poultry and game; and that brisk anonymous woman who supplies the fresh pasta for our Sunday night dinner. As I look at each one standing behind their produce, I see abundance and beauty, honest work, connection between producer and product, and a relationship with customers beyond conveyor belts, cash registers, and plastic cards.

The market itself is open to the elements. It is pungent and often chaotic. As I push my trolley from shed to shed there are puddles to navigate and overflowing garbage bins to avoid. There are no antiseptic aisles here, no piped music to sooth the consumptive spirit. And there in the thick of it are my provedores, rugged up in the winter and perspiring in the summer.

There is something about this that touches on the nature of God's work and being. In the creation story God's creating and providing are one: God creates life and God sustains life. There are no degrees of separation, no progressive movement away from creation on God's part: creator and provedore are bound. What's more, God the provedore is not the God of head office, the anonymous CEO of a global supermarket chain pursuing market dominance. This is God creating, choosing, handling, connecting, and feeding. This is the God of the pantry not of the boardroom, a perspiring God who does not manage supply chains from afar but is present to our lives in every course and every mouthful.

For those in search of God, the God of the table wrenches us back into the present with its pungent odors and cacophony of sound and demands that we pay attention. If it is stillness we are called to, it's stillness in the thick of things. "Be still and know that I am God," the psalmist admonishes (Ps 46:10). As the poet Milton Brasher Cunningham puts it, "Breathe deep. Sit still. Chew slowly."[5]

God as Presence and Mystery

It was on a road trip to Emmaus that the resurrected Jesus spent time with two travelers. Though they shared excitedly the story of one who had been crucified, buried, and whose body was now gone from the grave, they had no clue as to the identity of their companion. It was not until they stopped to share a meal together, when Jesus "took bread, blessed and broke it and gave it to them," that their eyes were opened "and they recognized him" (Luke 24:31). This awareness of Jesus through the breaking of bread and the sharing of meals became the regular experience of early Christians and remains so today. That God, made real in the person of a carpenter from a no-name town called Nazareth, should be experienced in the life of the church through a loaf of bread is an extraordinary truth, yet a truth with pedigree.

For the people of Israel, the presence of God was invoked through an annual cycle of feasts. There was the Festival of Passover and the accompanying Feast of Unleavened Bread, recalling the nation's momentous deliverance from Egypt. There was the Feasts of Weeks (Harvest or

---

5. Brasher-Cunningham, *Keeping the Feast*, 76.

First Fruits), a festival celebrating God's provision in the harvest. And there was the Feast of Booths (Tabernacles) remembering their story as tent dwellers in the wilderness. Typical to feasts in the Ancient Near East were animal sacrifices. This was good news in a time when meat-eating was a rare occurrence; feast and sacrifice went hand in hand. The ritual offering of the choice portions of fat up to one's chosen god was an accepted means of invoking a divine presence. For Israel it was an act of invitation through which the glory of God came down to dwell among the people (Lev 9:24; Judg 6:21; 1 Kgs 18:38). At these feasts God and people sat at table together and so reaffirmed the covenant bonds that bound them as family.

It was not only in the great moments of festival that Israel experienced God's table presence. It was experienced, too, through the daily provision of food in the wilderness (Exod 16), and anticipated in the promise of a land flowing with milk and honey (Num 14:8). In fact, the litmus test of God's presence was the degree to which the people experienced the abundance of the table (Lev 26:3–5). Concurrently, it was the imagery of famine and starvation that painted the perception of God's absence in the most lurid colors (Jer 52:6; Prov 13:25).

While not every meal we share today is one at which we formally invoke God's presence, each is a celebration of that presence and an embodiment of mystery. Each time we spoon potatoes onto the plate, butter the bread, and pour the water, we handle the mysteries of life. What's more, in doing so we hint at an essential truth beyond our comprehension: that all life is dependent on death. It is only in the surrendering of life that life's fullness is realized. We know it in our celebration of the Lord's Supper, yet it is at work in every meal. When we eat a bowl of porridge, devour an eight-ounce sirloin, or sip a glass of orange juice, we enact it: life for life. It is so ordinary, yet mysterious. It is this sense of mystery at the table and of God being with us as we eat that Thomas Howard affirms so beautifully:

> The idea that ordinariness should be thus fraught with heaven, and that a thing like mere eating should open out onto vistas that we thought were the province of religious mystery—it is all too heady. Not that we are transported every time we sit down to our cornflakes, any more than we are struck by Cupid's dart every time we come across our spouse. But the thing that forms from time to time and we are given to see when our vision is roused—that eating is a mysterious thing, or that our spouse is

fairer than Aphrodite—it is there all along, cloaked in the de-mure mantle of ordinariness.[6]

God as *Maître d'* and Servant

For twenty years, my friend George stood sentry at the entrance to the stately dining room of one of Melbourne's most prestigious historic ho-tels. He was a gentleman, short of stature but impeccably dressed, his dark hair slicked back and his moustache perfectly trimmed. His soft Belgian accent matched the tranquility of his presence. Gracious as he was, he was a man in charge.

George was the iconic dining room's *maître d'*, a consummate host whose eye for detail and memory for names were legendary. "Welcome to the Windsor," he would say to each guest as they arrived. His deep and resonant tone conveyed such warmth and certainty that you might have mistakenly assumed he owned the place. If guests had ever graced his dining room before, no matter how many years past, George would greet them by name. After taking their coats, he would show diners to their tables, pull out their chairs, and ensure their comfort for the evening. Throughout the night's service, George watched over every detail, antici-pated needs no one else could know, responded calmly to crises, eased the nerves of anxious members of staff, and ensured his dining room ran like a well-oiled machine.

As a young apprentice chef, I often watched George from a distance. In a room of grand pillars and chandeliers, his ability to make every guest feel at ease—from big spenders and socialites to those intimidated by the space—was extraordinary. Every guest was treated with indiscriminate grace. What's more, George understood his role. Guests arrived with a heightened sense of expectation, a desire to be transported, their vision lifted and their spirits comforted. Every night he was there to make it possible.

A good *maître d'* is a celebrant of ritual. Like a priest who leads her congregation through the movements of the liturgy, a *maître d'* is there to host the table as a place of transformation. Guests are moved progres-sively from the rituals of welcome to those of benediction and everything in between. While rituals may vary from place to place, their presence is universal; and no matter where it's located, the table is ritual's domain.

6. Howard, *Hallowed Be This House,* 66.

In the words of Akiko Busch, the table is a "small acreage of symmetry and ceremony."[7] We need it to be so, for in its rituals we communicate the importance of those who gather and the significance of the time we spend together.

On its own, eating can be a crassly biological affair. With all that chewing and swallowing, the enzymes and the gas, the way the body extracts what it needs and disposes of what's left, it is far from pretty. If this was eating's only purpose, we could just as well swallow a daily regimen of pills and dietary fluids. There is certainly no need for a table. However, our very humanness dictates that eating is more than biology and that tables are essential. For as long as we have inhabited the earth, we have been a people of ceremony. Ritual is part of who we are, for life is made to share and through ritual we live it most effectively.

The God we meet at the table is a *maître d'*, a celebrant of ritual. Alert to the deep human needs for form, tradition, and welcome—the need for ritual that invests life with a shared sense of rhythm and meaning—God provides means through which to celebrate the passages of relationship between God and humankind and between persons. The table is key. Of the voluminous law in the Hebrew Bible, a clear majority applies directly or indirectly to table fellowship and food. It reminds us just how important the table is to the mutuality and good order of society, and to ensuring all are included.

Some of the most compelling passages of the Hebrew Bible describe the work of God as *maître d'* in setting a table for humankind. Having been promised "a land flowing with milk and honey," the people of Israel were enticed with a picture of abundance that must have had them salivating:

> For the Lord your God is bringing you into a good land, a land with flowing streams, with springs and underground waters welling up in valleys and hills, a land of wheat and barley, of vines and fig trees and pomegranates, a land of olive trees and honey, a land where you may eat bread without scarcity, where you will lack nothing, a land whose stones are iron and from whose hills you may mine copper. You shall eat your fill and bless the Lord your God for the good land that he has given you. (Deut 8:7–10)

7. Busch, *Geography of Home,* 60.

Much later the prophet Isaiah anticipates a day when the great *maître d'* of heaven will lay an equally lavish table for all the peoples of the earth:

> On this mountain the Lord of hosts will make for all peoples
> a feast of rich food, a feast of well-matured wines,
> of rich food filled with marrow, of well-matured wines strained clear.
> And he will destroy on this mountain
> the shroud that is cast over all peoples,
> the sheet that is spread over all nations;
> he will swallow up death for ever.
> Then the Lord God will wipe away the tears from all faces,
> and the disgrace of his people he will take away from all the earth,
> for the Lord has spoken. (Isaiah 25.6–8)

What the majority of guests will never see, of course, is the humble work of service that sits just beneath the table's surface. For George and his team, the real work begins long before the guests arrive and will continue long after their departure, much of it invisible and less than glamorous. A good *maître d'* knows that despite his impeccable attire and the beauty of the tables he has laid, his work is first and foremost the work of service.

Just prior to his crucifixion, Jesus shared a table with his disciples. The meal is often referred to as "the last supper." This small group of men gathered in a private room for what turned out to be one of the most somber nights of their lives. The talk was of death and betrayal. According to John's account, it was as the meal was being served that Jesus "got up from the table, took off his outer robe, and tied a towel around himself." It was then "he poured water into a basin and began to wash the disciples' feet" (John 13:4–5). There were few acts of table service as humble, even demeaning, as this one. Peter's horror at the thought of his esteemed teacher doing such a thing was immediate, but Jesus persisted. Even more, he instructed his followers to "do as I have done for you" (John 13:15). It was a moment of commissioning that struck at the heart of the Christian calling: a call to the humility of self-giving.

Days later, the disciples still numb from the tragic events of Jesus' execution and now the baffling prospect of his resurrection, Jesus meets them in the early morning on a stretch of beach, having cooked them breakfast in a makeshift fire. Once again, it's in the context of such an ordinary act of table service that we have one of the most significant

moments of reconciliation and ordination in the Bible. Despite his auda-
cious failings, Peter hears from Jesus the healing words, "Feed my sheep"
(John 21:17).

If God is present to us at the table, God is present in the table's humility and its embodiment of service. It is somewhere in that everyday
humility, we hear God's persistent voice calling us to dine. "Listen! I am
standing at the door knocking; if you hear my voice and open the door, I
will come in to you and eat with you, and you with me." (Rev 3:20)

Cooking as a Spiritual Practice

It's an old school exercise book, "190 ruled pages" it says on the front,
with "nine-millimeter spacing." The cover is tattered from age, a faded
postbox red bound along its edge with a strip of woven tape. At the cover's
center is a box for the owner to insert name and subject. In hand-printed
uppercase letters and blue pen are the words MRS HOLT'S RECIPES.

It was my mother's book. She passed away not long ago. Amidst
the painful business of sorting through her life, my father took it down
from the shelf above the refrigerator. "I don't know who else would want
it," he said as he handed it to me. In truth, my mother had nothing to do
with its original compilation. As a boy of nine or ten, despairing at the
cardboard box stuffed with recipes at the bottom of her pantry, I set about
organizing them. With a set of colored pens and my best artistic flourish,
I created chapters: casseroles; main dishes; large cakes; small cakes, slices,
biscuits, and confectionery; soups; and desserts. Each page was carefully
numbered. Some recipes I handwrote, adding editorial comment here
and there: "this one is good." Most I stuck to the pages with adhesive tape.
Everything found its place and the cardboard box was thrown out.

Of course, my mother's style was never an ordered one. The book
today bulges with recipes randomly placed or stuffed. There are casseroles in the biscuits section and sweet and sour pork in desserts. There
are copious recipes scribbled down at someone else's table, each one a
good idea at the time yet never made. The recipes for curried sausages
and cod casserole—the ones I thought I'd gotten rid of—had reappeared.
Each time I hold the book, cuttings and scraps, even whole pages, fall to
the ground. It is everything she was: overflowing, erratic, generous, and
all-encompassing. I have nothing else as fragile and nothing as robust. It's
like holding a sacred text.

"The keepers of recipes," food historian Michael Symons writes, "are the makers of culture."[8] This is so collectively and individually. When I hold my mother's recipes, I understand better who I am, where I am from and, in part, who I aspire to be. Amidst the pineapple meatballs, the apricot chicken, and the egg and bacon pie with Carnation milk, is part of my story. From the perspective of my spirituality, Mum embodied the ordinary goodness of God for me each day. This tattered old book is testament to her priestly service. In making its recipes, she hunted and gathered on my behalf; she served me and fed me; she connected me routinely with God and those around me. In eating her food I was nourished, enfolded, forgiven, and enriched.

The idea that cooking can be a spiritual practice is not a stretch of the imagination; not if you think about it for any length of time. Only one who doesn't comprehend food's centrality to our lives—physically, culturally, socially, spiritually—could dismiss it as less. Regardless, as with all spiritual practices, to embrace the act of cooking in this way still requires intention and choice on our part.

1. Cooking as Ritual

As any home cook knows, most of what we do in the kitchen is mundane. It's routine and constant. There are some who view cooking as a grand act of flourish and creativity. Usually such people cook only on special occasions when there's a show to be had and an audience to impress. When it comes time for the dishes, they are nowhere to be seen. But most cooking is not like this. It's the day-in, day-out business of making dinner. There is no show and no audience, just a few tired people looking as done as the overcooked chops. Each night's routine is the much the same. The onions are chopped, the potatoes peeled, the carrots and celery diced, and the meat browned. There might be bread to slice, a salad to prepare, or rice to cook. There's the setting of the table with its plates and knives and forks and glasses, and a jug of water. There's the eating with its passing and sharing, its talking and its silences, sometimes its laughter or cross words. And then afterwards there's the clearing away, the washing of dishes, the scrubbing of pans and wiping of benches. It's done for another night.

No doubt, the routines of the kitchen can be drab, but somewhere in all of this is culture at its most raw, its most incremental. The routines

8. Symons, *The Pudding That Took a Thousand Cooks*, 126.

may change subtly as life proceeds, yet somehow there is momentum that continues. "The repeated round of cooks is staggering," Symons says. "Yet this endows human life with rhythm, which gets taken up in ritual, which grows into meaning."[9] Cooks are the keepers of ritual and the makers of meaning. Ritual is all about meaningful repetition. It's about repeating those things that help us remember who we are and whose we are.[10] It is so for the cook. It is so for those who eat and for those who wash the dishes and put the water jug back in the fridge.

Rituals have liturgies. There's the call to worship: the call to turn off the television and come to the table. There's the prayer of thanksgiving: the grace. There's the feast and the conversation, the sermons and reflections. There's the obligatory call and response: "thanks for dinner" and "you're welcome." There's the words of benediction and commissioning: the call to go in peace and do the dishes. But before it all begins, there is this simple prayer that I have used for more years than I can remember. With the day's provisions gathered on the benchtop, it only takes a moment:

> *May this food that you provide*
> *and that I prepare*
> *bring nourishment to our bodies*
> *and renewal to our souls.*
> *Amen.*

2. Cooking as Conversation with the Past

The Australian food writer Jill Dupleix has a sense of food I have long admired. Introducing one of her books, a collection of familiar recipes gathered from the past, she wrote these words:

> There are ghosts in our kitchens. You feel them at your back as you push the onions around in a little oil, when you crush the garlic or when you pull a cake from the oven and feel the heat against your face. These things have been done before, and will be done again: your actions are the actions of the centuries. You can hear them, too, in the whistle of a kettle, the gentle

---

9. Ibid., 32.

10. Brasher-Cunningham, *Keeping the Feast*, 11.

simmering of a stew, the sound of a broom sweeping the floor—the music of the kitchen, over the centuries.[11]

There is something about the preparation of food that ties us with the past. Bob Buford calls it "a conversation between the dead and the living."[12] And it's ongoing. It is as though we are surrounded by a great cloud of witnesses in aprons. Together they cheer us on, correct our mistakes, and remind us that, after all is said and done, it's just dinner. These ghosts, or spirits as we people of faith call them, are present to us in the recipes we use, the cooking implements we prefer, the ingredients we judge to be non-negotiable, and the events that call us together.

There's a recipe in my mother's book that is as telling as it is simple. She titled it "Chicken Casserole a la Jean." Jean was her older sister. As it happens I remember my mother writing it down at Aunty Jean's table. Neither Mum nor Jean was an enthusiastic cook. Life was too full to be distracted by detail, especially in the kitchen. The recipe is brief:

1 chicken pulled to pieces
Fry onions and peppers and champignons
Add 1 tin of celery OR asparagus OR chicken soup
Add to chicken and into oven

I have never made Chicken a la Jean, and I probably never will. But there is something in the spirit of this recipe that hovers over me today. I am a serious cook, more serious and even skilled than my mother was, but I am always conscious of her presence when I cook. "That'll do!" she would always say. When I am prone to make food more important than people, and to give the processes of preparation more time than I give to those who will eat it, I hear her say, "That'll do!" In calling to mind those who have gone before us and listening for their voices in our kitchens, we are choosing to make our cooking a continuous act of service. Ultimately, it is not just about us. It is not even about our recipes or the locally sourced ingredients, no matter how trendy or sustainable. It's about the continuity of love. And in that, it is about God.

3. Cooking as an Act of Confession

It was twenty years ago that I first met the late Father Rick Curry. My beloved and I showed up to a bookshop in Pasadena to hear the one-armed

11. Dupleix, "Ghosts of Kitchens Past," 3.
12. Buford, *Heat,* 25.

Jesuit speak about his book *The Secrets of Jesuit Breadmaking*. His un-expected ordination to priesthood was still a decade away. Content to be a Brother, he founded a school in New York City for disabled actors and the Dog Tag Bakery in Washington, DC to teach wounded veterans a craft. That evening, before a small and mostly unsuspecting crowd of onlookers, he created and kneaded a simple dough while speaking of his passions for bread, justice, and faith.

I was captivated that night, not by Curry's disability or even his skill as a baker, but by his presence. Here in a secular bookshop surrounded by an audience more interested in bread that religion, he spoke easily about his spiritual journey. There was not a hint of awkwardness on his part or discomfort in those who listened. It was as though his breadmaking and faith were a whole, and so naturally part of him. In the introduction to his book, Curry outlined his own daily practice in his making of a loaf:

> When I make bread, I make an Examen of Conscience. After reading the recipe, I take a deep breath, relax, and recall that I am in God's presence. I recall the last twenty-four hours and name the good things that have come into my life, and I thank God for them. After the dough has been mixed and begins to rise, I reflect on how I have participated in this new life, and beg God to show me how I am growing more alive in my spiritual life. I examine what my recent actions, omissions, thoughts, and desires tell me about my relationship to God, to myself and others in God. I examine how I have dealt with my family and coworkers. Have I spent any time in the last twenty-hours do-ing something generous for another? Did I harbor resentment? Have I held my tongue? Have I prayed for another's need? Has my conversation been hurtful? Am I part of the problem or part of the solution? Have I been kind? Have I remembered that God is lovingly watching over me?
>
> When the evaluation is completed, I take what I have learned about myself and place it in God's understanding hands. I bring to Him the larger needs that I feel at the moment. I speak to him as to a friend who delights in my company and under-stands and loves me. I talk to God about my fears, hopes, and joys. I ask God to let me be open to life and love. And when the smell of the fresh-baked bread fills my kitchen, I let my spirit be filled with gratitude and praise for God and for all the things in my life. I thank God for the gift of bread and the gift of life.[13]

---

13. Curry, *The Secrets of Jesuit Breadmaking*, 3–4.

There is something quite beautiful in this, and a reminder that in the routine tasks and ingredients of the kitchen are the most daily pointers to our dependence, our human need, our frailty, and the connections that sustain us. No matter what else our days hold—whatever is glorious and important, hard and defeating, fleeting and trivial—when we cook we are brought back to life at its most rudimentary. We bow our heads and confess again that all of life is gift. *All praise to you, Lord Jesus Christ.*

6

God in the Neighborhood

As I LOOK OUT from my apartment window on the eleventh floor, I see hundreds of other windows into living rooms and bedrooms, each one an entrée into households like my own, yet different. I have not met the people living behind them. In most cases I never will. In my building alone there are more than 120 homes. From where I sit I can see at least five buildings of similar size and density. There are familiar faces. Though we've not long moved in, already we've met Sam next door, Xavier across the hallway, the three affable young men who share the apartment opposite, and Jan at the other end of our floor who moved in with her husband on the building's completion fifteen years ago. He died last year and she is now alone with her parrot James.

Our building has just eleven floors. I say "just" because from where I sit I see apartment buildings that extend more determinedly upward than our own. The iconic Eureka Tower with its ninety-one levels dominates the vista. The height restrictions of our neighborhood require a more modest reach. Living in high rises close to the city's heart is something my family and I have done in various forms for nearly two decades. In Australia, once identified as the most "relentlessly suburban" nation on earth,[1] ours remains an uncommon choice. It is, however, increasingly familiar as patterns of residential life change. For a growing number of citizens, the old aspiration for a three-bedroom home on a quarter-acre block complete with clothesline and lemon tree has entered the realm of mythology. Expectations have shifted, helped along by financial realities, the rapid growth and diversity of population, and the new ascendancy of lifestyle over stability.

1. Goodman, "Comparative Urban and Suburban History," 65.

It is when I am on street level that many of the quirks of high rise living give way to the more pedestrian forms of neighborhood life. Yes, the landscape is different to the suburb of my youth, but what makes a neighborhood a thing of life is the same: there's the network of streets and sidewalks that we share; there are people out walking their dogs or pushing infants in strollers and with whom conversation comes easily; there are others heading out for a run or ducking into the convenience store for milk or cigarettes. A small collection of shops sits opposite our building. It includes an Asian grocery store where I go to get my shirts dry cleaned. The Chinese proprietor asks me the same question each time I go in: "You go for holiday? Where you go for holiday?" No matter what my answer, it leads to his confession that running a small business leaves no room for vacations.

Around the corner is a small café where people sit outdoors with newspapers, smart phones, or a friend. The proprietor there is a quietly spoken man whose coffee-making skills surpass his aptitude for small talk. If I sit outside the café for any length of time I notice two things: the constant movement of people within the neighborhood and the diversity of who we are. According to local government statistics, 65 percent of my neighbors were born outside of Australia. Fifty-one percent speak languages other than English in their homes. We are an eclectic bunch: Chinese, Malaysian, Irish, Indonesian, Kiwi, Japanese, Indian, Korean, Sri Lankan, Singaporean, American, Saudi Arabian, English, and Thai.

Technically our neighborhood is part of South Melbourne, a thoroughly re-gentrified inner-city suburb filled with renovated terraces, art galleries, and organic food stores. More honestly, though, we inhabit our own world. Ours is a thin wedge of a neighborhood. On its eastern edge is a tree-lined boulevard, a major thoroughfare for the city's trams. Beyond that is a vast swathe of parkland where children go to throw Frisbees. The neighborhood's western edge is marked by an eight-lane motorway that provides an exit from the city center to an endless stream of traffic. I often think it's like a fast-moving river that divides us from those who inhabit the real South Melbourne on the other side. To our south is a small wasteland of older, low-rise commercial buildings. It's an odd mixture of brothels, warehouses, and anonymous office blocks with a little sandwich shop tucked in between. To the north things go upmarket as you move closer to the city's heart, including the headquarters of the Melbourne Theatre Company and the Victorian College of the Arts. Sometimes it feels as though we are neither here nor there. We are just in between. But as with all neighborhoods, it is what it is.

Wherever our neighborhoods are, whatever they look like, and however they are defined, they are part and parcel of our everyday lives. We live in them. We make home in them. For many of us, they are communities we enter and exit multiple times each day. In many respects, they are the domestic containers of our lives, the places from which we launch ourselves each morning and retreat back into at night.

My congregation is made up of people from a diversity of neighborhoods. As an historic church at the center of the city, people come to us from near and far: some walk, some drive, others catch the train. They come from sprawling homes on the suburban fringe that open onto acres of bushland, to small city apartments barely large enough for one; from modest family homes in the middle-ring suburbs to council flats or rooming houses on the bay; from small worker's cottages in the inner suburbs to student housing on the northern edge of the business district. What I have discovered is that it's rare to hear a person of faith testify to being called to their neighborhood. True, they may tell stories of God's provision of a home in a particular place, but the language of religious calling is saved for other things. We may feel called to a particular city or country. Some tell of being called to a specific church. Others feel called to a relationship or career track. But very few tell of a call to where they live.

In preparation for an earlier book, I sat down with people of faith from more than sixty households to hear their neighborhood stories.[2] Amongst those there was a handful who did experience a calling to a specific suburb or street. They spoke confidently of God's leading and their continuing sense of vocation as neighbors. They were inspiring stories, but they were not the norm. More often than not, where we live just happens. If we have chosen it, we have done so as a matter of preference, family history, or budget. More commonly, there's a confluence of circumstances that find us in a particular locale for a particular time.

Perhaps it is because of this we struggle to make connections between life in the neighborhood and our spirituality. It's as though the two inhabit different spaces and warrant different responses. One speaks of intention, depth, and self-giving; the other of convenience, circumstance,

---

2. Holt, *God Next Door*.

and personal security. What's more, the sites we most easily associate with spiritual experience are often removed from our neighborhoods. The churches we attend are elsewhere, as are the places we go to for retreat or prayer. In fact, it is unusual today for people to attend church in the same neighborhood in which they live, let alone engage there in acts of mission. The neighborhood is the place to which we return when all of that is done. It's just where we live.

I met David in a state north of my own. We were speakers together at a conference for pastors. He is a gifted presenter, a wonderful storyteller and teacher of the Bible. For two decades he had served as a missionary in Southeast Asia and was now the head of an international organization for mission. He was confident and passionate if a little overbearing. As many of us are, he was better at speaking than listening. We shared dinner one evening and I listened. He told the most amazing stories of movements of the Spirit in different parts of the world and of the extraordinary things he had been able to achieve in his work. As the conversation lulled, I asked, "So where do you live now, David?" He mumbled the name of a suburb in Sydney. It happened to be one I knew quite well. "I have heard there's a growing Karen community there," I said. I knew of the Karen from my work in Melbourne, an ethnic minority group from Burma, many of whom are corralled in camps on the Thai-Burma border. They are migrating in significant numbers to Australia. He looked at me blankly. "We moved there to be close to my wife's parents. I don't know much about it," he concluded. He changed the subject.

The disconnect between David's passion and his neighborhood is not a thing for ridicule. There's a streak of this in all of us. With our spiritual eyes open to the world around us and our focus set on the far horizons of God's call, we fail to see what's right under our noses. Where we are feels too ordinary, too immediate to be of significance in things that matter. God is elsewhere, not here. If the call of Jesus to "follow me" is our passion, we assume we need to have our bags packed. No, the neighborhood is just where I live.

The call to love my neighbor is about as central as it gets to the expression of Christian faith. In fact, it's the most hands-on component of our spirituality. It is also the most difficult. The Desert Fathers, including Symeon sitting on his pole, identified loving one's neighbor as the hardest spiritual work there is. It is not the principle that's difficult, they would say; it's the practice.

In the Gospels, we are told of a conversation Jesus had with an expert in Jewish law (Luke 10:25–37). Keen to test Jesus' orthodoxy, this learned man asked Jesus to explain the pathway to eternal life. Jesus deferred to the questioner's expertise. "What does the law say?" His response was predictable. "You shall love the Lord your God with all your heart, and with all your soul, and with all your strength, and with all your mind," the inquirer answered, "and your neighbor as yourself." Indeed, the coupling of these two commandments was the accepted way to summarize the entire Jewish law, and it was a coupling Jesus backed with enthusiasm. He called them the "two greatest commandments" (Mark 12:31) upon which hang "all the law and the Prophets" (Matt 22:40). "You are right," Jesus responded. "Do this and you will live."

The principle is clear: loving our neighbor is up there with loving God. These two loves are entwined at the heart of our spirituality. But how does it actually work? "So who is my neighbor?" the inquirer asked. To answer, Jesus told a story. It turns out to be one of the most challenging stories in the Bible. We call it the story of the Good Samaritan. It's challenging because it takes a principle that is comfortably universal and plants it in the discomfort of a particular neighborhood. At one moment the commandment to neighbor-love has the pleasant aroma of holiness. At the next moment, it stinks.

The story Jesus tells is of a traveler who is on his way from one place to another when he is set upon by thugs. They beat him, strip him naked, and leave him to die by the side of the road. It's a popular thorough-fare and a steady stream of commuters pass by. The focus of the story is on who stops to help and who doesn't. As it happens, it's the religious insiders—a priest and a Levite—who avoid the man, and an outsider—a man of mixed race despised by the religious elite—who comes to his aid. "Which of these three do you think was a neighbor?" Jesus asked. "The one who showed him mercy," was the inquirer's subdued response. Jesus said, "Then go and do likewise!"

It is the particularity of this story that is so confronting. While there is other religious and cultural stuff going on in this story that we need help to unearth, it's the obvious stuff that smells. In answering the question of how neighbor-love works, Jesus tells a story of people his hearers know in a place they travel all the time. It's real. It's placed. Neighbors can never be abstractions because they are the people who live with us in neighborhoods. We know them. We pass them by every day, sometimes tripping over them in their need. It is certainly true that this story blows away neighborhood boundaries of culture and religion—Jesus' radically inclusive understanding of the kingdom of God is one of the most confronting truths of his ministry—yet the fact remains: for neighbor-love to have credibility, it has to be practiced where we are.

The New Testament scholar James Dunn identifies what he calls "delimiters" to the command to love our neighbors. The first delimiter is place: the neighbor is not everyone but "the person encountered in the course of daily life." The second is focus: the words "as yourself" point to a targeted and active concern that takes us beyond a general principle of love to the particular.[3] The ethicist Oliver O'Donovan makes a similar point. He argues that while Jesus' story is a slap in the face to exclusivism, the danger is that we take the story as an endorsement of an easy universalism. "The universal claim of every human being upon every other is, after all, more an ethical principle than a substantial one. To love everybody in the world equally is to love nobody very much."[4]

The uncomfortable truth is this: this story of Jesus is much more palatable if the identity of the neighbor is kept an abstraction, a universal catch-all for humanity as a whole. Without the neighborhood the neighbor is no threat. But then that slightly odd woman moves in across the street, the dispute over fence lines kicks in with the family on our right, or to our left the surly critic of our yard-keeping skills loses his wife. It is then that our noses pick up the scent and we are faced with a very specific obligation: "You shall love your neighbor as yourself."

We can paint a grim picture of neighborhood relationships today, especially in cities and suburbs. It's easy to do. Neighborhood caricatures abound, those of desolate places filled with small islands of isolation and of neighbors who instinctively pull up the draw bridges to keep the strangers at bay. But it's not true. What I have discovered over the years is that for every person of faith who struggles to name the people who live next door, there are two who move through their neighborhoods with varying degrees of grace. While they may not do so as an intentional expression of their faith, they still do it.

The reality is, neighborhoods today are a mixed bag, as are the levels of connection between neighbors. While there will always be some who keep the boundaries tight, there are others who crave connection. It is as

3. Dunn, *Word Biblical Commentary,* 783.

4. O'Donovan, "The Loss of a Sense of Place," 53–54.

true in a suburban cul-de-sac as it is in a city high-rise or rural town. It is also a fact that certain segments of the population need the neighborhood more than others. If you lack the means of mobility that commonly takes neighbors away from neighborhoods—as it is for the very young, the very old, and those who are physically disabled—neighborhood connections become more important. Often levels of neighborhood cohesion are higher in working-class suburbs, too, than in those of greater financial or educational means. The more social resources we have, the less we need the people next door.

Several years ago, my beloved led a residential institution for young people pursuing tertiary studies. Mary worked in the kitchen. Though she had dropped out of high school before graduating, she loved these students and treated them like her own. Before coming into the kitchen, Mary was a conductor on the city's trams. For two decades she sold onboard tickets to passengers. It was when the ticketing system was automated that she moved to food service. Her husband was Indonesian. They met and married in Bali before beginning their life together in Australia. He was a grave digger at one of the city's regional cemeteries. We knew that neither Mary nor her husband had family of their own. Apart from that, we knew little of Mary's life away from the kitchen.

Tragically, during our time at the college Mary became ill. After a long battle with sickness, she passed away. The entire community grieved her passing and my beloved and I went to the funeral. It was one of the more unusual and moving funerals I've attended. We gathered at the crematorium. There was no celebrant or clergy present, no formal liturgy or music. It was Mary's neighbors who led the funeral. For twenty-five years they shared a street in one of the northern suburbs of Melbourne. Stan from next door was the self-designated master of ceremonies and he handled the event with an understated but definite sense of style. The microphone was passed from neighbor to neighbor as they told stories, laughed, and wept together. It was clear these people loved Mary. As the ceremony meandered on, we recognized this slightly odd community of neighbors as her family.

While a neighborhood will not often function at the depth it did for Mary, the neighborhood remains an important stratum of social connection in the urban and suburban forms of our lives. What's more, it is one critical to the well-being of the wider community. What it needs from us is attention. In his book *The Art of Belonging*, social researcher Hugh Mackay presents a compelling case for this attention-giving in our neighborhoods. "Yes, we're sustained by our communities," he writes, "but they don't have a life of their own: we must nurture them. For communities to survive, we must engage with them and attend to them."[5] In Jesus' story of the Good Samaritan, it is in this attending that we are neighbors. When Sandeep offers to mow the lawns of the single mother of three next door, he is a neighbor. When Pam takes a hot meal to the elderly widower across the road as he recovers from a stroke, she is a neighbor. When Peter and Will offer to host drinks for everyone on their floor to say farewell to Ivy as she moves interstate, they are neighbors.

Certainly when it comes to experiences of community, our neighborhoods don't have today's playing field to themselves. There are multiple means through which we form and sustain relationships. Regardless, proximity and community are connected. Without those bricks-and-mortar neighborhoods of interdependence and relationship, our lives are poorer and, by extension, our cities are poorer too. There are many people of faith who get this, instinctively. They may not be able to articulate their motivations for investing in neighborly relationships, but they do it regardless.

In her Pulitzer Prize-winning book, *Pilgrim at Tinker Creek*, writer Annie Dillard offers an extended exploration of her rural surrounds in a place significant to her story. At the time of writing, Dillard lived by a creek tucked into a valley of Virginia's Blue Ridge Mountains. In captivating prose, Dillard explores the wonder, beauty, and terror of this isolated place, leading her to reflections on, among other things, the nature of solitude, the vocation of writing, and the mysteries of God. Inspired by the words of an unnamed muse, "Seems like we're just set down here, and don't nobody know why," Dillard sets about "to explore the neighborhood, view the landscape, to discover at least *where* it is that we have been so startlingly set down, if we can't learn why."[6]

A critical first step to embracing our neighborhoods as places of the Spirit is seeing them. The gift of a great writer is in her ability to see, and then to name what she sees. And in her seeing, well described, a reader finds truth for his own life. Perhaps the same is true for us. The *why?* of our neighborhood might elude us, and along with it a firm sense

5. Mackay, *The Art of Belonging*, 21.

6. Dillard, *Pilgrim at Tinker Creek*, 2, 12.

of calling, but in the act of seeing the neighborhood—in exploring and knowing it—we may find the seed of something divine takes root.

I met Judy in class. I was teaching a unit in mission for a local seminary, and Judy enrolled. For the most part she sat quietly in the back row, overwhelmed by the "intelligence" of her classmates. When it came to her thinking and writing, it was Judy who left others far behind. A year later Judy asked to meet for coffee. I arrived at the café early and waited. I had in hand the final essay that Judy had written for the class. I hoped for the opportunity to remind her of what an outstanding piece of work it was. As a research essay, it was a thoughtfully argued case for the neighborhood as mission. More personally, it was her neighborhood story, one through which she was able to articulate a theology connected to her life experience.

Judy had been back in Melbourne for just two years. Up until then her life has been a series of postings in far flung parts of the world. Her husband was a banker and they have lived in two Australian cities along with others in the UK, the US, Vietnam, Turkey, and Hong Kong. They were now retired to an apartment on the edge of Melbourne with a glorious view of the city parklands. In her essay, Judy recounted the neighborhoods in which she had lived and the gradual changes that came in her life as a consequence.

In the early years, it was a story of reluctance. "By our second posting in London, I was madly resentful," Judy wrote. "I felt like I was nothing of consequence, simply following along behind my husband. All I wanted to do was go home." At that point Judy described a random encounter in central London with a woman living on the street. "She was homeless. She was my age, my height, even the same color hair," Judy wrote. "Here's me waiting for a bus, carrying multiple shopping bags full of clothes I didn't need and returning to a home and a family, and there she is crouched down on the ground, with nobody. It was like I'd been slapped across the face. How pathetic was my own sense of injustice? I was ashamed."

It was a moment of change for Judy. "It wasn't a dramatic change, more a gradual one, but I began to look at my circumstances differently and to see other people more clearly. . . . At the same time, I remember reading the words of the seventeenth-century Quaker George Fox: 'Walk joyfully on the earth and respond to that of God in every human being.' Somehow it all came together." What followed from this was Judy's decision to embrace wherever she was as a gift and the people around her as opportunities. "Somehow I landed on this idea of being a good neighbor, of being aware of needs around me and doing everything I could to care. As much as I loathe the confession, I had seen it for so long in my own mother there was something instinctive about it." The remainder of Judy's paper was a description of the neighborhoods she called home: from an apartment overlooking Hong Kong's Victoria Harbor to a suburban home in Los Angeles; from a walk-up flat on the third floor in Istanbul to a gated community of villas in Hanoi. In each one, Judy identified three priorities: (i) to find simple ways to connect with those around her; (ii) to respond to whatever needs she saw; and (iii) to live in each place as though it was forever. Woven throughout the essay were significant reflections on the nature of faith, spirituality, and ministry.

Finally Judy rushed through the door of the café apologizing for her lateness. "I am so sorry. I got caught up!" Caught up, it turns out, with a neighbor who likes to talk: "She's just so lonely." We settled in with our coffees and began to discuss Judy's life since the submission of the essay a year earlier. "It was just so eye-opening for me," Judy said as we felt the afternoon sun through the windows. "And liberating." I smiled. "For all those years I had done what I felt was right," Judy continued, "being a good neighbor and a good friend, but with no real sense of its worth to God. It was writing this paper and discovering that my life's role was not just plodding along behind my husband. I had been loving my neighbors all the way through. I had been doing the very thing that Jesus identified as central to ministry. I had been living the gospel." Judy leaned forward in her seat. "Writing that paper was this amazing act of validation. It was bit like hearing God say, 'Well done, Judy!'"

Theologian Sallie McFague tables an important question: "Would it make a difference how we should live if we understood where we live?"[7] Of course, the answer is yes! The *where* and the *how* are connected. Fleshing out the call of God on our lives is not done in abstract. It is done in the places of our lives, the suburbs and neighborhoods in which we live. It is rare that we hear a call and then go to it. Rather, in living we discover it. The *where* of mission precedes the *what* and the *how*.

Just prior to Jesus' story of the Good Samaritan in Luke 10, Jesus sends disciples, seventy of them, into the villages and neighborhoods of the region (Luke 10:1–12). Importantly, they go as strangers, like lambs

---

7. McFague, *Blessed Are the Consumers*, 17.

sent into the territory of wolves; they go without supplies or security. Indeed, they will be the ones vulnerable to the thugs at the side of the road and to the vicissitudes of neighbor relations. They are the ones who must first receive hospitality before they can give it. Neighborhoods are places of mutuality before they are contexts for proclamation. Neighbor love is a relationship, not a program, and one that goes both ways. As a consequence, these disciples will return to their own neighborhoods having experienced what loving one's neighbor looks like from both sides of the fence.

In his book *Missional*, Alan Roxburgh reflects on this story of the seventy sent out in mission. "If you want to discover and discern what God is up to in the world just now," he writes, "stop trying to answer this question from within the walls of your churches. Like strangers in need of hospitality who have left their baggage behind, enter the neighborhoods and communities where you live. Sit at the table of others, and there you may begin to hear what God is doing."[8] This is partly what McFague hints at: in embracing where we live and those who share life with us, we understand better the life to which we are called. Our calling flows from our context. Because of this, it is a distinct possibility that our neighborhoods and our spirituality are more closely aligned than we think.

Walking as a Spiritual Practice

I like to walk. I walk to work. I walk around our local park for exercise, and to local cafés and bookshops. Wherever I can, I walk to meetings and pastoral appointments. Not long ago my beloved downloaded an app to my phone that tells me how many steps I've taken each day, how far I've walked in total, even how many flights of stairs I've climbed. The daily tally of numbers is extraordinary. That said, apart from adding to my sense of virtue in the late evening before I slice off another piece of cheese, I am hard pressed to find a connection between this and the well-being of my spirit. If walking is a spiritual practice, there has to be more to it than this.

In reality, walking is about the slowest form of movement we can imagine. For the philosopher Frédéric Gros, "walking is the best way to go more slowly than any other method that has ever been found."[9]

8. Roxburgh, *Missional*, 134.
9. Gros, *A Philosophy of Walking*, 2.

It is certainly not preferred by the driven or the busy; walking stands resolutely apart from things that propel. Commonly it's the priorities of productivity and efficiency that overrule walking as dead or wasted time. Even the term *pedestrian* reeks of the dull and unmotivated. Regardless, the act of walking remains a very human one. It is an act of the spirit. For as long as human beings have inhabited this earth walking has been an act of longing and aspiration: we have walked to find home; we have walked in spiritual pilgrimage; we have walked to celebrate, to protest, and to commemorate; we have walked as a form of rest and recreation, and in pursuit of better health; we have walked to discover new worlds, to conquer new heights, and even to pray.

Sadly, the commitment to walking is in decline. The head of Australia's Pedestrian Council has said, "While it took human beings a million years to learn how to walk, it's taken only fifty to forget."[10] Cars and boats and planes and trains have all promised, even delivered, a much more speedy arrival, as if arrival is the only good. The worth of walking is found in others things. It is not a practice of productivity, not even of transition, but one of presence.

Jesus walked. He walked his way into people's lives. He walked into deserts and through towns, between villages, and around lakes. He walked up hillsides, down laneways, and across fields. He walked into graveyards and by wells, in neighborhoods, and through temples. He walked alone and with others. He walked to his own death and away from his own grave. He even walked on water. And for what purpose? The writer Barbara Brown Taylor believes it was critical to his impact. Walking gave Jesus time to see things, she writes, "like the milky eyes of a beggar sitting by the side of the road, or the round black eyes of sparrows sitting in their cages at the market."[11] Indeed, if he had moved at a faster pace—on horseback, camel, car, or bus—it might all have been a blur. Instead, he walked.

For me, it's walking in my neighborhood that comes closest to a spiritual practice. It's something I choose to do at night once dinner is sorted and other commitments have been met. It's a routine that brings my day to a quiet end, like a plodding benediction. It's a kind of walking that has no sense of destination and no purpose other than the walking itself; yet there is a sense of place and belonging that comes with it. As a

10. Maunder, "Worth the Walk," 15.

11. Taylor, *An Altar in the World*, 65.

spiritual act, neighborhood walking is many things: it's a routine act of intention; it's a choice to be present; it's an acknowledgement of community and place; and it's a daily stride of contemplation. In all of this, walking is a prime candidate for a spiritual discipline.

To embrace walking as a spiritual practice, most especially where we live, is to engage with the practice routinely and intentionally as one of faith.

1. Walking for Awareness

If we want to see our neighborhoods, to truly inhabit them in the way that Annie Dillard inhabited her precious Tinker Creek, there's nothing like walking them. Walking is an act of awareness, a way of seeing, noticing, and being present to where we live. It's an immediate thing, very here and now. I can't walk my neighborhood and not be present to it. When I walk its streets I feel it and smell it. As I put one foot in front of the other, the neighborhood's contours become my own.

When I drive through my neighborhood, my destination is elsewhere. I am focused on the most efficient way in or out. I don't see it. When I walk my neighborhood I am aware of it. I notice the individual homes, the front doors and windows. I notice the little signs of life and those of struggle. I see the unkempt lawns beside those that are neat. I see the graffiti and the trash cans alongside the mail boxes and garden beds. At night, I can see the flickering glow of televisions through curtained windows and the momentary glimpses of life within. When I walk it, I can no longer ignore this place of mine. I see it as a human place, a place of God.

Writing in the 1930s, the Jewish philosopher and cultural critic Walter Benjamin described his youthful wanderings in the center of Paris. He suggested that to get lost in a city as a failure of navigation is nothing more than ignorance; but to lose oneself in a city "as one gets lost in a forest" is an entirely different matter.

> Then signboards and street names, passers-by, kiosks, or bars must speak to the wanderer like a crackling twig under his feet, like the startling call of a bittern in the distance, like the sudden stillness of a clearing with a lily standing erect at its centre. Paris taught me this art of straying. It fulfilled a dream that had

shown its first traces in the labyrinths on the blotting pages of my school exercise books.[12]

There is something about this "art of straying" that is key to walking in the neighborhood. It's about listening to its sounds, learning to interpret its sights and smells, and better understanding its pulse as a living organism. Such a practice takes time and the routine discipline of walking. It can be done alone or in company. Either way, it is a pathway to awareness.

2. Walking for Belonging

"When you give yourself to places," Rebecca Solnit writes, "they give you yourself back."[13] It is in walking that we give ourselves to our neighborhood. We walk ourselves into its story. By walking its streets and laneways we physically insert ourselves into it over and over again. In return, the neighborhood opens itself up to us and we become more consciously a part of it.

Neighborhoods are not large. In fact, by definition neighborhoods are defined by their proximity. In leading groups of people to think about their neighborhoods, I invite them into a simple exercise. I begin by giving each one a large blank sheet of paper. I then ask them to draw a thumb-sized picture of their own home in the center. It may be a stand-alone house, an apartment block, or something different. Whatever shape it takes, I ask them to represent it on the paper. Next I ask them to map out around it the streets and laneways of the neighborhood. "Imagine you take a walk around the streets that surround your home, just five minutes in each direction," I say, "what streets would you walk? What landmarks, shops, public buildings, or parks would you pass?" Once they have the neighborhood mapped out, I then ask them to identify all of the points of human connection they have on the map. It may be with the neighbor across the street or on the floor below. It might be the person at the corner store from whom you buy milk, the man who walks his dog in the same park, a café proprietor or a teacher at the local school. The only proviso is that the contact is within walking distance and on your map. For each of these connections I ask participants to add a smiley face to

12. Benjamin, *Charles Baudelaire*, 60.

13. Solnit, *Wanderlust*, 13.

the page. Some pages are filled with smiley faces, and others have just a few. Regardless, they are always there.

Walking the neighborhood is a discipline of both noticing and belonging. The more we notice the more we belong. We give ourselves to our neighborhoods when we walk them. We do it again and again, and in time, we find a sense of place and belonging takes root. In Solnit's words:

> Walking is only the beginning of citizenship, but through it the citizen knows his or her city and fellow citizens and truly inhabits the city rather than a small privatized part thereof. Walking the streets is what links up reading the map with living one's life, the personal microcosm with the public macrocosm, it makes sense of the maze all around.[14]

3. Walking for Contemplation

The Swiss philosopher Jean-Jacques Rousseau was a walker. "Never did I think so much, exist so vividly, and experience so much," he wrote in the eighteenth century, "never have I been so much myself . . . as in the journeys I have taken . . . on foot."[15] Sadly, we often think of contemplation as an act of zoning out, of freeing our minds from the constraints of where we are to inhabit a higher plane of zen-like meditation. This was not the case for Rousseau. What's more, it's a misunderstanding of contemplation's gift.

As I have said in a previous chapter, to contemplate is to look deeply into life in order to discern its truth. The life into which we look is the life around us, its objects, contexts, routines, and encounters. We do so assuming that life's sacredness is immediate, not far off. When we walk, we open our minds to this possibility. We are consciously on the lookout for the life and truth of God.

Granted, the neighborhood is not the first place we think of when it comes to "the beauty of holiness" and all things God. Perhaps walking amongst mountains, along rugged coastlines, or down country lanes has more an air of the Spirit. Writers like the nineteenth-century Henry David Thoreau influenced a generation to see the act of walking in the natural world as one of great virtue. Walks in the neighborhood are a harder sell. There are not many neighborhoods in our cities and suburbs

14. Ibid., 176.
15. Ibid., 19.

that allow the natural world to preside. Neighborhoods are constructed places, more full of concrete and asphalt than of grasslands and creek beds. Yet the fact remains, they are the place of our lives. In Mackay's words, our neighborhoods and suburbs are the places "where most poems are written, most cups of sugar borrowed, most flowers grown, most dreams fulfilled, most passions stirred . . . ."[16] As with our homes, neighborhoods are filled with the life we bring to them. Over time we fill them with this life and they become immeasurably more than a random collection of sleeping pods. They play host to the evolving truth of our stories. In walking, we open our ears to hear them.

16. Mackay, *The Art of Belonging*, 17.

7

God on the Sports Field

WHEN FIRST INTRODUCED TO the church of hockey, I was a Philistine. My eleven-year-old son was proselytized by a school friend and conscripted into the local mixed-gender team. Oscar's dad was a hockey devotee and the team's assistant coach; he spoke fluent hockey with an evangelistic zeal. I quickly learned that hockey dads are a breed apart. I was an outsider. They were pleasant enough standing shoulder to shoulder on the sidelines, swapping tales of their own days on the field and bemused by my ignorance: where had I been all this time?

It was a fair question. When it came to this game of bent sticks, shin guards, and those Michelin-men goalies stalking their circles of defense, I really had no idea. I had always imagined hockey as a game played somewhere else, like a distant religion of the sub-continent. News of a thriving, high-profile national body that governs the sport here in Australia was a complete surprise, as was the existence of the State Hockey Center in the suburb next door to my own. Who would have thought?

My son's hockey career spanned four years: training on Wednesday nights and games every Friday. Beset with his father's less-than-impressive sporting abilities, he never soared on the hockey field. He certainly played well—far better than I would have—and over the years his game improved immeasurably. Truth be told, his team was never the strongest in the pack. In four seasons we counted the number of wins on two hands with fingers to spare. The kids didn't mind; they just enjoyed the game.

Watching my son run from one end of the field to the other, his distinctive gait an undisciplined ode to freedom, brought a delight all its own. I spent most of the matches smiling at the team's boundless enthusiasm for the sport and each other. In time I was even bound to my fellow hockey dads as we cheered our kids on together, one ground to the next; shared water bottles and distributed orange segments at halftime; huddled together around an injured player; and rubbished the umpires under our collective breath. Granted, there were nights in the thick of winter when I paced the boundary in my woolen hat, trench coat, and scarf, secretly hoping for a speedy end to the season. Regardless, even on the coldest nights there was a hallowedness in the air: the expanse of green turf; the glow of floodlights standing sentry around the field; the distant echo of sticks clashing; the call and response of players like bird song. Standing at the field's perimeter exhaling clouds of breath into the cold as I cheered my boy, I understood this ninety minutes as different. It was a world entirely of its own.

Across the world, the sports field is one of dreams, an alternate universe at the edges of life into which we escape, commune, and imagine. From the slums of Bangkok to the rural villages of Somalia, from the playing fields of an ivy-league school in America to the dusty school oval of a small town in the Australian outback, children and adults kick, throw, tackle, and run. Wherever they are, these fields are home to aspiration and hope, physical exertion, elation and despair, victory and defeat. For participants and spectators alike, sport is a celebration of the human body, an expression of community, a routine reprieve from life's seriousness and productivity. The sports journalist Howard Cossell popularized the dictum that sport belongs to "the toy department of life."[1] That being so, sport is no less instinctive than our drives to love and to work. Should sport and play not exist, we would need to invent them.

I live in a sport-obsessed city. When it comes to sport, Melburnians lack discrimination. We watch anything and in extraordinary numbers. That said, our passions for cricket (the traditional sport of summer) and our own unique brand of football have an intensity all their own. It's football that paints our city in the most distinctive colors. What began as a league of local suburban teams battling it out for the annual Victorian premiership has morphed into a national competition, the Australian Football League, a business that contributes in excess of 4 billion dollars each year to the Australian economy. Annually AFL games across the country attract some 7.5 million spectators. That's not bad for a country of just twenty-three million people. Donald Horne, one of our best known public intellectuals of the twentieth century, once said that for

1. Cossell and Bonventre, *I Never Played the Game*, 16.

a large segment of the Australian population "sport is life and the rest a shadow."[2]

There are those who argue that this obsession with sport, mirrored in countries across the world, has a religious element. They begin by drawing parallels between spectator sport and religious ritual: the weekly pilgrimage and the religious trinket stands that line the way to the temple; the hallowed turf of the stadium and the symbols of devotion worn by the devout; the unchanging liturgy of the game; the distinctive language of the initiated; the common rites of passage for new converts and the baptism of children into the family of faith; the "heaven" of victory and "hell" of defeat and the near divinity of key players; the family of saints whose names and pictures line the clubroom walls; and the experience of transcendence sought by those who go to worship.[3]

Others identify the "spiritually evocative" elements of sport, those things that lead us to a higher state of consciousness.[4] These might include the physical and mental demands of sport that push the limits of human capacity, the absolute attention that sport demands, and the long-term discipline it requires. Of course, the argument runs deeper than these. It takes us beyond sport's behaviors to what Matthew Klugman calls its "interior." It is where we find the deeper longings that sport taps into, especially in its tribal nature: "a land where the experiences of past events and future hopes and fears sit side-by-side," Klugman writes, "where joys and heartaches are continually anticipated and remembered, where love and hate are so often intertwined."[5] It can be the place where the soul's need for transcendence is met; those moments when, for players and supporters alike, sport encapsulates things deeper and higher than the game itself. An unsuspecting convert to the Australian game, Manfred Jurgenson, recalls such moments:

> There were Saturdays when the game turned into poetry for both the team and the crowd. The ball was recited in a metre of inevitable beauty. For once there was precision, even among supporters. And I went home alone, kicking words, booed by the barracking of dusk. "Not a game," I began, "but old dreams reenacted. In its drama of endeavour, life becomes the ball game

2. Torre and Kirkpatrick, eds., *The Macquarie Dictionary of Australian Quotations*, 367.

3. Alomes, "Australian Football as Secular Religion," 49.

4. Murphy and White, *In the Zone*, 104–13.

5. Klugman, "Emotional Devotees," 216.

it reflected. High marks in the Never-Never. Suddenly meaning depends on a kick twenty metres out dead in front."[6]

In the midst of all this, it is the experience of being lifted from the banality of life, what Allen Guttmann once called an "ecstasis from the mundane," that's often identified among sport's spiritual gifts.[7] The journalist Amanda Smith describes her lifetime association with the city's iconic sporting stadium. "When I walk into the Melbourne Cricket Ground," she writes, "and become encased in that giant circle, the rest of the world can cease to exist. Nothing else seems to matter until the time comes to step outside of the magic circle again." For Smith, the experience of place and sport can be one of the most routinely "transporting" of our lives.[8] In more religious language, David Enticott describes the same experience. Both God and football, he says, "give us the opportunity to be lost in something; to be released from a sense of time; to appreciate the sheer beauty and wonder of life." At its best, Enticott argues, religious faith provides a context in which we can be free of the strictures and moorings of the self and find in God "something larger—a center that underpins."[9] Sport, he says, digs in the same burrow.

The ties between sport and religion named, the business of bringing them into a profitable conversation is fraught. Writing a decade ago in one of America's leading journals of evangelicalism, Mark Galli described the god of the sports field as an enticing but non-demanding one: "he offers splendid moments of transcendence while never demanding that we take up our cross, forgive our enemies, or serve the poor."[10] It is this disjuncture between the demanding convictions of religion, of whatever brand, and the easy obsessions of sport that Australian social commentator Hugh Mackay says limits the conversation: while claiming sport as an act of spiritual devotion might be "a nice idea," it can't be done. Mackay argues that spiritual and sporting impulses pull us in opposite directions: while sport is aggressively competitive—the epitome of the Darwinian struggle for ascendency—religion is committed to the values of humility, harmony, and cooperation; while faith preferences the weak and names

6. Jurgensen, "Highpoint Carlton," 130.

7. Guttmann, *From Ritual to Record*, 157.

8. Smith and Stoney, "The Name of the Game," 26.

9. Enticott, "God and Football," 7.

10. Galli, "The Prodigal Sports Fan."

every being as made in the image of God, sport preferences the strong and identifies winners as inherently superior. While each impulse may have much to say to the human condition, "they have almost nothing to say to each other."[11] In fact, Mackay says, it is in the tension between these impulses where humanity's greatest struggle lies.

When it comes to the world of professional sport, the existence of competing values is hard to deny. The corporate empires that now dominate the sporting landscape magnify the differences. Their drives for cultural dominance, financial gain, and a win-at-all-costs agenda for participating teams make for a harsh and unforgiving environment. What room is left for the Christian values of beauty, inclusion, grace, and redemption? One only has to review the controversies around illegal drug use in professional sport here in Australia or the extraordinary cover-ups attempted by Christian universities in the United States to protect their top athletes from the consequences of sexual violence toward women to see how jarring the comparisons can be. Shirl Hoffman, a leading commentator on sport and religion in North America, underlines the challenge. "Variously described by those inside and outside as narcissistic, materialistic, violent, sensationalist, coarse, racist, sexist, brazen, raunchy, hedonistic, body-destroying, and militaristic," Hoffman writes, "bigtime sports culture lifts up values in sharp contrast with what Christians for centuries have understood as the embodiment of the gospel."[12]

What remains, however, is the deep devotion great swathes of people feel toward particular sporting teams and codes across the globe. Whatever transpires within the business of sport and even among professional athletes, sport continues to harbor narratives powerful in scope and arouse tribal loyalties that run as deep as loyalties can go. In recent months we Australians witnessed, in one unforgettable season of Australian Rules Football, the meteoric rise of the Western Bulldogs from an impossible place on the ladder to winning the 2016 Grand Final. After sixty-two years since its last premiership, the only one in its history, the Bulldogs' extraordinary journey to victory was one of epic proportions and the fervor of Melburnians, especially the team's supporters in the city's working-class western suburbs, was nothing less than religious in scope. In the same year the Chicago Cubs baseball team ended a 108-year drought by winning the 2016 World Series. An estimated five million

---

11. Mackay, *Turning Points*, 235.

12. Hoffman, "Whatever Happened to Play?," 23.

people gathered at Chicago's Grant Park to celebrate the victory, the seventh-largest human gathering in world history. Whatever challenges the relationship between sport and religion presents, there is no doubt there are things going on in sport—devotion, fervor, and belonging—that are important to our humanity and difficult to overplay.

Historically, the church has struggled with sport. Though occasionally it has adopted sport as an evangelistic strategy or an alternative association of "fellowship" for the devout, the church has rarely been free to embrace sport as a good in its own right. Theologian Lincoln Harvey has traced the history of the church's attitude. The one constant, he concludes, is its vacillation: at one moment identifying sport as idolatrous and at the next coopting it as means to a higher end.[13]

The earliest Christians certainly experienced sport as a conundrum to their faith. This was because, in their day, the most popular forms of spectator sport were tied to religious ritual. To understand how deeply this was the case, we need only look at the origins of the Olympic games. In the world of ancient Greece sport was big business, evident in the size of Olympia's sporting stadiums. In 350 BC one was built to hold forty thousand spectators while the neighboring hippodrome for chariot races held up to one hundred thousand people.[14] The games themselves, beginning in the eighth century BC, were held in honor of Zeus, the so-called "Father of gods." They began with just one footrace but grew quickly to include wrestling, boxing, pentathlon, and chariot races. Every fourth year representatives of the various city-states converged on Olympia for a week of festivities. Originally the sporting contests were kept to a single day with the rest given to explicitly religious activities: the first day for opening ceremonies; the third to religious sacrifices; the fourth to the worship of Zeus; and the fifth for a feast to the gods. Indeed, Olympia was known as "the great abattoir" as hundreds of rams and oxen were sacrificed in the festival week. On the penultimate day the game's victors made their way to the temple in grand procession to sing a hymn of praise to Zeus as they received their laurel crowns.[15]

By the time of Jesus, sport, the gymnasium, and the spectacles of the arena remained deeply entrenched in religious and cultural identity. So

---

13. Harvey, *A Brief Theology of Sport*, chapters 1–5.

14. Guttmann, *Sports*, 19.

15. Harvey, *A Brief Theology of Sport*, 13–14.

much so that first-century Christians wrestled with the implications of their new allegiance to Christ for their participation. As they did with the consumption of meat offered to idols, in sport they struggled to discern the reach of their obligations. Come the third century, these dilemmas were eased when Christianity was adopted as the state religion of the Roman empire. Cast as a threat to the church's ascendency, the ancient Olympics were quashed in favor of a new allegiance to the Christian God. Though public sporting events continued, it would be a long time before the church's hierarchy or theology could accommodate sport in any positive light.

Fast forward a century and more, the predecessors to my own corner of the Protestant fold continued to hold sport in suspicion. The Puritans were a serious bunch who saw the frivolity of sport as unbecoming to serious Christian piety. From their perspective, religious life was honest, simple, and sober, with little room for fun. To be fair, their opposition to sport was more than an aversion to good times. They reacted, too, to the cruelty of blood sports prevalent at the time and to the drunkenness and immorality associated with the most popular sporting arenas. Regardless, it was in this milieu that the faith of my Baptist ancestors was nurtured.

John Bunyan (1628–1688) was an influential Baptist who suffered considerably for his faith and whose famed work *Pilgrim's Progress* would become one of the most-read books in the English language. As it happens, Bunyan first heard the call to conversion on the sports field. It was a Sunday and he was engrossed in the team game of tip-cat, a precursor to the modern games of cricket and baseball. It was when he was up to bat that he claimed to hear the voice of Jesus: "Will you leave your sins behind and go to heaven or have your sins and go to hell?" According to Harvey, "the implications were as obvious as the answer was clear."[16] Bunyan walked away from the sports field never to return.

It was not until the eighteenth century that sport saw a glimmer of light in the church. In the great Christian revivals that swept across countries on both sides of the Atlantic, a new theology of pleasure emerged, one that offered sport a lifeline in Christian thinking. Influential preachers like Jonathan Edwards gave new weight to the "affections" in religious life, reclaiming happiness and well-being as part of God's intent for humankind; the pursuit of God and the pursuit of joy were no longer alienated. Flowing from this, sport's physical discipline could be claimed a

16. Ibid., 50.

means to religious development. The burgeoning movement of so-called "muscular Christianity" claimed the body as a "vehicle of virtue" through which one could pursue the disciplines of endurance, self-restraint, fairness, courage, and honor.[17] As Christians began embracing physical activity into the nineteenth century, so movements like the YMCA flourished as did religiously inspired sporting clubs and associations. Newly invigorated by "the manliness of Christ," young men in particular found integration between fitness of the body and the enrichment of the soul. What transpired in many cases, however, was the ultimate demise of spiritual aspirations in favor of a toned physique. It was partly what the church had feared all along: put sport and religion together and ultimately the interests of the soul are subsumed by the more immediate and tantalizing interests of the body.

Of course, there is much more to the story than this, but the briefest review gives us a glimpse into the church's struggle. What is interesting is that despite this vacillation in the church's attitude through history, individual Christians have continued to run, kick, throw, and play as an expression of their humanity and in aid of their well-being. Despite the conundrums, there remains an innate sense among the ordinary people of faith that life on the sports field—a life of recreation and play in whatever forms it comes—has its own reward. While connecting this with spiritual well-being might be challenging, it is certainly possible. Indeed, I believe it is more than possible; it is important for the people of God.

Some years ago, I taught a unit on spirituality at a state university. Rick was one of my students. In his mid-twenties, he was pursuing a postgraduate qualification in psychology. It was his long-term dream to work as a therapist, especially with children suffering trauma. Rick was able to take this unit as part of his elective requirement. In the course of the semester, we read together many of the classics of Christian spirituality as well as exploring resources and traditions external to the church. Rick was a fine student who worked diligently throughout. Nearing the end of the semester, we met together to review plans for his final essay.

In our conversation I learned that Rick lived in a community house with other students and worked twenty-five hours each week in a café to help pay his rent. He also carried a full load of classes, a non-negotiable requirement of his academic program. Even more, he did his best to be in

---

17. Erdozain, "In Praise of Folly."

church every Sunday morning. When I asked him what he did to relax, Rick sat upright as though we had finally gotten to the important stuff. He told me that every Saturday morning he strapped his surf board to the roof of his car and traveled to the coast to surf. "Alone?" I asked. "Yeah, mostly," he said. His eyes danced as he told me of his first surfing lesson from his uncle when he was just twelve years old, and of what it feels like to ride a wave so much bigger than himself. "It's amazing," he continued. "I feel more alive out there than I do anywhere else."

As we kept talking, Rick confessed his confusion around the things he had been learning in the class and his struggle to apply them in his life. His pastor has asked him to run a Saturday morning Bible study series on the spiritual disciplines for the younger people in the church. "It's time to step up, Rick," his pastor had challenged him. "I know this is really important," Rick said to me, looking down at his notebook, "but I would have to give up the surfing trip to do it. I can't do it all." After exploring the options a while longer, Rick finally looked up and said, "To be honest, Simon, saying yes to my pastor's request feels like saying no to my spirit."

To embrace the sports field as a context of God's presence—be it an expanse of ocean, a running track, or a basketball court—we need a theology of play; one that helps us place the recreational activities of our lives within the purposes of God. This broader category of play also reminds us that while not everyone participates in or follows a sporting code, we all engage in activities that are playful: from throwing a Frisbee to a game of chess; from tackling a jigsaw puzzle to playing computer games; from running to surfing. The category is wide; we all play.

The most commonly quoted definition of play is provided by the Dutch historian Johan Huizinga. He proposes play as "a free activity standing quite consciously outside 'ordinary' life as being 'not serious', but at the same time absorbing the player intensely and utterly."[18] This idea that play stands apart from the "serious" stuff of life and absorbs us periodically into another reality is an essential part of its gift. While work takes us toward an end, play is an end in itself.

The truth is, our everyday lives are unrelentingly obligating. Rick knew it. We all know it. The "musts" and "shoulds" of life are part of our productivity. On any given day there are commitments to meet, targets to reach, tasks to complete, and schedules to keep. Amidst all this, play

---

18. Huizinga, *Homo Ludens*, 32.

provides an interval free from obligation. What's more, it is "entirely dispensable" as an activity of life, "the icing on the cake of existence," Hoffman calls it.[19] Frankly, a well-ordered and productive life can proceed without play just as a well-made cake can be presented without frosting. That said, it is this dispensability of play that takes us to its reward, for in it we express desires deeper than obligations can name. "At leisure," Hoffman continues, "released from the crushing demands of daily life, the Christian has a few moments of freedom to shed the camouflage of natural man, to polish up the *imago Dei*, to regain spiritual balance, and to recover a sense of who he or she really is."[20] Perhaps this is what Rick experienced when he surfed, what he described as an experience of being "more alive" than he was in other parts of his life. It was on the waves that his spiritual center of gravity was restored.

In a similar vein, theologian Lincoln Harvey positions play as a "radically unnecessary" part of our lives, yet one that is "deeply meaningful."[21] For Harvey, it is this "unnecessary" and "meaningful" dynamic in play that takes us to the heart of God's grace. Creation is an act of freedom on God's part. God has no need of anything or anyone outside of God's self, yet God chooses to engage in the playful act of creation for the sake of love: "The Christian doctrine of creation allows us to understand that our being . . . is best described as the unnecessary-yet-meaningful reality of being freely loved into existence in Jesus Christ." This would suggest, Harvey argues, that when we are at play "we are living out our deepest identity as unnecessary but meaningful creatures."[22]

What all this points to, of course, is the worth of sport to our spirituality is far more than its instrumentality. That is, it is more than what it leads to or makes possible. In fact, if we only ever applaud sport as a means to an end—be that evangelism, physical fitness, or character development—its reach is seriously diminished along with our spiritual imagination. As Hoffman says, justifying sport instrumentally is as misguided "as trying to justify symphony orchestras on grounds that they develop endurance in the muscles of violin players."[23] We simply miss the point: "Just like art, dance, and music, athletic experiences can be spontaneous

19. Hoffman, *Good Game*, 265.

20. Ibid., 266.

21. Harvey, *A Brief Theology of Sport*, 69.

22. Ibid., 83–84.

23. Hoffman, *Good Game*, 267–68.

outpourings of inward spiritual feelings that reach their highest religious potential as offerings rather than as agents of something else."[24]

My son's hockey days are well and truly over. He has graduated to other things, pursuits that draw similarly on his needs for physical challenge, camaraderie, and playfulness. As he and I traverse our neighborhood, we are reminded routinely of sport's centrality to life. Its fields, stadiums, courts, and tracks are all around us. There are those who run the perimeter of the city's parklands, those who ride bikes along the river's edge, while others row its length competitively. There are those who swim laps at the aquatic center, play soccer at the community park, hit tennis balls on the local courts, or run marathons through the city streets. Countless others make routine pilgrimage to stadiums and fields across the suburbs to watch others compete.

Sport is part of life. It is the life of the body in its most visceral form. Some 60 percent of people in my own country participate in it each year, while 28 percent are involved regularly in organized sporting clubs and games. There are certainly as many people, if not more, playing on sports fields each year as there are sitting in churches. The amount of energy invested in sports, the coverage given to it in all forms of media, and the amount of money invested in it, all point to its continuing priority in our lives. Certainly its dangers are real: its potential for emotional and physical abuse; its crass commercialism; the glorification of violence; its fiercely competitive spirit; and its bent to idolatry. When it comes to spirituality, all of these call for caution. That said, we remain embodied people and our participation in sport, as participants and spectators, touches life at its most physical.

Perhaps it is this bodily aspect of sport that has made the church so resistant to it as an expression of spirituality. Though old divisions that render the flesh less dignified are rejected in our theology, they are alive and well in our practice. In his provocative book *To a Dancing God*, philosopher Sam Keen argues that while we may have rejected the idea of the human person as "a mind to which a body was accidentally attached," our dismissal of the body remains deeply embedded in our visions of the spiritual life.[25] It is when we go looking for God at the sports field that this dismissal is most troubling. Body, mind, soul, and spirit are one. In every

24. Ibid., 271.
25. Keen, *To a Dancing God*, 46.

expression of who we are, God is richly present. That God inhabits the sports field as much as God inhabits every other sphere of life is a truth we can depend on.

Play as a Spiritual Practice

According to the prophet Zechariah, the great city of God is one where "old men and old women" sit together on the sidewalks watching "boys and girls playing in its streets" (Zech 8:4–5). There is something about the free play of children that conveys life at its most harmonious. Images of children playing amidst the rubble of cities torn apart by war are images of hope; life goes on. Certainly, one of the great delights of my life is to watch a child play.

I recall watching my son play alone in the backyard sandpit when he was a child. His rich imaginary world and his dedication to careful construction came together in his tunnels and towers of sand. I remember, too, watching my daughter play games with friends at the local playground, her lifelong preference for people management to the fore. At the same time she learned the painful art of compromise in favor of a shared world of imaginary scenarios. Though with different personalities, both children were completely consumed by their world of play. Observing such children, educator Micheline Wyn Moriarty concludes that the worlds they inhabit are those of "wonder and delight for their own sake" and in which they develop "inner spiritual resources" and "forge connections" with the earth and each other.[26]

There is something in this that sounds like the beginnings of a spiritual practice, no matter what our age or stage of life. It is in play that various truths are affirmed, values cemented, and discoveries made. It is in playfulness that we discern afresh God's creativity, beauty, laughter, and delight. In what ways, then, can we embrace play as an intentional spiritual practice, one that leads us deeper into the way of Jesus? There are many possibilities, but I begin with those that follow.

26. Moriarty, "Sport and Children's Spirituality," 106–7.

1. Play as an Act of Pleasure

Jesuit theologian Hugo Rahner describes play as our participation in the divine, "a way in which our spirits return home to God."[27] In play, he says, we take the inviting hands of God and together we dance. It is a dance of pure pleasure, one entirely without purpose other than the dance itself: "In play, earthly realities become, of a sudden, things of the transient moment, presently left behind, then disposed of and buried in the past." In play "the mind is prepared to accept the unimagined and incredible."[28]

There is something of this pleasure with God that is embodied uniquely in play. It is a pleasure captured in the Douay translation of Psalm 8, an English version of the Vulgate dating back to the 1500s:

> The Lord possessed me in the beginning of his ways, before he made anything from the beginning. I was set up from eternity, and of old before the earth was made . . . I was with him forming all things: and was delighted every day, playing before him at all times; playing in the world. And my delights were to be with the children of men. (Ps 8:22–23, 30–31)[29]

This idea of playing in the presence and pleasure of God was very much in the mind of the Scottish athlete Eric Liddell, whose run in the 1924 Summer Olympics was celebrated in the 1981 Oscar-winning film *Chariots of Fire.* Molded by a dour Presbyterian faith, his sister was concerned that the trivial pursuits of running would lead him away from the mission of the church. "God made me fast, Jenny," Liddell responded reassuringly, "and when I run I feel God's pleasure."[30] It is this sense of pleasure in play that I hear people name routinely. First, of course, it is their own pleasure but, when prodded to take it further, it becomes a window into the pleasure of God. It is there on the hockey field and in the quilting circle; on the running track or the tennis court; in the spectator stands at the football stadium and the walking track through bushlands; in the children's sandpit and the dance hall. In all of this is the opportunity to play before God, to rediscover the exuberance of what is unnecessary yet truly life-giving.

27. Rahner, *Man at Play,* 12.

28. Ibid., 65–66.

29. Quoted by Huizinga, *Homo Ludens,* 239–40.

30. For a fuller account of the story, see Preece, "'When I Run I Feel God's Pleasure,'" 25–26.

Isabell swims. With a squad, she trains three mornings each week at the Melbourne Aquatic Centre. On Saturdays she swims alone and for much longer. I serve as a supervisor in her training for hospital chaplaincy and we meet routinely. Recently, we sat together on the banks of the river that winds its way through the city center, and Isabelle described the role swimming plays in her life. She called it a meditative act. Lap after lap, she said, her body and mind move in sync with each other: "There has always been something about it that calms me. When I swim I feel my body as so much a part of me, like an extension of my spirit." Isabell told me of the prayer that has become part of her Saturday morning ritual in the pool. As she touches the wall and turns at one end of her lane she says, "This body is your gift to me, O Lord" and touching the wall at the opposite end, "I receive it with thanks." As we watched a solitary rower pass by on the river below, Isabelle reflected on ways swimming blends with her spirituality. "The pleasure of it goes far deeper than the outcomes," she said. "It's not so much about speed or fitness or anything like that. It's more to do with a deeper well-being that I feel in the pool, a peace of mind that envelopes me. It's a beautiful thing. I can't imagine life without it."

2. Play as an Act of Surrender

At its best, a spiritual practice is a routine means by which we offer our lives to God and open ourselves to the transforming work of God's Spirit. We do so in our regular reading of the Bible, Sunday worship, habits of prayer and meditation, and even in periodic commitments to fasting or silence. Of course, the concurrent danger of practices like these is that they become works of righteousness, means through which we seek to prove our spiritual mettle or justify ourselves as worthy of God's acceptance: if only I pray longer, confess more tearfully, or fast more stringently, then I might graduate to a higher level of perfection. How easy it is to fall into what John Coe calls "the temptation of moral formation," seeking growth in our own power, purity, or achievement. [31]

There is a particular danger of this in embracing physical exercise or training as a spiritual discipline. As you watch a young man in a gymnasium lift weights in front of a full-length mirror, interrogating his every move and muscle in the reflection he sees, the dangers become clear. If all

---

31. Coe, "Resisting the Temptation of Moral Formation."

we can see in the reflection is ourselves—our successes and our failings in bold relief—then our spirituality becomes an obsession of self-interest. Worse still, we miss the true gift of being gathered up in the beauty, goodness, and grace of God.

It is here that play as a spiritual practice shows its worth, for play is an act of freedom not obligation, one of delight not seriousness. The French sociologist Roger Caillois calls it "an occasion of pure waste."[32] As such, play allows pleasure to come to the fore. As in the pursuit of music and art, so through the playfulness of life we give expression to freedom and allow laughter and pleasure their place. "Unmitigated seriousness betokens a lack of virtue," Thomas Aquinas once said, "because it wholly despises play, which is as necessary for the good human life as rest is."[33] A regular commitment to play has the potential to heal and release us from what Rahner identifies as our "idiotic earnestness" and "senseless preoccupation with the things of this world."[34]

To embrace play as a spiritual practice is to be reminded of just how ridiculous our own self-justifying efforts are, as serious as they may be. The truth is, spiritual practices were never intended as means to salvation, but, as Michael Austin has said, as a way of "opening ourselves up to God and his transformative power."[35] In acts of play we surrender ourselves to the foolishness of grace.

3. Play as an Act of Reclamation

If we were to stand in a field together and you threw a ball or a Frisbee for me to catch, I would be an awkward recipient. Though I am now a man in my fifties, the prospect of shame associated with the childhood business of throwing and catching lingers. I may be able to name that fear for what it is and the toothless beast it always was, but my awkwardness at the sight of a ball has not budged.

Like many children, my memories of games in the schoolyard are filled with associations of inadequacy. I always preferred the library. The only physical activity I did not loathe was in the swimming pool, and then with only moderate levels of success. I learned early to mistrust my

32. Caillois, *Man, Play, and Games,* 5.

33. Quoted by Rahner, *Man at Play,* 2.

34. Ibid., 2.

35. Austin, "Sports as Exercises in Spiritual Formation," 75.

body, to wish that I was built differently, to judge it as weak and deficient. I learned, too, that games are rarely separate from competition and the drive to win among those who naturally excel. If my body is in possession of a competitive bone, I have not discovered it yet. What's more, the competiveness of others leaves me mystified and intimidated.

I was well into my twenties when I first tasted play untouched by competition or the ascendancy of winners. I was a young pastor-in-training and posted to a small congregation in rural Queensland. The church building was a small wooden chapel that stood alone in a field far from the nearest town. There was not a street light to be seen. After an evening service one Sunday, the congregation dispersed into the night. The last to leave, I turned out the lights and locked the main door of the chapel behind me. As I walked out in the surrounding field that served as the church parking lot, the only light came from the moon above. Standing by my car was a small group of young people, just five of them. As I came closer I could see one was holding what looked like a basketball, though it was difficult to make out. "Ever played dark ball?" one of them asked. "Um, no!" I said. That familiar sense of dread was immediate. "C'mon then!" With that one of the young women grabbed my arm and pulled me out into the center of the field. I could not see the others but I could hear their voices. "What do we do?" I called out. "You don't want to get hit by the ball," one said excitedly. "Just try and catch it so you can hit someone else with it." "But I can't see anything. It's too dark!" "That's the point!" the young woman exclaimed as the ball suddenly appeared between us. For the next thirty minutes, we ran and threw and dodged and tripped over ourselves and each other. All we could hear were our shrieks of laughter, and the constant cry, "I can't find it!"

The most liberating thing of that night's play was that no one could see me. No one could see my lack of coordination or my clumsiness. There was just uproarious laughter as we tripped and fell into tangled heaps on the ground. I had not laughed so hard or moved so fast in all of my life. And it was glorious! No competition, no judgement, no fear, no glaring inadequacy for all to see. It was just fun, the most wonderful and uninhibited fun. I drove home that night exhilarated, feeling alive in a way I had rarely experienced before.

The very word *play* implies something free and liberating. Whether it's on a sports field or a stage, on a basketball court or sitting at a board game, the designation *play* reminds us that we are embodied people. The reclamation of our bodies and the playfulness inherent to them is a practice as freeing as it is routine.

Theologian Stephanie Paulsell writes of her own adult rediscovery of running. Like me, she recalls with ease the humiliations of the school yard and the taunts of other children mocking her flailing arms on the running track. For years she avoided running and its shame and assumed her body to be a thing best hidden. Even in the early days of relationship with her husband-to-be, himself a seasoned runner, she managed to send him off on his own. It was only when he insisted that she join him that Paulsell was faced with a choice. Committed to her new relationship, she ventured tentatively onto the pavement. Gradually, emboldened by his belief in her, Paulsell decided to leave her past narrative behind and to feel her body again. It was her spiritual awakening.

> I sprinted down the last half of the track, Kevin matching me stride for stride, and felt in every muscle the pleasure of exertion, of pushing my body beyond its boundaries. It was a physical pleasure, the pleasure of feeling myself wholly embodied, of feeling blood and breath moving through me. It was a spiritual pleasure, the relief of feeling old fears and inhibitions drained of their power, a feeling of freedom and possibility. And it was a sexual pleasure, the pleasure of feeling someone I love drawing out my strength, urging me on, matching his body rhythm to mine. It is one of my husband's enduring gifts to me that he reintroduced me to the joy of bodily exertion. Through honoring my body and its strength, he helped me begin to do the same.[36]

There is something about play embraced as a spiritual practice that enables us to reclaim our bodies as temples of the Spirit and of God's abundant creativity; to reclaim God's gifts of pleasure through the sun on our backs, the air in our lungs, or the consuming focus of games into which we disappear for intervals of time. Like birdsong that has no purpose other than the simple pleasure of sound, or flowers that fill a garden with nothing but color, play is a reclamation of all that is spare and surplus to life. It is the reclamation of grace.

---

36. Paulsell, *Honoring the Body*, 116.

8

God at the Supermarket

I MET JESUS IN the supermarket. He was in the fresh produce department at HEB restocking the onions. I didn't notice him at first. I was consumed with picking over the tomatoes when two fell to the ground. Just as I was about to collect them, he appeared beside me. "I'll get those for you, sir," he said. As he stood again, tomatoes in hand, I saw his name tag, *JESUS,* with the store's motto underneath: *because people matter.* He was a quietly spoken young man with olive skin and an accent that betrayed his roots elsewhere.

This was central Texas. We were staying with my beloved's family in Belton, a town bordered by the Leon and Lampasas rivers with the Interstate 35 running through its center. The Hispanic community makes up one-quarter of the county's population. As I received my tomatoes, my eyes lingered on the nametag and then on the young man's eyes. "Thank you," I said. "You're welcome," Jesus replied with a shy smile, and returned to his onions.

I never met Jesus again. Our stay in Texas was brief, and, to be honest, I preferred the Albertsons further up the highway. But I'll never forget our encounter and the slightly odd but intriguing idea that Jesus worked at HEB. Directly opposite the supermarket stood the First Baptist Church of Belton, the largest church in town, their grand buildings crowned with spire and bell tower. Though we attended services every Sunday of our stay, I never saw Jesus there. He was across the road working weekend shifts for minimum wage.

No matter where we live in western societies, supermarkets are a given. So much so, they've become part of the taken-for-granted landscape of our lives. From where I live, I can access five major supermarkets within

114

a five-minute drive from my home. Here in Australia, population twenty-three million, there are 4,500 supermarkets in operation with an annual turnover of $89.5 billion.[1] Fifteen million of us visit them every week. In fact, we do so an average of three times a week or 135 times every year.[2] In the US, population 319 million, the numbers multiply. There supermarkets number in excess of 38,000 with an annual turnover of more than $668 billion.[3]

While other options exist for keeping our pantries stocked, supermarkets account for over 90 percent of our grocery spending.[4] Despite the rise in farmers' markets and, in some places, the re-emergence of specialty food stores, it's still the supermarket that rules in the sourcing of food. As with anything so pervasive in our lives, the relationship to supermarkets is one of alternating love and resentment. We love the convenience and choice they embody; the carnivalesque display of colors and goods from across the world in easy reach. We loathe their mundanity, the trolley wheels that never work, the queues, the crowds, the impersonal service, and that interminable muzak. In his study of the supermarket's place in our lives, the sociologist Kim Humphrey describes it as straddling a divide between "consumption as fantasy and consumption as necessity." In wandering its aisles, he says, we enter "a continuum between enjoyment and tedium, contentment and anger."[5]

Perhaps it is the pervasiveness of the supermarket that renders the idea of Jesus being there an awkward one. In a place so intimate to the mundane appetites of our bodies, it seems crass to imagine a divine presence. To be honest, I am not even sure we want to. For many years now I have been teaching a class titled *Table Spirituality: Hospitality, Community and Mission*. In one session I send students in small groups to the local supermarket for an hour's reconnaissance. Armed with a list of prompts, their task is to look for evidences of God. Almost uniformly, students are bemused. Though some might be intrigued that this task is included in a curriculum for spirituality, most are bewildered, even irritated by the assignment. How on earth can this be relevant? What I ask them to do is quite simple: to pay attention; to notice what they usually

1. Nagaratman, "Supermarkets Sweep," 1.

2. Langley and Hogan, "Research Survey Reveals More Australian Grocery Shopping Habits," 2.

3. Food Marketing Institute, "Supermarket Facts 2015," 1.

4. Langley and Hogan, "Research Survey," 2.

5. Humphrey, *Shelf Life*, 143.

don't see; and to ask questions of this context they normally reserve for more "spiritual" places.

As pervasive as the supermarket is today, it has not always been so. In fact, it's a recent invention. The modern supermarket made its first appearance in the United States as late as the 1950s while Australian supermarkets followed suit in the sixties. To understand their advent, we need to go back further.

The word *shop* has a long history in both its English and Germanic forms. For centuries it described a lean-to, booth, stall, or porch attached to a building made for another purpose. For much of history the shops we know today simply didn't exist. The trading of particular goods and services happened most commonly from homes or outdoor marketplaces. In this context, to go shopping was simply to secure from a neighbor or fellow villager a staple one couldn't provide alone. Most household needs were met internally. The word *shopping* first appeared in English in the middle of the eighteenth century, with another hundred years before the word *shopper* emerged. It was in the early 1800s when London's Burlington Arcade was opened to great fanfare that the first purpose-built shop appeared, a space that had no other end than the display and sale of particular goods. It was the precursor to the shopping malls of today. Suddenly shopping appeared as a fashionable past time for the wealthy, those who could parade their social standing and peruse luxury goods in a public yet secure place. From here shopping as both leisure and aspiration took off. The nineteenth and twentieth centuries saw arcades and department stores thrive as the growing middle classes shopped their way to respectability.

Shopping as a domestic chore was another business entirely. In the forms we understand, its beginning was spurred by industrialization—the movement from agrarian to industrial economies—which took root from the mid-eighteenth century and progressed full steam in the two centuries to follow. For much of history, the primary task of the home-maker was to produce, prepare, and organize all that was necessary to feed, clothe, and house a family. Much of this fell to the woman of the home and the majority of a household's needs she met in-house. With the advent of industrialization and the rapid urbanization that accompanied it, the lion's share of this activity was taken over by large-scale producers and their factories. Between 1880 and 1930, historian Charles McGovern observes, Americans came to a new dependence "on the commercial marketplace, with few feasible alternatives, for the necessities of daily life."[6] Increasingly, it was the duty of the "housewife" to shop for most of the goods her family required, and to do so with as much thrift and prudence as she could manage.

For the most part, this domestic shopping was centered on the local grocer who sourced a selection of goods—bottled, canned, packaged, and fresh—and sold them on to his captive constituency. With transport non-existent for the majority, daily trips to the corner grocer or local market were standard. Small businesses operated in small spaces and there was a limit to what could be stocked, but relationships were key and attentive service part of the exchange. In the latter part of the nineteenth century, pre-orders with local grocers were encouraged and home-delivery options emerged. The early twentieth century saw chain operators begin to flourish, offering larger spaces and greater levels of choice. Still, the typical grocery store of the 1940s had two counters, one for groceries and one for provisions, with an array of shelving and ladders behind them to which only the grocer had access.

It was not until the end of the world wars that the concept of self-service finally took root. The combination of war and economic depression had schooled a population in the virtues of thrift. Fueled by the mass production of standardized and relatively inexpensive goods, systems of nationwide distribution, and the flourishing of brand-name advertising, consumers' expectations and patterns of consumption changed rapidly. With the flourishing of suburbs far from city centers and increasing access to personal forms of transportation, new forms of shopping found fertile ground. As historian Beverly Kingston notes, the architects of the new large-format self-service store had a clear brief:

> Plenty of parking, a square plan for the layout, enough checkouts and a system whereby customers could have their purchases conveyed to the car park by conveyor belt or where all doors were operated by a magic eye were considered essential. Wire trolleys soon replaced baskets for shopping 'the easy way'. Besides, they carried more with less effort. The customer was encouraged to collect her trolley at the entrance and really stock up for the home shelves.[7]

6. McGovern, *Sold American*, 10.

7. Kingston, *Basket, Bag and Trolley*, 87.

So began the modern supermarket. Its growth as the favored venue for grocery shopping was rapid. The form came to represent all that was modern about a technologically advanced society; and modern it was. It was 1963 when my home suburb of Dandenong saw the opening of its brand new Coles New World supermarket, boasting a retail space of 10,000 square feet (930 square meters) surrounded by parking for three hundred cars. I was just an infant and my parents new arrivals in the neighborhood, but the local press reported on the expectation that filled the suburb. This stand-alone temple to modernity stood proudly on the rise out of the main street, the words *A NEW WORLD OF SHOPPING* arced over a piece of the earth's surface rising over the roofline. The best thing was the life-sized rocket ship standing launch-ready on the rooftop. Opening day was chaos as local housewives flocked through the doors for one of the most exciting days our suburb had known. As the years went by, I was enamored by that rocket ship pointing skyward, so much so I barely noticed the twin flags of nation and empire unfurled on poles in the foreground. The supermarket was our future.

Fifty years on, our infatuation with the big-box supermarket has dulled but only as our dependence on it has set like concrete. The truth is, what began as the sign of a new dawn in domestic shopping has become the yawning norm to the near death of anything different. While residents of the inner city might still relish their fresh produce markets and independent organic grocers, the outlying suburbs and new housing estates know few alternatives to the supermarket monopolies. Their mushrooming megastores, morphing from an average floor space of 1,700 square meters to the preferred 3,000 square meters (or 33,000 square feet), are now part and parcel of our lives. The question of how we connect with the Spirit in them is fraught, yet their pervasiveness urges that we do.

A good place to begin is to table the challenges presented by the modern supermarket, challenges that press in on our values and commitments as people of faith. There are many of them. I name just three.

Eradicating the Local

The supermarkets of today are predatory beasts. Indeed, they have been that way from the beginning. Their success in a particular location depends heavily on dominating the market and eradicating opposition. While competition between the big-name retailers is intense, it is the smaller local businesses that fall prey to whatever brand of large-scale supermarket appears. On a number of levels—price, size, convenience, brand recognition—they simply cannot compete with the retailing giants and are routinely brushed away like lint on a pullover.

Here in Australia it's Woolworths and Coles that control the market with the German discount retailer Aldi snapping at their heels. In the US, the traditional dominance of grocers like Krogers, Safeway, and Albertsons is now challenged by the retailing juggernauts of Wal-Mart and Costco.[8] In the UK it's a savage war between Tesco, Sainsbury's, and the Wal-Mart subsidiary Asda, and a handful of smaller players.[9] In each of these contexts the fight is not first and foremost to lure the customer, but to ensure the customer's choice to go elsewhere is curtailed: devour the competition and secure the market. "Although based on the notion of abundance and choice," writes Humphrey, "the growth of the supermarket in fact stems from the logic that increasingly narrows the range and number of retail environments the consumer can visit."[10]

The impact of these monopolies on locally owned businesses is well documented. As with the near extinction of the local hardware store, driven by the relentless growth of retailers like Bunnings in Australia and Lowes in the US, so the local grocer, butcher, and fishmonger struggle to breathe under the weight of the regional supermarket. It is in my beloved's home state of Texas where I see this most starkly, a place where the independent butcher, green grocer, and baker are virtually non-existent. For the vast majority of Texans there are no alternatives left to the supermarket megastores that line the highways.

As an example, the retailing phenomenon of Wal-Mart has been breathtakingly successful. Today Americans spend $35 million every hour at Wal-Mart stores, with more than 100 million of them shopping at Wal-Mart every week.[11] Now the largest single corporation in the world employing in excess of 1.5 million people,[12] Wal-Mart receives half of its annual revenue from grocery sales, cornering 25 percent of the market nationwide and still growing at an extraordinary rate.[13]

8. See Plunkett Analytics, *Supermarkets, Grocery Stores, Food Stores and Convenience Stores Industry (U.S.)*.

9. See Seth and Randall, *The Grocers*, and Bevan, *Trolley Wars*.

10. Humphrey, *Shelf Life*, 77.

11. Murphy, *Consumer Culture and Society*, 66.

12. Lichtenstein, "Wal-Mart," 3

13. Plunkett Analytics, *Supermarkets, Grocery Stores, Food Stores and Convenience Stores Industry (U.S.)*, 5.

Facing a similar pattern of growth in the large format retailers in the UK, residents of villages and rural areas watch the closure of their local shops at a rate of 300 per year. The nation has seen independent grocers fall from 62,000 in 1977 to fewer than 24,000 today. Similarly, local butchers shops have fallen from 25,000 to just over 8,000 in the same period.[14] Here in Australia the uniquely named milkbar—the corner store that traditionally sits at the center of neighborhoods across the nation—is an endangered species. Thirty years ago, the suburbs of Melbourne were home to 1,600 of them. Today there are less than four-hundred left.[15] In her book *No Logo*, the Canadian cultural critic Naomi Klein describes the relentless expansion of the mega retailers as akin to the spread of molasses across a neighborhood, "slow and thick," drowning all competitors as it goes.[16]

Minimizing Choice

It's no wonder we often feel overwhelmed when we enter a supermarket. Its aisles are stocked with an average of 20,000 distinct items. In American supermarkets that figure rises to 39,000.[17] Many of the items come from other parts of the world and sit alongside those trucked in from all corners of the home nation. Really, we have never had such a carnival of choice within arm's reach. Compared to what was available to my grandparents, the contrast is stark. That said, this array of choice comes at a cost.

If I walk down the breakfast cereal aisle (and yes, it is an entire aisle), I am overwhelmed with possibilities. I am faced with no less than 152 options: from Cornflakes and Fruit Loops to Nutri Grain and rolled oats of every description; from twenty-four varieties of muesli—natural, toasted, and clustered—to an array of handy breakfast bars and so-called "liquid breakfasts" with names like Up & Go. Dig a little deeper, however, and see that the majority of these 152 varieties come to us from just four manufacturing companies: Kellogg's (an American multi-national), Sanitarium (wholly owned by the Seventh Day Adventist Church), Nestle (a Swiss transnational, now the largest food company in the world), and

14. Blythman, *Shopped*, 6.

15. Sexton, "Are You Being Served?," 8.

16. Klein, *No Logo*, 133.

17. Food Marketing Institute, "Supermarket Facts 2015," 1.

Uncle Toby's (an Australian company now owned by the American giant General Mills). The fact is, it is almost impossible for an independent, local manufacturer to secure space on the megastore's shelves without crippling costs and the most screwed-down profit margins ruled entirely by the retailer. This situation is mirrored in the US.

What's more, once an audience is captured and the shopping alternatives minimized, the retailers do all they can to steer consumers to the products that maximize their profit and further secure their control of the market. What appears to be an abundance of choice is a carefully constructed narrowing of options to the retailers' advantage. Indeed, the minimization of freedom in place and product is key to the logic of the supermarket's strategy for growth. The sociologist Zygmunt Bauman makes a similar point more generally. Modern day consumers, he writes, are "not so much free as they have the obligation to choose."[18] Increasingly, our shopping choices are made for us, and those we still make are made within the parameters set by the retailers.

Disconnecting Shopper and Source

No matter which way you look at it, the modern supermarket is an extraordinary thing, for better and worse. I can travel just five minutes from home, no matter how suburban the context, and be surrounded by the aromas and flavors of the world. There are navel oranges from California, dates from Mexico, and a selection of cheeses from France and Holland. There is muscovado sugar from Mauritius, tea from England and Japan, and canned tomatoes from Italy. There are artichoke hearts from Spain, avocados shipped overnight from New Zealand, fresh crab from Chile, and defrosted prawns from Thailand. There are smoked mussels from China, mangoes from far north Queensland, and mineral water from Fiji and Vietnam. The tragedy is that we barely notice, nor often do we care.

In most cases, it is only the small print on the back of the can or packet that reveals a product's origin. Unless the retailer is keen to emphasize locally grown produce with a "grown in Australia" insignia slapped on the signage, origins are considered unimportant. Eggs are eggs, no matter where or how they were farmed. It's more the price we are interested in than the state of the chicken farm. And, to be honest, we would prefer not to know just how the beef mince nestled under plastic

18. Bauman, *Consuming Life*, 74.

film got that way. It's on special this week and perfect for the spaghetti bolognese we've planned for dinner. Of course, it is not the supermarket alone that nurtures this disconnect between shopper and food source— the impacts of industrialization and large scale agribusiness predate the supermarket—but it certainly thrives on it.

In his book *The Pleasures and Sorrows of Work*, philosopher Alain de Botton follows the path of a tuna caught in the Indian Ocean surrounding the islands of the Maldives to the appearance of one of its steaks on the plate of an unsuspecting eight-year-old in suburban Bristol, a coastal city in southwest England. In between, the tuna is processed and packaged for transport in a state-of-the-art fish processing plant on the mainland, then crated and stowed in the cargo hold of a Qatar airways Airbus alongside vegetables and postal items bound for London. There the tuna is warehoused briefly just outside of Heathrow before being transported by lorry to the supermarkets of Bristol. Along the way de Botton meets numerous players in the tuna's story: the Maldivian fishermen whose livelihoods depend on the catch; the fish processing plant workers widowed by the Sri Lankan tsunami of 2004; the English lorry driver whose life on the road has impacted his family and his marriage. Standing in the supermarket aisle watching a stream of shoppers amble by, one who occasionally glances at the tuna's flesh tucked neatly under plastic, de Botton concludes that we are now as "imaginatively disconnected" from the source, processing, and distribution of our groceries as we are in reach of them, "a process of alienation which has stripped us of myriad opportunities for wonder, gratitude and guilt."[19]

Of course, there is more to this supermarket story than I've outlined here. Add to these the systemic issues that flow from feeding the ever-ravenous supermarket: issues of food waste, unsustainable farming practices, exploitation of suppliers, unfair working conditions, and more. If we are concerned for the well-being of the earth and the good of society, there is much about the modern supermarket that we should critique. In fact, there are activists like Michael Pollen, theologians like Norman Wirzba, and journalists like Malcolm Knox who do so, each from different perspectives and to great effect.[20] However, to explore the idea of connecting with God in the supermarket requires more than a critique of its shad-

19. de Botton, *The Pleasures and Sorrows of Work*, 35.

20. Pollan, *The Omnivore's Dilemma*; Wirzba, *Food and Faith*; Knox, *Supermarket Monsters*.

ows. Whatever we make of supermarkets and however we evaluate them, they remain one of the primary spaces of consumption in our lives. For many of us they are unavoidable. Should we have the resources of time, focus, and finance to do so, we may work to minimize our dependence upon them, but the fact is, supermarkets remain part of our domestic landscape as they do for the vast majority of people living their faith in the world.

I am the primary shopper in our family. As the one who cooks, I am responsible to keep our pantry and refrigerator well stocked. Every Friday morning I head out to gather the resources we'll need for the week to come. I have confessed already that I am one of those who has easy access to a fresh produce market, including green grocer, fish monger, butcher, baker, and delicatessen. Regardless, when it comes to the cans, packages, and bottles that supplement my weekly haul of freshness, I push my trolley along the aisles of a supermarket along with everyone else. Indeed, supermarkets have been part of my life for as long as I can remember. When I was a boy my mother worked on the cash register at the local Safeway. During school holidays I would hover at the store front and watch her interact with the customers as her fingers worked the keys of her register at the speed of light.

Having spent years in supermarket aisles, the thing I have noticed is the act of shopping in them is far from straightforward. It is a complicated business, one that is not easily dismissed or glorified. "Supermarkets are not simple places," sociologist Kim Humphrey writes in his landmark study of Australian food stores. "On the contrary, in all their everyday mundanity they embody some of the enormous complexities of living and consuming in a society such as ours."[21] He continues:

> The supermarkets explored here, then, are not cathedrals of a manipulative and unproblematically domineering consumer capitalism, but nor are they carnivalesque arenas of playful consumers. They are not simply palaces of commodity fetishisation and the site where the richness of the life-world is hollowed out, but nor are they sites of endless permutation, personal empowerment and everyday pleasures. The supermarkets explored here, and the people who move within them, are understood to be embodied within certain social and cultural settings, to be

21. Humphrey, *Shelf Life*, 6.

subject to certain locational frustrations, and to be the creators
of certain pleasures and strategies for survival.[22]

As Humphrey observes, there is no simple equation of good versus
evil in today's supermarkets. The most significant things that go on in
them arise out of the interplay between store, shopper, and the culture
in which they reside. What the shopper brings with him or her into the
store is as important as the values and priorities of the supermarket itself.

If our only evaluation of the supermarket is of the store and the
corporation that embodies and feeds it, we risk reducing the shopper to a
mindless, manipulated pawn who, by walking through the doors, surrenders all agency to the will of the corporation. That is not the case. What I
see as I shop each week are householders diligently, though often wearily,
meeting their obligations to provide for, to love, and to serve those within
their care. The truth is, they bring with them an entirely different set of
priorities than those harbored by the supermarket and a different set of
questions than those asked by the critics of supermarket culture.

In my view, too many of the books written on the systemic issues
of consumerism, those in which the supermarket is implicated, are essentially blind to this. This is especially so of the Christian literature.
It happens, too, that most are written by men. While it is true that the
supermarket is no longer the female environment it once was—males
now account for 35 percent of supermarket customers—the fact remains
that in the majority of households grocery shopping remains a female
task.[23] My guess is that as the author sits at his desk writing his books
on the perils of a consumerist society and the evils of the supermarket
multinationals, his spouse is out pushing a trolley along the aisles of a
local store doing her best to provide nutritious menus for her household
within a limited budget. Shoppers are the domestic pragmatists, the ones
who have to make life work.

If we are to discern God's presence in the supermarket, we must begin
by giving the act of consumption a break. The truth is, consumption is
an essential aspect of our humanity. To identify as consumers is not to
identify as sinners. To consume is an act of necessity. While the hazards
of consumption in supermarkets are real—those of waste, manipulation,

---

22. Ibid., 17.

23. Langley and Hogan, "Research Survey Reveals More Australian Grocery
Shopping Habits."

excess, and disconnection from the sources of life—consumption itself remains a good, for in it we are about sustaining and nourishing life.

A negative attitude to consumption, especially among those who are religious, has been shaped significantly by theorists who have helped us think about how we best live in a consuming society. Two of those, the economist Thortein Veblen (1857–1929) and the sociologist Max Weber (1864–1920) consistently viewed consumption as an inferior activity to that of production. Veblen disparaged what he called "conspicuous consumption" as an "unproductive" act that does nothing to serve the good of human life.[24] Weber contrasted consumption as frivolous and impulsive with production as sensible and practical.[25] In Weber's view, consumption is tied to greed and waste while production is tied to efficiency and frugality. What's more, as this thinking developed in the early to middle decades of the twentieth century, activities of production were most closely aligned with the male-dominated, public realm of work, while activities of consumption were those of the female in the private realm of home and shopping mall. The so-called "housewife" did not fare well.

As with many theories, there is a dose of truth in the contrasts of Veblen and Weber, but swallowing them whole is not a lot of help. In fact, doing so does a great disservice to what is a significant part of our lives. In the words of sociologist Wendy Wiedenhoft Murphy, the act of consumption forms "one of the most visible and salient aspects of contemporary society" as we buy, sell, use, and dispose of products and services every day.[26] Indeed, we do it over and over again. We are consumers. Whether we push a trolley though a supermarket megastore or carry our eco-friendly tote to the farmers' market; whether we shop the sales at Macy's or scour the racks of a secondhand clothing store, consumption takes a good deal of our time and energy. We can devote that time to doing it with flourish and style, to limiting its impact, to doing it justly and modestly, or to avoiding it as best we can. However we approach it, consumption matters. When it comes to our relationship with God, dismissing it just doesn't fly.

---

24. Veblen, *The Theory of the Leisure Class*, 69, 97.

25. Weber, *The Protestant Ethic and the Spirit of Capitalism*.

26. Murphy, *Consumer Culture and Society*, 1.

Nearly twenty years ago, the ethnographer Daniel Miller conducted a groundbreaking study of the daily shopping habits of women in the northern suburbs of London. For the most part, these women worked outside the home, often for long hours, but held primary responsibility for the care of their households. Over an extended period of time Miller observed these women, shopped alongside them, and talked with them. What he found was that the women's role in supermarket shopping was a complex negotiation between providing what their family members wanted and what they needed for good health and well-being. There was certainly nothing selfish or self-serving about their actions. Their domestic shopping was an outworking of love, the desire to provide for and be in good relationship with those they were most connected to in life.

Miller argues that daily shopping, far from being mindless, frivolous, or unproductive, is a mundane act based deeply in the practices of love, sacrifice, and care. This is language, he argues, reminiscent of the devotion that undergirds a religious rite. The commodities we purchase do not have meaning in and of themselves, "rather they are meaningful—they come to matter as a means of constituting people that matter."[27] Through the acts of shopping, these women were validating the worth of those whom they loved and nurturing the relationships that held them together.

The fact is, supermarket shopping is just one part of the much larger phenomenon of consumerism. We are all gathered up in it. No matter how trivial it may seem, or how beside the point it feels to our deepest aspirations, consumerism as a whole is a meaning-laden and meaning-making activity. Consumerism is "not only a pattern of behavior that characterizes an individual life," writes ethicist Bruce Rittenhouse, "but a way in which an individual organizes his or her particular life to seek to give it meaning."[28] For Rittenhouse, consumerism's motivation is religious. In whatever form it takes, from the momentous to the mundane, our practice of consuming seeks to answer questions "posed by the nature of human existence."[29] In truth, we take those questions and their associated longings with us into the supermarket as much as we do into a luxury car showroom or fashion boutique. We long for connection, affirmation, and well-being; we long to love and to be loved; we long for

27. Miller, *The Theory of Shopping*, 152.
28. Rittenhouse, *Shopping for Meaningful Lives*, 3.
29. Ibid., 132.

beauty and delight; we long to live in a just and equitable world. Those longings may not be at the forefront of my mind as I select the local brand of canned tomatoes I prefer, the bottle of hot sauce that my daughter requests, the chocolate biscuits that my son will devour as quickly as I buy them, or the flowers that my beloved will cherish, but they are there no less. The desires that undergird our shopping are worth naming from time to time, for they speak of things good and right as much as they do of things that need challenging.

In her book *Not Buying It,* the New York-based writer Judith Levine reflects on her "year of frugality," a year in which she and her partner shopped for nothing but the most basic necessities of food and personal hygiene. In diary form, Levine tracks her personal experiences alongside reflections on the global issues of consumerism. While providing insightful critiques of consumerist culture and its impacts upon our world, Levine is also able to affirm the hope that undergirds much of our domestic shopping. Indeed, she is wary of those unable to name that hope. If chastity is the puritanism of the Right, Levine says, then anticonsumerism is the puritanism of the Left, each equally destructive to the human soul. "Part of me is disgusted by America's sense of entitlement to vast quantities of everything," she writes. "At the same time, I am loath to ally myself with any movement, right or left, that starts by telling people not to desire."[30] Though not religious herself, Levine affirms religions as those which give their adherents permission to "desire wildly, to want the biggest stuff—communion, transcendence, joy and freedom."[31] Perhaps if we are able to name those desires—our desires for the big stuff—as part of what sits beneath our weekly trip to the supermarket, we might find the presence of Jesus there less awkward than we imagined.

Shopping as a Spiritual Practice

The idea that shopping could be a spiritual practice—one that disciples us more deeply into the way of Jesus—may be as challenging to get our heads around as any other I suggest in this book. By shopping, of course, I refer to far more than what we do in a supermarket. We shop at department stores, on high streets, in shopping malls, craft markets, big-box retailers, and corner stores. We are lured to spend our money at the online

30. Levine, *Not Buying It*, 91.

31. Ibid., 254.

mega-marts of Amazon and Costco and in the open digital marketplaces of eBay and Gumtree. The question is, in what ways can we embrace our shopping as a routine and intentional expression of our Christian faith? As a spur to your own thinking, let me suggest three.

1. Shopping for Connection

Chris and Maria have run a small corner store in a neighborhood close to my own for just on thirty years. We Australians call it a milkbar. They carry a basic selection of groceries, milk, bread, and cigarettes; there are snack-foods and newspapers, toiletries, and a modest display of stationery. They make sandwiches and have a see-through display of hot pies and pastries, a freezer full of ice cream, and a glass-fronted refrigerator full of drinks. As it happens, Chris and Maria live behind their shop in a small three-bedroom flat in which they raised three children. For fifteen hours each day, seven days a week, you'll find the door open and at least one of them standing behind the counter.

Sadly, shop owners like these are a dying breed. Stores like Chris and Maria's milkbar struggle to survive in today's marketplace. A twenty-four hour 7-Eleven has opened just two doors up and two national brand supermarkets are just five minutes' drive away. When I see them, I wonder how much longer they can last. While I suspect that a nostalgic yearning for what used to be has a limited shelf life—our lives are full, and the lure of the convenient one-stop mega-store is hard to resist—it is worth noting what we are losing in the process. Honestly, I know full well that the sixteen-year-old casual who scans my groceries at the supermarket is someone I'll most likely never meet again. Next week there will be someone else in her place. In contrast, the Chris and Marias of this world will always be glad to see me, always ready for a chat and good for some neighborhood gossip. They will have little handwritten notices stuck to the window: a lost kitten; a neighborhood reading group; a bike for sale. In a world of constant movement and change, their shop remains a stable and enduring presence.

There are certain values we bring to our shopping, often unarticulated but present no less. They might include priorities like value-for-money, convenience, status, or quality. What if one of the values we prioritized was connection? This might well be expressed in the choice to shop at a local business wherever possible, or to build relationships with particular retailers over the long haul.

My beloved has gone to the same hairdresser now for twelve years. No matter where we have lived, her relationship to Tony and his team remains. So, too, she takes her shoes to be repaired at the same store, no matter how inconvenient the location compared to closer options. Choosing to make the local corner store, butcher, green grocer, or boot maker a regular part of our routine will not always be the most convenient or cheapest option available. Perhaps in doing so, though, we make a small investment in the neighborhood or in other relationships in everyday life that pays important dividends in the longer term.

The Catholic writer Vincent Bilotta identifies the search for intimacy as one of the fundamentals of living. He describes it as the everyday task of seeking intimacy with ourselves, with others, and with God.[32] The intimacy he writes about is an "ordinary intimacy," one that is fostered most effectively in the rounds of daily life and in the encounters we have in the mundane spaces of our lives. It's an intimacy different than that of family or close friends, but one no less important to our formation in the world. It's the intimacy we foster in line at the grocery store or as we interact with the salesperson at the service desk in the department store. It is not about becoming best friends, nor about sharing the deepest secrets of our lives. It is more to do with honoring the person with whom we interact as a fellow human being, a person with a story, a history, hopes and fears as real and complex as our own. It is this sort of ordinary intimacy that the writer Barbara Brown Taylor calls us to.

> The next time you go to the grocery store, try engaging the cashier. You do not have to invite her home for lunch or anything, but take a look at her face while she is trying to find "arugula" on her laminated list of produce. Here is someone who exists even when she is not ringing up your groceries, as hard as that may be for you to imagine. She is someone's daughter, maybe someone's mother as well. She has a home she returns to when she hangs up her apron here, a kitchen that smells of last night's supper, a bed where she occasionally lies awake at night wrestling with her demons and angels.[33]

If connection was to become one of the guiding values of our shopping—honoring and nurturing the relationships that shopping

---

32. Bilotta, "Originality, Ordinary Intimacy, and the Spiritual Life," 83–91.

33. Taylor, *An Altar in the World*, 94–95.

provides—we may well find that its impact helps to keep in check some of the more alienating forces of consumerism in our lives.

2. Shopping for Sustainability

There is a language that has entered the retail environment in the past decade that points to a renewed awareness of consumerism's impact upon our world. It's the language of Fair Trade, organic, free range, palm oil free, FAD free, No Sweat, and more. It highlights a rising consciousness among shoppers in developed economies that our purchasing choices have impacts beyond our own tables. Indeed, through our shopping we are connected with people and communities we will never know face to face. What's more, we are connected afresh with the earth beneath our feet and the air we breathe. These connections are played out in the food we eat, the clothes we wear, and the transport we use.

My friend Jonathan Cornford, a writer and teacher with Manna Gum—an organization that promotes practices of ethical and sustainable living—writes persuasively about the importance of ethical consumption to our spirituality. Ethical consumption, he says, is founded on two principles: (i) the need to reduce unnecessary or frivolous consumption so as to reduce the strain on the earth's resources and all those who inhabit it; and (ii) the need to encourage production processes that take better care of the earth and its people.[34] The challenge, of course, is in the doing. How do we translate principles likes these into the daily choices we make in our shopping? It's a challenge Cornford wrestles with, along with many other people of faith.

As difficult as these challenges are, the fact is we have never been so well served in the provision of information and resources to address them. Today I can open an app on my smartphone as I stand in the aisle of the supermarket and have a wealth of information at my fingertips.[35] In seconds I can determine which of the tinned tuna on the shelf best meets the concerns of sustainable and ethical harvesting of tuna across the world. I can stand before the canned tomatoes and choose those harvested and processed locally and by a company that operates according to acceptable commercial standards. What's more, I can do the same

34. Cornford, *Coming Back to Earth,* 93.

35. The app I use is called Shop Ethical!, a development of the Ethical Consumer Group headquartered in Melbourne, Australia.

with footwear, electronics, clothing, and more. Granted, it takes some effort to begin with, but no matter where we are in the world there are organizations and resources, often just a click away, that help us to make purchasing choices that reflect our values.

Amidst his reflections on these issues, Cornford provides a simple list of principles to guide our shopping more generally.[36] These include: (i) buy less stuff; (ii) choose longer lasting and better quality; (iii) where possible, buy pre-used items; (iv) choose products with certification systems that provide protection for people and environment; (v) preference products made locally; (vi) get informed about the origins of products and the ethical commitments of the companies who produce and distribute them; (vii) use your role as a consumer to agitate for change in the work practices and environmental impacts of corporations. The fact is, our daily shopping lives are full to the brim with choices, many of them minor and apparently insignificant on their own, but as they accumulate they not only make a difference to the world, they shape our faith and character in the most important ways.

3. Shopping for Attachment

The word *detachment* features prominently in historical writings on spirituality, and for good reason. Inspired by the Psalmist's spiritual obsession with "one thing" (Ps 27) and by Paul's testimony of pressing on toward the goal of full union with Christ, "forgetting what lies behind and straining forward to what lies ahead" (Phil 3:13–14), we have understood the need to detach ourselves from priorities, obsessions, and preoccupations that distract us from the most important spiritual aspirations. Symeon sitting on his pole in the Syrian desert had a strong sense that this included detachment from material possessions and the ties they represent.

While there is a profound dose of truth in this assumption, it fails to acknowledge the full story. The truth is, when it comes to the nature of the spiritual life lived out in the world, a good deal of attachment is presumed; attachment of the right kind to the materiality of God's world, one that leads us to embrace life in its fullness. Reflecting on this form of attachment, theologian William Cavanaugh writes:

> In this spiritual universe there is no such thing as an isolated commodity confronting an isolated individual. All created

36. Cornford, *Coming Back to Earth,* 103.

things sing and dance and shout of the glory of God. People and things are united in one great web of being, flowing from and returning to their Creator. Our dissatisfaction with things does not lead us endlessly on to the next thing but to our true end in God. The Christian view elevates the dignity of things by seeing them as participating in the being of God, but simultaneously causes us to look through and beyond things to their Creator.[37]

At its darkest end, the ill of consumerism is in its preoccupation with the wrong sort of attachment. In fact, as a values system consumerism is built on a profound sense of detachment. It proceeds on the belief that we will find our salvation and fulfillment in the pursuit of things we do not yet have and apart from relationship with the Creator of those things. Like the woman standing at a counter in a department store depicted in a *New Yorker* cartoon: she looks at the salesperson and asks, "What would you suggest to fill the dark, empty spaces in my soul?" Consumerism's drive is in the wanting, not the having. It is the outworking of a restless and dissatisfied spirit, powered by a profound discontent with what we have and a belief that what we do not yet have will bring us the contentment we crave.

In light of this, there is something to be said for engaging in the practice of shopping as a proactive nurturing of genuine attachments: nurturing deeper and more sustained connections to the material possessions we purchase, cherishing their worth, craftsmanship, history, beauty, or practicality as the gift of God. Sometimes we face a genuine need to purchase a product or service, or to replace a possession that is past its use-by date or simply worn out. There are many other instances, however, where the need is more a whim or the outworking of a deeper discontent within our lives.

Recently the company product manager for a major furniture and homewares retailer in Australia reflected openly on the attitude of today's consumers: "Young shoppers aren't buying for life anymore," she said. "Fifteen years ago people were likely to change their curtains every ten to twelve years, but now it's every five to six years. It's the same with furniture, they can afford to do it and, more importantly, what looked good six years ago is just so . . . six years ago."[38]

If we are to embrace shopping as a spiritual practice, we need to bring to it a good dose of self-awareness and a willingness to critique our

37. Cavanaugh, "When Enough Is Enough," 12.

38. Barrowclough, "Out of the Frying Pan and into the Wok," 19.

own engagement in practices that run counter to the values of our faith and discipleship. I once heard it said that the statement, "I am content; I have what I need" is one of the most countercultural affirmations a disciple of Jesus can make in daily life. The challenge to bring into sync the deep contentment that characterizes a life in God and our God-given identity as consumers is a life's work.

9

God Among Friends

DARREN AND I MET in first grade. Our hooks in the school corridor were next to each other. As I hung my bag up on the first day, feeling desperately anxious about this strange new world and fearful of my mother's leaving, Darren pushed his way in next to me as though he belonged. He always belonged, no matter where he was. His skin was pale and freckled and his hair an unruly knot of blond curls, but his confidence was boundless. It made my shyness look bland and uninteresting. He took my hand. "C'mon," he said, "let's go in."

For five years Darren and I were best friends. We lived in the same neighborhood and shared other friends in common. He was a small boy, shorter than others in the class, but with a big personality and a temper to match. We swore heartfelt allegiance to each other for the rest of our lives, had sleepovers at each other's houses, and rode our bikes through the vacant land at the edge of the housing estate. Darren's family were recent immigrants from England, his father a brick layer and his mother a factory worker who swore like a trooper. Their house was always a mess and their family life chaotic and loud. Unlike my own family, they were not religious; not at all.

Darren wanted to be a jockey. It was an obsession he confessed on that first day. Though he had terrible asthma, he was determined. I was not surprised years later to hear that his riding career had begun, and shattered, too, to read in the paper of a terrible riding accident. Darren was thrown from a horse mid-race and trampled on the track. He spent the rest of his years a paraplegic.

Our friendship did not last beyond fifth grade. We drifted apart, our sworn allegiance like a faded note at the bottom of a school bag. Darren began to hang out with boys who were too rough for me and I couldn't go along; but I loved Darren. He was always full of life, full of boundless declarations of hope and loyalty. For a time I was gathered up in his world and I liked it. I fed on his confidence and, in large part because of him, was able to find my own way.

Graeme and I have been friends for just a handful of years. He's a decade older than me, a clergyman too. In fact, he's a bishop in a tradition different than my own. We first met as a consequence of an article I had written. Having read the piece, Graeme invited me to speak to a clergy conference in another state. He was not what I expected. I had spent a good deal of time with leaders from his tradition and had learned a wariness in their presence. Right or wrong, I perceived in them a strong sense of ecclesial superiority served with a good spoonful of entitlement. What I found in Graeme could not have been more different. He is one of the most gracious and generous men I know, deeply respectful of traditions and perspectives different than his own. At our first meeting I was taken aback and, in time, rebuked in my prejudice.

Today Graeme and I minister in the same city, in fact in adjoining neighborhoods. His return to Melbourne has meant we catch up for coffee regularly. He always initiates. In time I have come to appreciate his frailties alongside his strengths, his uncertainties amidst his assured presence. He reads widely and voraciously, pushing himself to sit with theological viewpoints divergent with his own. Though his instincts are conservative, he is open to being challenged and prodded.

Graeme entered my life at a critical point. My disillusionment with the church was significant, my own branch of it and others. Here was a man so deeply aware of the institution's failings, yet one who embodied such a considered loyalty to it. I found in him an expression of faith that was like a well weathered rock: solid, wise, and constant, yet open to the elements around. To this day I leave our times together feeling better about myself, more certain about the church, and more aware of life's goodness.

Between my friendships with Darren and Graeme are fifty years of life. In that time I've known a steady trickle of friends. Most have been for a season while some have lasted longer. Together these friendships weave a blanket that surrounds and identifies me. In significant ways, these friendships have shaped who I am. They have sustained my faith and challenged my living. What's more, as I listen to the stories of others—students, parishioners, family members, and colleagues—I hear the same testimony over and over again. Friendships matter. In recalling them, we are enriched. In having them, we are enabled and stretched. In their absence we grieve.

From the perspective of our spirituality, friendships play a significant role. Those who share life with us in friendship shape the contours of that life, including the lines of our faith. Canadian writer R. Paul Stevens suggests that the history of our spiritual pilgrimage is most commonly traced from the history of our friendships.[1] They may not tell the full story, but friendships form a significant part of our spiritual development. Sadly, though, friendships are not often given the place they are due. This is so for many reasons, but two in particular: first, we minimize friendship's importance and thus deprive it of the oxygen it needs to thrive; second, we imagine friendship in such idealized ways that we dismiss what's in front of us as unworthy.

Friendships Minimized

Writing in the mid-twentieth century, the English novelist C. S. Lewis described the prevailing attitude to friendship as "something quite marginal." "It's not a main course in life's banquet," he observed, but "a diversion; something that fills up the chinks in one's time."[2] It is interesting that Lewis wrote this not in his early years as a student but in the last decade of his life. As it happens, Lewis was a man who invested deeply in friendships throughout his life, friendships he named as sustaining to his humanity and critical to his development as a writer. But this is not what he observed in others of his generation; real friendships were thin on the ground.

The same is true today. As we age, our focus moves necessarily to nurturing our own households and to furthering our professional lives. The friendships we once valued take a back seat. In the words of philosopher Jeannette Kennet, as life proceeds "friends start shedding like leaves on a plant."[3] Sometimes they disappear altogether. The typical formula is this: if we have time to spare we have time for friends; if time is short, friendships are the fluff that can be flicked away. In a theoretical sense, we

1. Stevens, "Friendship," 435.
2. Lewis, *The Four Loves*, 55.
3. Quoted by Evans, "The Buddy System," 17.

might identify friends on our list of lifelong priorities, but in the practical allocation of our time week by week it is friendships that are most easily sidelined.

How many times have you expressed regret to a friend? "I am sorry it's been so long. Life has been busy!" Lewis suggests that sitting underneath this regret is a more telling truth. We minimize friendship, he says, because we don't truly value it, and we don't value it because we have so rarely experienced it.[4] These truths feed off each other: the less oxygen we give to friendships, the less life they give to us in return; the less we feel their gift, the less inclined we are to sustain them. Before we know it, they have vanished.

This minimization of friendship plays out in our spirituality as well. If we are about nurturing a deeper connection with God, we have been well schooled to instinctively think of more prayer, more Bible reading, more worship or acts of witness. We rarely think of drinking more coffee with friends. In fact, alongside more "spiritual" activities, hanging out with a friend sounds almost frivolous. Honestly, I am much more likely to declare to my congregation that I am going on a three-day silent retreat than that I'm meeting a friend for lunch. However, when we appreciate the role that friendships play in the development of our character, our formation as people of faith, and our discipleship as followers of Jesus, this marginalization of friendship is suspect.

Friendships Idealized

At the other end of the spectrum is a challenge quite different to the first. We fail to give friendships their place because we're paralyzed by an idealized picture of what they should be like. What friendships we have look shabby in comparison.

The glorifying of friendship has a long and noble history. The founding thinkers of Western philosophy took friendship seriously. In fact, they understood it in its purest form as one of life's peak experiences. In their pursuit of "the good life"—an aspiration that drove much of their thinking—they were deeply concerned with the development of virtue. In this, they understood true friendship as a rich resource. At its best, friendship is the coming together of two people of virtue into one unified expression of heart and mind.

4. Lewis, *The Four Loves*, 55.

For Socrates (469–399 BC), this elevated "unity" of friendship was an act of subversion: a relationship of true freedom standing above the corruptions, restraints, and obligations of other connections. In fact, the relationships of family, the civic square, and the marketplace could barely compete. Aristotle (384–399 BC) unpacked this further. He distinguished between friends of utility, friends of pleasure, and friends of virtue. While the former serve particular needs external to the friendship, friends of virtue are about the relationship itself. In this is its purity. True friends rise above the basic needs of life, free to find and admire the good in each other. In this my friend becomes another me, a mirror in which to see myself more clearly. The trouble is, so elevated was this view of friendship it rendered it elite, accessible only to those of the highest virtue. In the words of philosopher Graham Little, such friendship is "the property if not of the gods then of the implausibly pure in heart."5

Early Christian thinkers picked up on these ideas, though influenced significantly by the Roman philosopher Cicero (106–43 BC). Cicero's esteem of friendship as a state of virtue equaled his predecessors'. Where he differed was in his assessment of the friend not as another self but a different self. The purpose of friendship is not in the merging of two identities but in those identities standing side by side, made one in their aspiration, not in themselves. It was on this basis that Augustine of Hippo (354–430), the most influential theologian in the early development of the church, came to understand friendship as a divine gift—a route through which we come to know the love of God side by side. Furthermore, true and pure friendship is instrumental to this love: we experience the love of God in it; we are directed to the love of God through it. "Two things are essential in this world," Augustine said, "life and friendship . . . . We were created by God that we might live; but if we are not to live solitarily, we must have friendship."6

It was this meeting of minds in God that Augustine valued deeply in his own relationships. In his *Confessions*, one of the earliest autobiographies of faith, he is almost lyrical in his personal affirmation of friendship's gift:

> All sorts of things rejoiced my soul in their company—to talk
> and laugh and to do each other kindness; to read pleasant books
> together; to pass from lightest jesting to talk of deepest things

---

5. Little, *Friendship*, 12.

6. Quoted by Grayling, *Friendship*, 66.

and back again; to differ without rancour as a man might differ with himself; and when, most rarely, dissension arose, to find our normal agreement all the sweeter for it; to teach each other and to learn from each other; to be impatient for the return of the absent and to welcome them with joy on their homecoming; these and suchlike things, proceeding from our hearts as we gave affection and received it back, and shown by face, by voice, by the eyes, and by a thousand other pleasing ways, kindled a flame which fused our very souls together, and, of many, made us one.[7]

It's a beautiful description of friendship; for many years I had it pasted into the cover of my journal. That said, it's an idyllic picture. Augustine describes a level of leisurely intimacy that leads to an almost mystical unity of souls. This elevated sense of friendship was picked up by later writers in the church. In the twelfth century, the English Abbot Aelred of Rievaulx wrote of friendship emanating from the love of God; so much so, he argued, it cannot exist apart from God: "God is friendship, and whoever abides in God abides in friendship."[8] The thirteenth-century theologian Thomas Aquinas felt similarly, suggesting that the love of a friend—a love simply and purely for its own sake—is a model for the love of God. Through it we are transformed into the likeness of God.

So much of this thinking, both philosophical and theological, is rich in its affirmation of friendship's potential. What is dispiriting is its idealism. With all this talk of virtue and godliness, of the mystical unity of spirit and soul, friendship's bar is set high. Add to this today's sentimentalized understandings of friendship, those that stagger for breath under a weight of expectation, and it can all feel beyond us. Little identifies these as friendship's internal enemies: "so ideal and so imagined" is friendship that we are beaten before we begin.[9] "So much hushed writing about it removes it from us rather than bringing it closer," he writes, "the authors forgetting that friendship is an everyday accompaniment to buying and selling, to whoring and warring, working or just worrying how we'll vote."[10]

If I look at my own friendships and assess their worth based on ideal criteria, I might well conclude I have none—none that really count.

7. Augustine, *Confessions*, 52.

8. Aelred of Rievaulx, *Spiritual Friendship*, 66.

9. Little, *Friendship*, 245.

10. Ibid., 4.

And yet I do. If we are exploring friendship as an expression of our spirituality, we do well to put idealism and imagination in their place. Some friendships will lead to a unity of souls that is deeply felt; most won't. Some will include an experience of the Spirit that is tangible; others will not. Friendship is a real state, not an ideal one. It is an ordinary connection between ordinary people. This ordinariness is actually critical to its worth. "Friendships are living things," writes theologian Paul Wadell, "graced by unpredictable adventures." What this means, he concludes, is that "friendships don't always soar; sometimes they plod along, sometimes they stall, sometimes they stop for a while and sometimes they die."[11] None of this negates what is present in friendship. Whatever form it takes and however long it lasts, friendship is shared between people who are flawed and fractured and yet in whom there is the image and presence of God. That is enough.

In the midst of Augustine's elevated view of things, he did call friendships "schools of love," avenues of God's saving and sanctifying work in our lives. It's an idea worth exploring further. In what ways do our friendships, in their ordinariness, take us deeper into the life and love of God?

Friendship as a Forge for Character

There is a strong theme that runs from Aristotle to Cicero, from Augustine to contemporary writers on friendship, that our experience of what it means to be a good person—a person loved and loving—is directly tied to how we conduct ourselves as friends. Friendship and character are entwined. As philosopher Ray Pahl says, it is friendship that provides "the most durable anvil" on which we beat out our particular understanding of "the good" and "the right."[12]

This is especially so because of the space that friendships inhabit. As relationships go, friendships are unique. They exist without institutional support or legal obligation. They are marked by freedom. When it comes to family relationships, there are the institutions of marriage and family, and family law to support them. Workplace relationships are negotiated in institutions, corporations, and businesses with the backing of workplace law to ensure equity and fairness. In the marketplace there is consumer

11. Wadell, "Shared Lives," 12.

12. Pahl, *On Friendship*, 85–86.

law and in the public square, civic law. When it comes to friendships, there are no institutions and no rules. We choose our friends, and we are free to un-choose them without legal cost or constraint. It is because of this that friendships rely entirely on trust. Without trust, friendships fail for there is no other net into which they can fall.

As I have watched my own children mature into adulthood, I have seen them learn the most painful lessons amidst the ups and downs of friendships. What is heartening is to see their character forged along the way. I see my daughter sit with a friend in a hospital ward several days running when her own family is too far away to be present. I see my son go to the aid of a young friend from China who, with minimal English, must negotiate the unjust withholding of a rental deposit by an unscrupulous agent. In neither case is there a requirement that drives them, only friendship and the character it takes to act selflessly in aid of another. We are not obligated to do right by a friend. We choose to do right. We are not legally bound to seek the welfare of a friend. We choose to put them first. It is because of this that Dietrich Bonhoeffer identifies friendship as "the rarest and most priceless treasure" and the act of being a friend the mark of a true Christian.[13]

Friendship as a Mirror of Self

For all of Aristotle's idealism regarding friendship, there is a wonderful truth to this idea that we see ourselves in our friends, and conversely, our friends see themselves in us. "If then it is pleasant to know oneself," he said, "and it is not possible to know this without having someone else as a friend, the self-sufficing man will require friendship in order to know himself."[14] It is this mutuality of knowing that is one of friendship's richest benefits. The biblical command that we love our neighbor as we love ourselves presupposes self-knowledge and self-love in the one who cares. These are the gifts of friendship.

A child is not born an island. We come into the world with the desire and capacity to seek ourselves in other people and, in turn, to mirror for them a sense of who they are in our eyes. One only has to hold a newborn infant in their arms to know the truth of this. We are born for connection. The only way we can be fully human is to be in relation with

13. Bonhoeffer, *Letters and Papers from Prison*, 64–65.
14. Quoted by Pahl, *On Friendship*, 83.

others, to see ourselves in them and they in us. It is in friendship where this mutuality of knowing is at its best.

In my early twenties I left home to begin tertiary studies in another state. I had grown up in a large family, our lives enmeshed. As one of six sons, my identity was subsumed by the family name and the connections we shared. As a younger member of the clan, I was shy. I preferred my place in the shadows while others shone or spoke on my behalf. Beginning a chapter of my life without family connections or reputation and without any voice other than my own, I was completely lost; but with a new sense of freedom.

In the first week I met Leigh, a tall, lanky Tasmanian with an unruly beard and a farmer's drawl. Our rooms were in the same dormitory and Leigh would come across the hallway, sit on my bed, and talk. He was older than me and it took me a while to understand that his interest was genuine. He saw me as a peer, not a younger brother. He wanted to know me, and not because of my family name. He liked me. We spent two years in rooms on opposite sides of the corridor and in that time Leigh was a mirror in my life. As I came to love him so I came to know myself. Graham Little writes:

> To have a friend is to have a particular self that somebody else recognises. It means having someone know you as something other than somebody's child, not just a Koori or a Turk, an accountant or the driver of a tram, not just a woman, an adolescent, one of the unemployed, a middle child or a Virgo. A friend is someone interested in discovering there's more to you than what you are made of. And more than there seemed to be yesterday.[15]

Friendship as an Expression of Love

While self-understanding is a wonderful benefit of friendship, it's not the end game. To stop there is to miss the essence of friendship from a Christian perspective. If friendship takes us deeper into the life and love of God, it takes us into the realm of self-giving love. At its heart, friendship is a state of self-giving. It exists first for the sake of the other.

There are narratives prevalent today that limit friendship's capacity as an expression of love. There are three in particular. The first is

15. Little, *Friendship*, 6–7.

what's called the quest for *self-actualization*. It's an end-game that fills the self-help manuals in our bookshops. In it we are admonished to seek friendships that strengthen our personal goals of self-flourishing and, simultaneously, divest ourselves of those that hold us back. From this perspective, relationship with those whose needs overshadow our own is a diversion costlier than it is worth. The second is the high priority our society gives to *personal freedom*. Consequently, we place a premium on staying available to new experiences. The prospect of being held in one place or one community for too long is a trap to be avoided, and so with friendships. We can bear the brunt of this in the most pedestrian ways. When I talk to someone amidst a crowd of people whose eyes are constantly diverted elsewhere, I know they are more alert to the prospect of other encounters than they are to me. The third is the *commodification of life* that overflows into all corners of our experience. As we come to expect the expiry of goods and services once they have passed their use-by date, so friendships can be disposed of when they are no longer useful, entertaining, or rewarding in the way they once were.

Though narratives like these affect Christians just as much as they do anyone else, we are called to account in our friendships by a different starting point: we are befriended by God, enfolded into the generosity of God's embrace through Christ. It is this that holds, sustains, and feeds us, and it's here that our friendships with others begin. Our best efforts in friendship do not arise from places of insecurity, fear, or self-interest. Instead, we give ourselves to friendships as our most natural instinct. What's more, as followers of Jesus, "the friend of tax collectors and sinners," we understand our vocation as one of embrace and inclusion. For us, friendship is even more than an overflow of relationship with God; it is our calling.

In John 15 we listen in on a conversation between Jesus and his disciples just prior to Jesus' death. In it Jesus paints the most extraordinary picture of friendship, both its origins and reach. He speaks first of the love God the father has lavished on him, God's son. It is this enfolding friendship that leads him to the cross. He then goes to the love by which he embraces the disciples, calling them his friends and enfolding them into the friendship of God. "You did not choose me," Jesus says to them, "I chose you." From this place of eternal friendship with father and son, the disciples are called to "abide in love" and to "love one another." We offer friendship because we know it in our deepest selves.

Lest this all begins to sound as heavenly as the pictures painted by Aristotle and Augustine, we do well to remember that this call to friendship is lived out within the constraints of our humanity and the odd communities we inhabit. Jesus may well have called the disciples to an extraordinary standard of love, yet we know the story that played out once their supper conversation was over. As Jesus made his journey to the cross, most of these men were nowhere to be seen, and those who were failed the tests of friendship miserably. From there, of course, things did get better. Some of these disciples went on to have a substantial impact in friendships with all manner of people, but not often with halos intact. This business of abiding in love, especially in relationship to friends as fickle as we are, is always a work in progress and one that feels more ordinary than wonderful most of the time.

A few times each year, my beloved and I go away for a weekend with a small group of friends. We have been friends for a long time, around thirty years in fact. Our lives first converged through a church in the suburbs of Melbourne. I was a young, inexperienced pastor finding my way in ministry and we were all involved in the church in various capacities. For five years we lived and breathed life together. There was an intensity to our relationships at a formative period in all of our lives. The friendships we formed went deep and have lasted to this day.

In our thirty years together there have been marriages, divorces, children born and raised, and overseas appointments for work and study. We've known experiences of illness and depression, death and grief, times of great achievement and others of failure. We've navigated challenges to belief and losses of faith, shifts in careers and copious changes of address. All of this we have shared with each other. It has not been thirty years of intimate involvement in each other's daily lives. For all manner of reasons there have been periods of absence, the times between reunions longer than others, and occasions when one or other of us should have picked up the phone and didn't. But when we are together there is something about the story we share, the history that we have made together or alongside each other, that is the most precious gift.

There are some within this circle of friends who are better at friendship, some who initiate more naturally and work harder to keep the wheels turning. To my shame, I am not one of those. Chronically introverted, my instincts are wired differently. Regardless, I have tried, not only because I believe in it theoretically, but because I would not choose to live my life apart from these people. In fact, I cannot imagine my life, or even who I am, without them. In the most incremental, even imperceptible ways, these friends have shaped who I am and how I am in the world. To this day I am challenged by their lives, sometimes as I brush up against attitudes or perspectives I do not share, but more often in the way we navigate our lives alongside each other. As sporadic as they can be, these friendships are a gift.

In his book *Leap Over a Wall,* Eugene Peterson reflects on the life and spirituality of David, the first king of Israel. In doing so, Peterson explores David's relationships with key figures in his story. One of those is Jonathan. The connection between the two men is one of the great friendships of history. "The soul of Jonathan was bound to the soul of David," the story tells us, "and Jonathan loved him as his own soul" (1 Sam 18:1). Such was their friendship, Jonathan initiated a covenant through which he promised loyalty and faithfulness to David for the rest of their days. The circumstances of their friendship were as tough as they could be. Jonathan's increasingly deranged father wanted David dead for reasons of jealousy and political power. After helping David escape a particular trap set by his father, Jonathan never saw David again face-to-face. Regardless, the love of their friendship remained. Even more, David's future as king was directly dependent upon Jonathan's belief in him. The relationship shaped David's life and vocation.

As much as this story of friendship is steeped in religious history and has within it grand and melodramatic elements, you can't help notice the more pedestrian signs of friendship common to us all. There are moments of deep feeling and others that are bland. There are flashes of jealousy, pride and hurt; moments of clarity alongside those of confusion and fear. There are heartfelt reunions and long absences, foolish decisions, and ones of heroic loyalty. In Peterson's reflections on the story, he identifies the extraordinary worth of friendship both then and now. When it comes to friendship's impact on our spirituality, he says, friendship's role is typically underplayed. "It's every bit as significant as prayer and fasting, " Peterson writes. "Like the sacramental use of water, friendship takes what's common in human experience and turns it into something holy."[16] I, for one, have experienced that holiness. Common as it seems, friendship is a gift of immeasurable worth.

16. Peterson, *Leap over a Wall,* 53.

Conversation as a Spiritual Practice

Talk is cheap: so the saying goes, and it's mostly true. Our world is full of talk; loud, persistent talk that never ends. Too much of it self-serving, self-aggrandizing, self-justifying. We attend talkfests where "expert" voices are privileged over others. We visit political chambers and church sanctuaries where pulpits and lecterns give voice to those in power while the majority is silent. And we sit before our televisions watching panels where the cleverest and loudest voices win. Too often they sound like a gathering of egos shouting, "Look at me!"

No doubt, this sort of talk can be cheap. What's more, talk like this rarely changes things. Rather than transforming the minds of those who participate, it simply confirms the views they already hold and the choices they have already made. It is not altogether different in the talk of our everyday lives. How many times have you left an exchange with an acquaintance or colleague wondering if your presence was really necessary to it? We can be talked at, talked over, talked down to, or talked around, but rarely are we talked with. Rarely are we genuinely listened to, and seldom do we listen to others.

At its best, conversation is different. Conversation is a meeting of minds, memories, and stories. It is a mutual meeting of spirits distinguished by its openness to the possibility of change. There is always the chance in conversation that we will be shifted, prodded, challenged, or moved to think and act differently. It is this, I suggest, that sets conversation apart from talk. In fact, if we do not come to conversation open to its transforming potential then all we have is talk. Open conversation is the oxygen of true friendship. It is the oxygen by which we breathe together, and it is good.

The proposal that conversation between friends can be a spiritual discipline—a routine practice embraced with intention that leads us to the likeness of Christ—is, at first blush, as difficult as the others we have proposed so far; but its potential is rich. If conversation is allowed to be a tool in the deepening and transforming of our spirits, it may well impact our spirituality in significant ways.

1. A Practice of Attending

"I don't know exactly what prayer is," the poet Mary Oliver confesses, but "I do know how to pay attention."[17] This is surely where all spiritual practices begin: they are disciplines through which we pay attention to our own lives, to the lives of those around us, to the world we inhabit, and, in all of this, to God. The more ancient spiritual term for this practice is *attending*. It is what I do when I engage in intentional conversation with a friend: I attend; I listen in the most deliberate way I can.

To understand the impact of attending in friendships, philosopher Graham Little asks us to recall those moments when we have been "recognized, attended to and listened to well." It is in those moments, he says, "those magnificently human moments" in which we feel "exhilaratingly alive" that we touch on the transformative power of attending.[18] To be attended to is to experience the depth of what we give to others when we listen attentively to them.

The practice of attending is built on a cardinal respect for the humanity, integrity, and worth of our friend. She embodies the truth of God in her story in a way I'll not encounter in any other place. In my attending I honor that truth and I listen for it. I do not come with judgment or the need to convince or cajole. I only come with a sense of inquiry, a desire to hear, understand, and care. I want my friend to know again that I am here and that my support is genuine and ongoing. I want to see what she sees, to feel what he feels, and to know what she knows. And if he is lost, I want him to know that he has company.

In recent years, I have experienced events that were isolating in ways I had not previously encountered. It had to do with public issues about which there is strong disagreement in the Christian church and in which I have a pastoral investment. I felt pressed to take a role that was more public than I was naturally comfortable with. The toll was considerable. I struggled to know what to do with that toll and how to carry it as I needed to. In the course of things, a friend invited me into conversation. He went out of his way to make generous time and to convey his concern for me. As I settled in to that conversation—what felt like a wide and open space—I realized its gift. The hours we spent together were some of the most healing I have experienced. He gave no advice, had no agenda

17. From the poem "The Summer Day" in Oliver, *New and Selected Poems, Volume 1.*

18. Little, *Friendship,* 255.

other than to care, and no particular wisdom to share; but he attended to me with such generosity, I came away feeling both comforted and challenged. It was a small but significant turning point in my own well-being.

Attending is not a complicated thing to do. There are only two rules that apply. Rule #1: shut up. Rule #2: listen. Really, it is not complex; but it's not easy either. Good attending is a practice that takes some learning. If we think listening is easy, it is often because we've never done it. Good attending is a pastoral act that takes discipline and practice; the more we give ourselves to it, the more instinctive it becomes. That said, it is a practice we are all capable of. As a practice of our faith, it includes no secret pathway but is open to all.

In exploring this practice for myself, I came across a book that had in its title the enticing phrase "conversation as ministry." In the early chapters, the author defines the sort of conversation he has in mind, including its twelve essential components. As I waded my way through them, including such things as a grounded ecclesiology, a biblically informed character, a reflective self-awareness, I began to have a sense of something more complex than I had imagined, more the business of secret church squirrels than of regular people. None of the author's twelve points are wrong. In fact, each is spot on and worth exploring. That said, conversation between friends is surely the most accessible and immediate business we are in. Perhaps all we really need to begin is the author's final point: conversation gives body to the realm of God on earth. There is something about attending in friendship that makes the presence of God tangible.

2. A Practice of Investing

The real beauty of conversation between friends is that it's ongoing. There is nothing momentary about it. Friends have history. They have shaped a story together. No matter how long-standing or recent a friendship might be, it builds one encounter at a time, one conversation after another. These conversations, building incrementally, sit within the context of our story and add to it. In time they develop a grammar all their own. The more we converse, the less there is to explain or divulge and the more we make room for challenge and depth.

The idea of a spiritual practice as an investment is a helpful one. In all spiritual disciplines there is something about slow, persistent practice that is key. The practices of prayer, meditation, confession, worship, or Bible reading build over time. Not every deposit we make feels significant in its own right, but in time the worth of those investments grows into something substantive. To be honest, there are moments in my prayer life where I feel nothing of substance, where the rote and ritual act feels nothing more than that; and there are others when my heart soars. Yet I look back and know that the practice of prayer—the mundane and the exhilarating—has shaped my relationship with God like nothing else.

Conversations with friends can build slowly into a transformative practice, each one an investment into something larger. There will be conversations that sing and others that are monotone; encounters that thrill the spirit and some that are dreary. There will be intentional conversations that burrow away at particular challenges; and others that meander with no sense of purpose or destination. To use Augustine's words, such conversations can "pass from lightest jesting to talk of deepest things and back again." But, in all of this, we are investing, one conversation at a time, in something of greater worth.

What investments need is time, time to mature so as to reward the investor with the greatest returns; so, too, with conversation. For relationships to flourish and for conversations to have their impact, there is no substitute for time. "Relationships are not best founded on efficiency," Hugh Mackay observes, "nor are they best nurtured through the exchange (no matter how frequent) of inherently impersonal digital data." When you surrender the art and discipline of face-to-face conversation, he says, believing that text messages and emojis can fill the void, "you've begun to lose your grip on what it means to be a social creature."[19] When it comes to spiritual practices, there are no shortcuts. In the practice of conversation between friends, the incremental investments require intention and time. There is no other path.

3. A Practice of Confronting

In the opening paragraphs, I proposed conversation as a meeting of minds, memories and stories. In that meeting the possibility of change flourishes. The English writer and philosopher Theordore Zeldin argues that such change is not only possible within each participant, but can flow between and out of the conversation they share. "When minds meet,"

19. Mackay, *The Art of Belonging*, 187.

he writes, "they don't just exchange facts: they transform them, reshape them, draw different implications from them, engage in new trains of thought." "Conversation doesn't just reshuffle the cards," he continues, "it creates new cards."[20] In this form, conversation is more than attending to each other's stories. It is more than an incremental investment over time. It is found in the willingness of those who converse to tread territory that is risky, even confronting. It takes trust to flourish. "What matters most," Zeldin concludes, "is courage."[21]

Geoff and I have been friends for over twenty years. We met as students in the States, initially bound by our common status as "aliens" in a foreign land. Quickly, though, the relationship moved to firmer ground. We come from different traditions and different states. Our personalities are a study in contrasts, yet over two decades our friendship has remained. This has much to do with Geoff's persistence and grace; he does friendship better than most men I know, and I have reaped the benefits. That said, we remain different, shaped by disparate contexts and communities. Apart from our years in California, we have rarely lived any closer than a day's travel apart. Even more, there are issues about which we disagree and hold very different views. While I am accustomed to standing in the minority on some things, there are few people in my life, those with whom I disagree, with whom I can have conversation on these issues that is not marked to some degree by mistrust. With Geoff it is different.

Friends have time on their side. When friends disagree, there is always more to the relationship and its conversations than the issue of difference. I cannot dismiss Geoff as merely "the opposing view." There is more to him than that. There is more to our relationship than the disagreement at hand. What's more, I cannot marginalize his viewpoint as I can with an acquaintance on Facebook. The respect we share more broadly touches everything about which we converse. Zeldin proposes that it is in these moments of difference we are faced with a choice. The direction the conversation takes from this point will shape us as much as it shapes the relationship. As friends we can choose to focus on our past—the memories and experiences that have made it—and keep on saying, "this is the way we are," or we can set out to explore new and risky

20. Zeldin, *Conversation*, 14.

21. Ibid., 16.

territory.[22] That territory will necessarily include confrontation as we wrestle intentionally with what sets us apart. It is not an easy path to take.

Of course, the practice of confrontation is more than negotiating differences of opinion. It also means allowing conversations to name things that are difficult to name and to put our finger on things that are painful, even shameful, in our lives. When friends find the courage to traverse this territory, openly and sensitively, they touch on a spiritual practice that has as much capacity for transformation as any other practice we can name.

22. Ibid., 46.

10

God in the Workplace

As DAYS OF THE week go, Sunday is a standout in my memories of childhood. It's not because it was the sabbath but the day my father wore a suit. Dad looked fine on Sundays: important, almost regal. With broad shoulders and a straight posture, he carried a suit with elegance. Of course, it was church day. As the youngest I sat next to dad during the morning service. As the sermon dragged on, I passed the time playing with his hands.

Dad's hands were one of my favorite things about him. They were large and calloused, and I could lose myself amongst the lines and crevices. I imagined tobogganing down the slopes or hiding from trouble in a dark ravine. Underneath Dad's nails was always black. We had one of those plastic nailbrushes sitting beside the bathroom sink. Every Sunday morning Dad would scrub vigorously, but the grease was embedded. No matter how hard he tried it was there to stay. I liked it. Dad's hands were strong, familiar, and secure.

By trade, my father was a turner-and-fitter. Before I can remember, my parents left behind a small dairy farm in the Gippsland of southern Victoria. With a large family to provide for, the farm was no longer viable. My parents decided Dad would look for work in the factories of an industrial suburb on the edge of Melbourne. For the next twenty years, six days a week, I woke to the familiar sound of the front door closing as my father headed off to work for another day. I understood little of the responsibility he carried and even less of the price he paid to meet it. Supporting a large family on a tradesman's wage made overtime essential. To dwell on his personal fulfillment or need for advancement was a luxury beyond his budget. Work was a necessity; it simply had to be done. The factories were noisy and impersonal. Dad was one of many workers who shared the factory floor; their work was hard and the hours long. He would come home tired and smelling of the factory. He was always glad to be home. Work could be forgotten until morning.

Sundays were different. Dad was an important man in the church. He served as a deacon and elder for all the years I can remember. His gentleness, piety, and compassion drew respect from his fellow church members. In matters of concern he was called upon for his wisdom. He was always busy on boards and committees, and spent countless evenings visiting, pastoring, and praying. The Sunday suit seemed more than appropriate to me. In church my dad was somebody.

Despite this, no one in the church seemed to notice Dad's hands. Nobody asked him why his nails were black. The truth is, it didn't matter who my dad was outside the church. His value and spirituality were measured by who he was in it. As far as I know, never in twenty years did another church leader ask him detailed questions about his work, the factory, or the people he worked with. Never did a pastor visit him at the factory, curious to see what he achieved. I cannot recall a single sermon on the subject of work. It was as though Dad lived in two different worlds with two outfits: the world of the blue overalls and the world of the suit and tie. His hands, however, always stayed the same, his blackened nails a constant reminder that whatever he was called in the church, he would always be a worker.

When we think of the word *spirituality*, certain images come easily to mind: images of solitude, hushed Sunday gatherings, or candlelight. The word *ministry* is similarly blinkered. We think of preachers and pastors, Sunday school teachers or missionaries. Beyond these, we might think of ministry including an act of service offered through the programs of the church. Rarely do these realms of spirituality and ministry accommodate a laborer standing over a lathe, an accountant with a spreadsheet, a plumber mending a broken pipe, or a parent running a child to school. We have been conditioned to view the spiritual as a realm of separation and ministry as a tightly defined expression of gospel proclamation.

It is when I think of my father's hands that these conditioned responses fall short. It is not right that people like my father live life in two worlds with no apparent connection. They are deprived of resources to discern the presence of God—including God's purposes and calling—in the activities that take up much of their lives. The great reformer Martin

Luther (1483–1546) was driven by a similar dissatisfaction as he saw the priesthood of ordinary people denied by the attitudes of the church:

> The idea that service to God should have only to do with the church altar, singing, reading, sacrifice, and the like is without doubt but the worst trick of the devil. How could the devil have led us more effectively astray than by the narrow conception that service to God takes place only in church and by works done therein . . . . The whole world could abound with services to the Lord . . . not only in churches but also in home, kitchen, workshop or field.[1]

Work is many things. Luther's vision for "home, kitchen, workshop or field" is inclusive. Though it includes the paid labor of people like my dad, the category of work is more than this: from standing at a lathe to leaning over a kitchen sink; from voluntary service in the community to the business of searching for employment; from studying toward a qualification to caring for one's grandchildren. In his theology of labor, Richard Higginson defines work as "any activity undertaken with a sense of obligation to oneself, others, one's community, and God."[2] Whatever form it takes, Luther's words remind us that work demands a more central place in our spirituality.

Hundreds of years after Luther's rebuke, Pope John Paul II made a resolute call to the Roman Catholic Church to revalue the work of its people and to nurture a "spirituality of work" that draws them closer to God in the midst of it.[3] Inspired by this call, writers like Gregory Pierce and William Droell set about resourcing the church for the task. One of their concerns was with the language of the church. It needed reinterpreting, they argued, so that the great themes of salvation, creation, redemption, and sanctification could be made tangible in the work of the people. Without this, the gulf between faith and work would remain.

> If lay people cannot find any spiritual meaning to their work, they are condemned to living a certain dual life; not connecting what they do on a Sunday with what they do the rest of the week. They need to rediscover that the very actions of life are spiritual,

1. Quoted by Feucht, *Everyone a Minister,* 80.
2. Quoted by Jensen, *Responsive Labor,* 3.
3. *Laborem Exercens* (On Human Work), 1981.

and enable lay people to touch God in the world, not away from it.[4]

The final sentence is compelling: how do we "touch God" in our work? How do those who inhabit workplaces far more than they do places of worship respond to God's presence and calling each day? No matter what brand name the church carries, the majority of its resources and programs continue to call people out of the world in order to engage with them. Consequently, today's church can be as guilty of marginalizing the priesthood of the common people as the one Luther condemned centuries before. People like my father deserve better.

This idea that we can touch God in our work is one worth chasing; but the chase is fraught. To pursue it, we need to avoid two equally hazardous starting points: romanticism and cynicism.

The stark realities of work are shot through with human failing, struggle, and injustice. If we are to discern our way to a spirituality of work with substance, we'll have to relinquish romantic notions of work that ignore these realities. Work today is a messy and compromised business. Our workplaces are full of corruptions large and small, inequities immediate and systemic, and injustices local and global. My grandparents' idea of "an honest day's work for an honest day's pay" is almost anachronistic. To discern the presence of God in our work means first confronting the godlessness of much of it. In other words, we have to proceed with our eyes open. Conversely, surrendering to easy cynicism—dismissing all talk of touching God in our work as fanciful—does nothing to encourage an all-of-life response to God for those who fill the church's pews. Frankly, both romanticism and cynicism land us back where we began: with an otherworldly preoccupation that says nothing to our life experience.

Hazards aside, the idea of seeking God in our work begins with good theology. From a biblical perspective, there are two important theological statements that we make with confidence. Both have their beginnings in the creation story of Genesis.

4. Droel and Pierce, *Confident and Competent*, 26.

God Works

The God of the Judeo-Christian tradition is a working God, a God of overalls and calloused hands. From the beginning of the biblical story, God is revealed as worker. In the opening chapters of Genesis, we meet God as creator and provider. Indeed, God's daily productivity is extraordinary. As the story of God and God's people unfolds, we see God as rescuer, redeemer, teacher, parent, protector, warrior, healer, judge, reconciler, administrator, and servant. Further to these, the biblical scholar Robert Banks has explored multiple images of God in the Bible that reveal the nature of God and God's work: God as composer and performer, metalworker and potter, garmentmaker and dresser, gardener and orchardist, farmer and winegrower, shepherd and pastoralist, tentmaker and camper, builder and architect.[5]

This image of God as worker stands in contrast to the Greek idea of gods existing above the realm of human work, removed from the compromised realms of physical labor. The God of the Bible has his hands in the dirt. Indeed, it is by God's hands that we are made as with the whole of creation. The psalmist proclaims it again and again: "For you, O Lord, have made me glad by your work; at the works of your hands I sing for joy" (Ps 92:4–5); "The works of his hands are faithful and just" (Ps 111:7); "Your hands have made and fashioned me" (Ps 119:73); "I remember the days of old, I think about all your deeds, I meditate on the works of your hands" (Ps 143:5). Equally we are roused as we sing that great hymn of faith: "when I consider all the works thy hands have made, then sings my soul, 'How great thou art.'"[6]

We add to this the powerful truth that God is embodied in the person of Jesus, born of a woman's labor and apprenticed to a carpenter. In this we have evidence of the kingdom of God lived and breathed in the midst of human work. "This workman's jacket," Alan Richardson writes, "was a fitting garment for the God whom the biblical revelation had all along represented as himself a worker."[7] The redemptive work of Christ is as grounded in the stuff of our lives as God's work was in the garden of Eden. Even more, the ongoing work of God's Spirit—the renewal of creation—is a work that embraces the whole earth and all human experi-

5. Banks, *God the Worker*.

6. Based on the Swedish traditional melody and poem written by Carl Gustav Boberg in 1885.

7. Richardson, *The Biblical Doctrine of Work*, 48.

ence. The wonderful truth is that work is more than something God does. Work is intrinsic to who God is. If we are looking for dignity in human labor, we find it in God.

We are Created to Work

This second statement follows from the first: we are made to work. Yet it's a truth we stumble over. Early in my training as a pastor, I was posted to a small church in southern Queensland. German immigrants had settled in the region a century earlier. These were hardworking people. The years on the land had been harsh, but they valued physical labor as a sign of good character. My soft, uncalloused hands made them wonder what I had to offer.

I recall spending a day with Harold, a cattle farmer. As we worked together in the afternoon sun gathering hay bales and stacking them on the back of his truck, Harold described the drought he had battled for a decade. The financial and emotional hardships were severe; a neighboring farmer had taken his own life the year before. I soon realized how little I understood. As Harold threw the last bail up on the truck, he removed his hat, wiped his forearm across his brow and said matter-of-factly, "But then, work was never meant to be nothin' but a curse. As long as there's sin around, there'll be hard work."

Harold's theology of work comes from his reading of the creation story. God's words of judgement to Adam and Eve in Genesis 3—words spoken as a consequence of their disregard for God's commands—include these:

> . . . cursed is the ground because of you;
> in toil you shall eat of it all the days of your life;
> thorns and thistles it shall bring forth for you;
> and you shall eat the plants of the field.
> By the sweat of your face
> you shall eat bread
> until you return to the ground,
> for out of it you were taken;
> you are dust,
> and to dust you shall return. (Gen 3:17–19)

The Contemporary English Version has it, "from here on you will have to sweat to earn a living." For Harold, this resonated, as it does for many people in the world. Yet his conclusion that work itself is a result of human failure misses a vital part of the narrative. What we see in the first two chapters of Genesis is that work is a part of God's creation and gathered up in what God declares as "good" and "very good." Work is not just instrumentally important; it is intrinsically so.

> God created humankind in his image, in the image of God he created them; male and female he created them. God blessed them, and God said to them, "Be fruitful and multiply, and fill the earth and subdue it; and have dominion over the fish of the sea and over the birds of the air and over every living thing that moves upon the earth." God said, "See, I have given you every plant yielding seed that is upon the face of all the earth, and every tree with seed in its fruit; you shall have them for food. And to every beast of the earth, and to every bird of the air, and to everything that creeps on the earth, everything that has the breath of life, I have given every green plant for food." And it was so. (Gen 1:27–30)

In the retelling of the creation story in Genesis 2, "The Lord God took the man and put him in the garden of Eden to till it and keep it" (Gen 2:15). However difficult our work can be, it remains a part of God's design. What's more, work is part of God's eternal future for humankind. Isaiah's magnificent picture of this future anticipates a day of eternal peace and prosperity that ripples out through the whole earth. He describes the nations "beating their swords into ploughshares and their spears into pruning hooks" (Isa 2:2–5). As Ben Witherington observes, Isaiah's vision of this ultimate shalom "is not of a workless paradise, but of a world at peace worshipping the one true God and working together . . . ."[8] To embrace our personhood in God's image is to grasp our identity as workers, an identity central to our narrative from beginning to end.

These two theological statements are simple yet important: God works; we are created to do the same. Together they form a vital first step in reclaiming work as part of our spirituality.

As we move from these statements to particular expressions of work that help us touch God, we do so with equal parts realism and hope. In the

---

8. Witherington, *Work*, xiv.

face of all that is troubling about work, the purposes of God remain, as does God's agenda for the renewal of all creation—work included.

In the next few pages, I want to suggest aspects of the work of God that are potentially present in the work we do. There are far more than I can list here. I choose just a few. But in doing so, perhaps we'll be inspired to see our work as a legitimate act of spirit, one gathered up in the work of God's Spirit.

The Creativity of God

"Be fruitful and increase in number; fill the earth and *subdue* it" (Gen 1:28). It is with these words that God blesses and commissions human-kind in the creation story. This designation of privilege and responsibil-ity is key to the flourishing of creation. That said, this call to "subdue" is harsh to the ear. In its English form it infers domination, control, or the breaking of something into submission, and sounds anything but creative. In contrast, the Hebrew word from which it comes, *kabhash*, has among its meanings "to knead" or "to tread." Given my professional background in the kitchen, I immediately think of the work needed to create two culinary staples. They just happen to be the two elements of the church's sacred meal: bread and wine.

Seasoned bread makers know that successful baking relies heavily on the fermenting miracle of yeast. It's a temperamental ingredient. You need to understand its chemistry to work with it. When it comes to the baker's act of kneading, there is no domination involved. It's not as though you can beat the dough into submission. Rather, it's about working with the essential ingredients and gently, slowly, and skillfully kneeding them to their potential. The same is true for the grape and the nurturing of good wine. "Treading" those grapes is one part of a creative process by which we work the ingredients to their optimal end.

At its best, this is what much of our work is about. We are co-creators with God. Think of a musician or carpenter, a teacher or parent, a metal worker, gardener, or architect. Each one takes basic ingredients provided by God—music, wood, metal, plants, even a human mind—and through various means nurtures those elements to particular ends. Of course, there are corners in the modern world of work where this is a challeng-ing connection to make. Large-scale industrial systems of production have so incrementalized work that many of those on work's production lines struggle to identify the end result. Regardless, we are made to be co-creators with God. Humane work makes those connections clear.

The Providence of God

Genesis 1:30 speaks of God providing food for "everything that has the breath of life in it" as Paul describes the God who "richly provides us everything for our enjoyment" (1 Tim 6:17). This is one of the most empowering evidences of continuing relationship between creator and humankind. The God of the Bible does not create and walk away but stays intimately connected with all that is made. God as provider is not simply a descriptor of role or function. It describes God's being.

With God, we are co-providers. Providing is our God-ordained responsibility in the world. In many aspects of human work, we are the conduits of supply and service. Human need is unending. We need sustenance, support, light, warmth and security, housing and nourishment. There is need for education, power supply, protection, healing, governance, and leadership. We need the services of communication, administration, organization, and logistics. There are needs for cleanliness and the disposal of waste, direction, design, forward planning, and the recording of past events. We need the maintenance of order and the repair of things that break down. We need tending to when we are sick, support when we are in crisis, comfort when we grieve.

The work of providence encompasses so much of what we do in our work each day. The more taken for granted our provision, the more necessary it is to everyday life. The truth is we do not notice the rubbish disposal trucks that prowl our streets in the early morning until they stop coming. We barely notice the magical service of the home laundry until our dirty clothes are left to pile up on our bedroom floors. It's the work of providence that keeps the world turning, even in the most imperceptible ways.

Providence is also connected to our care for those in our own households who depend upon us. It is here that our co-providence goes to the heart of our Godlikeness, a responsibility we carry as bearers of God's image. This is partly why Paul speaks so directly to Timothy: "And whoever does not provide for relatives, and especially for family members has denied the faith and is worse than an unbeliever" (1 Tim 5:8). The connection between our role as providers and our identity as followers of Christ is a crucial one.

The Community-Making of God

In the doctrine of the Trinity, Christians profess faith in a God of relationship. The God of Father, Son, and Holy Spirit has community at heart. In the birthing of Israel as an infant nation, God names a community of faith into being: "When Israel was a child, I loved him, and out of Egypt I called my son" (Hos 11:1). This work of birthing community lies at the heart of the gospel: "You are a chosen race, a royal priesthood, a holy nation, a people belonging to God. . . . Once you were not a people, but now you are God's people" (1 Pet 2:9–10). Our call to conversion is a call to enter into the community of God. As we become part of the "body of Christ" and the "household of faith," we are born again into relationships of identity and purpose.

The mission of the church is to embody this community—one that reveals the presence and purposes of God in the world. As the people of God scatter into their workplaces and neighborhoods each week, they take this mission with them. Anywhere in society that we are about extending the hospitality of God and nurturing human community, we are expressing that mission. In some cases, the work of community-making is explicit to a worker's role. Urban planners, classroom teachers, community workers, even café proprietors, have community-making built into their job description. For others, the work of nurturing community is more a choice in the way they work than it is a required task. Either way, nurturing community is an outworking of our faith.

This activity of community-making at work takes on a more urgent character when we understand that for many people the workplace is one of a shrinking set of contexts in which they experience human intimacy on any regular basis. Writing at the end of last century, the workplace sociologist Jim Channon anticipated this as a critical phenomenon in our time, one he was urging corporations to take more seriously:

> When people had tribes to go home to, or villages where they could share the seasonal festival, or even neighborhoods with some personal intimacy, the spirit of community was a part of the natural order of life. But as we approach the 21st Century, our business cultures have become our tribes, our villages and our neighborhoods . . . if there is no experience of spirit in our

corporations, then there may not be much spirit in the civilization at large.[9]

If Channon is right, and more recent research suggests that he is,[10] then the business of community-making at work is more significant still. To nurture it, to fan it into flame, to celebrate it, to protect its well-being: all of this is work worth doing.

The Justice of God

The story of God's covenant with the people of Israel begins in earnest in the brick-making kilns of Egypt. Enslaved by the Egyptians who had become "ruthless" and tyrannical in their demands, the lives of the Hebrew people were "bitter with hard service in mortar and brick and every kind of field labor" (Exod 1:13–14). God's liberation was to free the people from this enslavement and lead them to a land where their work would be life-giving and life-affirming.

The God of our faith has justice at heart. This justice flows from God's being, the "lover of justice" (Ps 99:4), the one enthroned in righteousness and robed in equity (Deut 32:3–4; Ps 89:14). Justice is the foundation of God's rule and the heart of God's continuing work (Ps 97:2). God judges the world in righteousness and champions equity. God is a stronghold for the oppressed (Ps 9:7–9), a protector of the poor, the widow, and the downtrodden (Ps 10:17–18). God bends down to listen to the cries of the meek and liberates the ones most vulnerable to oppression (Ps 10:17–18; 82:3–4).

> Who is like the LORD our God,
>   who is seated on high,
>   who looks far down
>   on the heavens and the earth?
> He raises the poor from the dust,
>   and lifts the needy from the ash heap,
> to make them sit with princes,
>   with the princes of his people.
> He gives the barren woman a home,
>   making her the joyous mother of children. (Ps 113:5–9)

9. Channon, "Creating Esprit de Corps," 53–54.
10. Pocock, Skinner, and Williams, *Time Bomb*, chapter 4.

As the people of God, we are called to clothe ourselves in justice and to robe ourselves in righteousness (Eph 6:13–16) and to be engaged in the same work of liberation. It is now our work to champion and embody the liberation of God in the world. Expressions of religious piety devoid of the work for justice draw God's condemnation (Amos 5:21–24; Mic 6:6–8). Justice lies at the heart of our vocation.

There are arenas of work that have explicit connections with the pursuit of justice. There are those who seek justice in courts of law or in the development of public policy. Others advocate for those who are mistreated, misunderstood, or disadvantaged. There are workers who defend rights, pursue fairness and equity, and work to ensure the dignity of others: social workers; practitioners of law and law-enforcement; workplace advocates and union representatives; providers of aid and development; investigative journalists and conflict mediators. The list is long.

In other fields of work the connections are less obvious. Regardless, commitments to justice, fairness, inclusion, and equity can sit beneath our work. These commitments inform our relationships, determine our choices, and color our responses in daily settings. Choosing to wear the distinctive robes of justice in our workplaces and our wider community may mean we stand apart from the crowd, even harm our chances for advancement or acceptance. At times it may even mean we must walk away from a company or institution we can no longer support, or to stand resolutely with others who do so. In today's workplaces the commitment to justice can be costly, yet the call of our faith persists.

The Grace of God

When all is said and done, to speak of the work of God is to speak of grace. It is the undeserved favor of God that infuses God's work in all its forms. Grace is in the creation, the calling, and the redemption of God's people; in their healing, protection, sustenance, and homecoming. It is the work of God's undeserved kindness, a work that is of God's essence, the one who abounds in steadfast love and faithfulness (Exod 34:6). It is this same grace embodied for us in Jesus Christ, a love that knows no boundary and no end (Rom 8:35–39), the grace that sustains and enriches our lives.

This grace is embodied in our work in any number of ways, not least in the grace of work itself. To have work is a gift. I have never suffered the challenge of long-term unemployment, but my work in the city with those who are without home and work for prolonged periods of time has taught me that to have a job is a very tangible experience of grace. The deprivations of unemployment are many and scarring. Partly it has to do with the values of our society. Sociologically and psychologically, we are defined by our ability to produce, provide, and purchase. To be without work is be diminished in all of these and therefore lessened in our sense of self and the worth attributed to us by others. From a Christian perspective, there is much to challenge in these measurements of worth, but we do so acknowledging the human needs to produce and provide are God-given. The novelist and broadcaster Dorothy Sayers once observed, "Work is not, primarily, a thing one does to live, but the thing one lives to do."[11] Work and identity are closely linked. When we are deprived of work, the experience cuts at the heart of who we are.

Grace is also evident in the nature of our work and the ways we engage with it. Grace is redemptive, reconciling, healing, restoring, and forgiving. Where we work to redeem what has failed or fallen into disrepair, we exercise grace. Where we work to reconcile what is broken or in conflict, we embody grace. Where we work to heal what is sick or distressed in people, systems, or communities, we demonstrate grace. Where we work to restore order, dignity, or worth, we offer grace. Where we work to make forgiveness possible or tangible for the sake of new beginnings, we communicate grace. From the cubicles of office buildings to classrooms and hospital wards, from factories to shopping malls, from grain fields to highways and workshops, our days are filled with opportunities to embody and live the grace of God. It is our work.

Campbell's workbench is an old, laminated tabletop removed from its legs and balanced across two tea-chests that have known better days. His workroom sits behind a shop front on a suburban street, a veterinary clinic on one side and convenience store on the other. The room is small, the walls painted in apple green with just one window looking out onto a rusted drainpipe. The space is filled almost to the ceiling with bags and boxes, each one full to overflowing with donated clothing and household goods. Campbell's work is to sort the donations for the thrift shop out front, to decide what is kept and recycled for sale and what is thrown away. Sometimes he does a shift on the counter helping customers. Once each month he organizes a morning tea for the volunteers, and each week

11. Sayers, "Why Work?," 53.

he does a run to a warehouse to collect an overflow of goods from larger stores. There have been times when he has joined a rally or demonstration in the city center calling for more just responses to the poor or those seeking asylum in Australia. Mostly, though, he stays at his bench in the back room.

What Campbell does each day is a mixed bag. Like the one's overflowing on his table, there's a good deal of stuff that should be binned alongside things that are worthwhile. There are moments when he is conscious of what he is doing and how it helps or contributes to the work of the organization or the community; there are others when he's on autopilot and doesn't think about much at all. In amongst it all is the work of God. In Campbell's work, God is present as creator, provider, and community maker. Indeed, the God of justice, grace, and redemption is as present to Campbell at his sorting bench as God is to the priest standing at the communion table. It is all the work of God.

Work as a Spiritual Practice

There is much about our work that is gathered up in the work of God and much that is not. Sometimes we have to navigate our way through the dross of our workplaces to find what is of God, but we can be sure it's there. To move from here to embracing our work as a spiritual practice requires more than discernment. It calls for intentionality and choice. A spiritual practice is one we engage routinely and with purpose to lead us more deeply into the way of Jesus. As with the more traditional disciplines, the movement to transformation is gradual. It begins in choosing, over and over again.

1. Choosing to Serve

One of the defining images of spirituality in the New Testament is in the account of Jesus washing his disciples' feet. At the conclusion of this act, Jesus makes it clear that the humility of service defines the essence of Christian ministry: "Now that I, your Lord and Teacher, have washed your feet, you should wash one another's feet" (John 13:14). When we place this story in the context of Jesus' life, we appreciate afresh the premium God places on the humility of service and self-giving in the life of the disciple. Just as it was a choice for Jesus to kneel, so it is for us.

Of course, there is a contrast between the humbling, selfless embodiment of grace evident in this act of Jesus, and the profit-driven nature of "customer service" in today's commercial world. This contrast is a reminder to people of faith that we have another standard of service against which we measure our work. It is a standard that will never feature in the corporate manuals and policies that govern our workplaces. It cannot be mandated by management. It must be chosen. For Christians working in service industries, there are daily, tangible opportunities to reclaim the notion of service as vocation, that it is a calling that undergirds their work each day. But this vocation of service enfolds all of us, no matter where our work is done. We are all confronted with the choice to serve or to withhold that service.

By walking out the front door every morning, my father chose to serve me. Why did he work? In large part, he worked for me. Six days a week for all of those years my father took off his outer garments, knelt down, and washed my feet. This is not an overly romantic assertion. I am not suggesting that he left each day with a divinely inspired sense of purpose, or that a stream of heavenly light circled his head as he stood at his lathe. The service of foot washing is not like that. It's ordinary, routine, dirty, and domestic. Tomorrow it will need to be done again. The choice to serve is daily. It is in the choosing and the re-choosing that we are transformed.

2. Choosing to Persevere

On a recent visit to one of the islands of Indonesia, I stayed by a river that rose and fell with each day's rain. In the late afternoon the river would swell. It filled with the water rushing downstream from the mountains above. By morning, the riverbed was close to dry, its rocky contours exposed. Each day I watched a middle-aged woman crouched down on the riverbed gathering rocks she placed in a basket. Once her basket was full she would balance it on her head as she climbed her way back up the riverbank. From there she made her way slowly to an unseen destination. As she passed I could see her weathered face and hands as she smiled and nodded her greeting. This continued for hours each day. When I asked my host where she was taking her rocks, I was told she sold them to a stonemason in a neighboring village. "It's hard work," he said, "but she is without a husband and has three children. Somehow she gets by."

In a beautifully observed book, the veteran Australian journalist Jana Wendt tells the story of nine different workers—including a priest, a forensic anthropologist, a CEO, a sculptor, and an acrobat—with a view to understanding what drives them in their work.[12] What is common in these stories is a passion, a deep sense that what these people do is part of who they are. To some degree I am one of those. I am gifted with a sustaining sense of vocation in what I work at professionally, but this is not the case for everyone in today's marketplace. For a significant number of people, like this woman with her rocks, work is necessity, nothing more.

In truth, it is a challenging task to find God connections in menial and so-called "unskilled" labor. They are there, of course, but in much less grand and obvious ways. That said, there are signs of the Spirit in the character that we bring to work. Perseverance is one of those.

The writer of the letter to the Romans asserts that "suffering produces perseverance; perseverance, character; and character, hope" (Rom 5:3–4). It is an important link in the chain of spiritual maturity. It speaks of our faithfulness to God and those around us. It mirrors the image of God, the one whose persevering grace holds human existence together. Daily work—especially work that is routine, mundane, or difficult—demands perseverance in good measure. When we choose to persevere in difficult or tedious circumstances for a greater good, we touch the character of God.

3. Choosing to Celebrate

In the creation story, there is a time when God steps back from the work of creation and celebrates the results: "God saw all that he had made, and it was very good" (Gen 1:31). This form of celebration, gathered up in the origins of Sabbath rest, is an expression of our spirituality. It's a time to contemplate and enjoy the worth of who we are and what we have achieved with God. The people of Israel followed an annual calendar of celebratory feasts, each one marking a particular act or provision of God. In their celebrations, the people reaffirmed their dependence upon God and their bonds as the people of God. Even more, these celebrations were an opportunity to enjoy together the fruits of their labor.

By its nature, celebration is seasonal. The depth of celebration is directly proportional to the effort extended in working toward the goal.

12. Wendt, *Nice Work*.

In many cases, our work affords us seasonal opportunities to find joy in what we do—an occasion to say with God, "It is good." Think of the teacher who works day in and day out with her students, explaining, inspiring, exhorting, and prodding—sometimes reveling in the privilege, other times longing to walk away from it—who once every year watches with pride as her students graduate to the next stage in life. Think of the carpenter who labors month after month in rain and heat, hammering, sawing, lifting, negotiating, and constructing a home. There comes the day when he stands back and admires what he's achieved. Think of the therapist who meets week after week with a struggling client: the tears, the anger, the ups and downs, two steps forward, three steps backward. Finally, maybe months or even years later, she watches her client walk out the door for the last time, significantly more whole or stable than before. In each case, there is a God-given opportunity to step aside and name what is good and worthy in our work. We can take it, or simply move on. To take it is a practice of the Spirit. It is a moment to be claimed as one of spiritual worth, for in it we touch the goodness of God.

4. Choosing to Pray

"To work is to pray." So said the monks centuries ago. As lovely as it sounds, it would meet with raised eyebrows in most workplaces today. Certainly, those who have lived in monastic communities are people who've taken hard work seriously but within the context of a worshipping community. Even today, the daily schedule of the cloistered order involves the routine movement between physical labor and the ancient liturgies of prayer. Frankly, there are few secular workplaces that look anything like this. Finding time to sit with co-workers over a cup of coffee is challenge enough. Looking out for spaces to pray is akin to hunting for dinosaurs on company time.

Still, there is truth here, and the opportunity for choice. The exhortation of the Apostle Paul to the Christians of Rome, from merchants to carpet weavers to domestic servants, was compelling. "I urge you, in view of God's mercy," Paul writes, "to offer your bodies as living sacrifices, holy and pleasing to God—this is your spiritual act of worship" (Rom 12:1–2). Similarly he says to the Colossians, "Whatever you do, work at it with all your heart, as working for the Lord . . . it is the Lord Christ you are serving" (Col 3:23–24). It may sound clichéd, but it's clear from these directives that offering our lives to God, including our work, is itself an act of prayer. When we offer up to God who we are in our fullness, everything that issues from our hands, hearts, and imaginations is sanctified.

Prayer comes in many forms. Through the shared liturgies of the church, the solitude of our prayer closets, the aching of our hearts in times of struggle, we reach out for God and God reaches out to us. To claim our work as a means of prayer is to add to these practices, not replace them. For the past decade I have offered a simple prayer at the beginning of my workday. Printed on a small white card, it sits in the drawer of my desk. To be honest, I don't know where it came from, what words are mine, and what comes from other sources. But that no longer matters much. They are words that have become my own in the praying:

> God, I offer myself to you today
> for the work you want me to accomplish,
> for the people you want me to meet,
> for the words you want me to say,
> and for the silences you want me to keep.
> I confess my need of you.
> Grant me the humility to know my limitations,
> the wisdom to discern your voice,
> and the courage to do what is right.
> In the name of Jesus my Lord,
> Amen.

The purpose of such prayers is not to lift our work to a higher spiritual plane. It's more ordinary than that. It is going about our daily routines with the confidence that God is present with us, listening, prodding, and guiding. It is our choice to name it.

11

God on the Weekend

I have long cherished an imaginary world. It is not my own but the creation of cartoonist Michael Leunig. His simple line drawings of ducks, teapots, and little characters with big noses have graced the pages of our city newspaper for decades. His ruminations of whimsy and wisdom have amused, challenged, even infuriated readers. Of all his characters, it is two I love most: the intrepid voyager Vasco Pyjama and his sagacious mentor Mr Curly.

While the driven Vasco circumnavigates the globe in his amphibious armchair, accompanied by his ever-faithful navigating duck, Mr Curly is back in tranquil Curly Flat. There he leads a contented life watching birds and tending his vines on the shores of Lake Lacuna. The adventurous but often fragile Vasco is always on the go, constantly exhausted by his endless pursuit of truth and self-discovery. Periodically he returns to Curly Flat to join his mentor for a picnic at Lacuna, but for the most part these longtime friends correspond via handwritten letters. Luenig calls them *The Curly Pyjama Letters*.

In one letter, Mr Curly responds to a question that troubles his anxious friend. "What is worth doing and what is worth having?" asks Vasco. To this Mr Curly's reply is simple: "It is worth doing nothing and having a rest." In the paragraphs that follow, Mr Curly describes a world "sick with exhaustion" and "dying of restlessness," one where an ecology of evil flourishes as the need for rest is repressed or ignored. A "great mass mania" has taken hold of this world, Mr Curly says, and the consequences are deathly. He concludes with an exhortation:

> I gently urge you Vasco, do as we do in Curly Flat—learn to curl
> up and rest—feel your noble tiredness—learn about it and make

a generous place for it in your life and enjoyment will surely follow. I repeat: it's worth doing nothing and having a rest. Yours sleepily, Mr Curly xxx[1]

Despite Mr Curly's sleepy salutation, there is an urgency to his words: "You must rest, Vasco . . . you must!" The truth that resonates here is that the human need for rest touches things deep in the soul and its lack has serious implications—implications that ripple out to the world beyond. In the town of Curly Flat, rest is a profoundly spiritual issue.

I traveled recently to Sydney for two full days of meetings. The months prior to this trip were overflowing. My family had moved house; my beloved's work had changed; my father was unwell and my pastoral load in the church was unusually heavy; I had accepted more teaching commitments than was sensible, and several deadlines pressed in unforgivingly. I recall sitting in my window seat in the aircraft staring out at the drab grey tarmac as the pilot waited for our turn on the runway. In equal parts I felt dread and relief: dread at the energy the next two days demanded and relief to be leaving Melbourne behind.

After the first day of meetings I returned to the hotel and entered the lift from the lobby. I was headed for my room on the ninth floor. As the doors were about to close, a woman rushed toward the lift wheeling a large purple suitcase behind her. I pressed the button to hold the doors open. She huffed her way in, one wheel of her case running straight across my big toe. I winced. She didn't notice.

The woman was well dressed, a black pants suit with heels and her finger nails painted bright red. As the doors closed she leaned against the lift wall, her head tilted back and her eyes shut, and let out an audible sigh. "A busy day?" I asked as we ascended. "Oh, God yes," she said, opening her eyes but avoiding mine. "I've been *on* since six this morning." She paused. "And it's not over yet." At that the lift door opened. It was her floor. As she wheeled her case out through the doorway I was sure to keep my toes well in. Without thinking, I said to her, "Peace be with you." With that she turned to look directly at me, at first with the most quizzical look as though I might have two heads. But then, just as the doors were about to close, her face softened: "Thank you." She was gone.

As I lay in my hotel bed that night, I recalled the weariness that marked the woman's face, the lines of fatigue that had gathered under her

---

1. Leunig, *The Curly Pyjama Letters*, 26–28.

eyes. Most confrontingly, I saw myself. Her words of lament, "I've been *on* since six this morning," sounded in my head and the graceless state of my own soul was as evident as those bright red nails. The truth is, I had been *on* for so long I barely knew where the *off* button was.

For many of us, life is marked by busyness. It may be the busyness of particular days or weeks. Sometimes busyness comes in waves: seasons in which life feels overwhelmingly full. In its place it can be a constructive part of life. Periods of busyness are pathways to productivity and achievement. But as Mr Curly so pleadingly reminds us, when busyness becomes the standard by which we live—the unrelenting state of our souls—we tread dangerous ground. To live in the constant grip of activity and the desperate weariness that comes with it is to open ourselves to two life-decaying possibilities.

First, it is to verge on a state of violence. According to the *Macquarie Dictionary*, violence is "an unjust and unwarranted exertion of force or power." To live without pause is just that: an unjust, unwarranted force that does violence to ourselves, our families, and ultimately to our world. Second, to live in this state is to live in a state of spiritual deprivation. In it, some of the most fundamental values of our faith are compromised: contemplation, beauty, community, hospitality, gentleness, and generosity. All of these things take time, the very thing we do not have when busyness is the norm and productivity our addiction. Truth be told, sustained deprivations like these sicken the soul.

If we are in pursuit of God, we must understand that the weekend—that routine and defined period of rest, wherever it falls in the week—is as filled with sacred purpose as our days of work and productivity will ever be. Despite the persistent demands of our culture and the urgings of our inner voices to press on, to suppress our natural rhythms in favor of *more, harder,* and *faster,* we people of faith are called to live in a different way. For us, rest is not an addendum to the way of Jesus but a vital expression of it.

The call to rest sits deep in the theology of our Christian tradition and in the Jewish faith that undergirds it. Indeed, it sits at the heart of the creation story we share. The first chapter of Genesis is an account of the extraordinary work that God did to bring this world into being. According to this account, after causing winds to sweep across the face of the earth God calls light out of darkness, separates land from the oceans and plants gardens with fruit trees and seed-bearing plants. God then creates wild animals to roam the land, fills the air with birds and the waters with fish. He sets cattle on the hills and sheep in the pasture, creates a world of insects and a hidden realm of organisms invisible to the human eye. And then God makes humankind to govern and nurture it all. If ever there was an award for productivity, surely God wins.

And yet at the end of all this, Genesis 2:2 tells us, "God finished the work that he had done, and he rested on the seventh day." Not only so, but God blessed this seventh-day rest and proclaimed it "hallowed" forevermore. This picture of God resting is not just a religious quirk at the end of the story; it is the story's culmination, the moment to which the creator and all creation moves. As God rests, so we rest. We who engage in the *imitatio Dei*, the imitation of God, rest with God because rest is *of* God. What's more, God sets this pattern of rest apart as holy. No other aspect of creation is revered like this. Clearly, the call to rest is important.

The Jewish people understood this. As their laws and customs developed, so this practice of sabbath-keeping became the organizing principle of their lives. As sabbath is unpacked in their codes and practices of community, we begin to understand the comprehensive nature of this divine call. It touches not only the weekly schedule of the individual but of the entire community under God: "You shall not do any work—you, your son or your daughter, your male or female slave, your livestock, or the alien resident in your towns" (Exod 20:10). By necessity it moves from the broad principle of creation to the particular patterns of life in households and neighborhoods; and from there to the good of the earth and all that depends on it.

> For six years you shall sow your land and gather in its yield; but the seventh year you shall let it rest and lie fallow, so that the poor of your people may eat; and what they leave the wild animals may eat. You shall do the same with your vineyard, and with your olive orchard. Six days you shall do your work, but on the seventh day you shall rest, so that your ox and your donkey may have relief, and your homeborn slave and the resident alien may be refreshed. (Exod 23:10–12)

Clearly, this Sabbath rest is an all-encompassing one. It includes the rest of God, the rest of humankind, and the rest of the earth. It is a social, economic, and environmental rest enfolding the complex ecosystems of life. Why? Because the divine call to rest is essential to the sustainability of all things. Without rest there is only death.

At the heart of this call to sabbath rest is the invitation of God to a particular rhythm of life. It is a rhythm that allows for the routine movement from one pace of life to another: from one that is fast, productive, and life-demanding, to one that is slow, present, and life-restoring. The distinctive pace of sabbath is one that prioritizes presence over productivity, delight over demand, stillness over progress. It is a pace that invites us to notice, name, and celebrate.

Sadly, among religious people both Jewish and Christian, the laws of sabbath-keeping have a checkered history. In many religious childhoods, the sabbath was a day of "thou shalt nots": thou shalt not work; thou shalt not go the cinema; thou shalt not play sport; thou shalt not polish thy shoes or wash thy car. Regardless, the essence of sabbath is nothing to do with negative legalism. It is a resounding affirmation of life, beauty, and delight.

Theologian Frank Rees points to the refrain in the Genesis story "It is good!"—repeated no less than six times in this first account of creation—as a rich affirmation of God's intent for sabbath. This rest is defined not by what God doesn't do, but by these routine declarations of wonder in what has been achieved. For people of faith, sabbath-keeping is not about negating life but the celebration of life in its fullness. It's about the practices of "engaging positively with God's creation, affirming life, valuing the good things achieved and reflecting on what needs to be put right. It is about recreation, reflection and renewal."[2] Theologian Jürgen Moltmann agrees:

> The celebration of the sabbath leads to an intensified capacity for perceiving the loveliness of everything—food, clothing, the body, the soul—because existence itself is glorious. Questions about the possibility of 'producing' something, or about utility, are forgotten in the face of the beauty of all created things.[3]

Sabbath's gift to us is the routine provision of time in which we slow down long enough to do this very thing: to perceive or notice—to take in all that is good in our world, our lives and our relationships, and ultimately, in God. Tragically, in an age that idolizes speed and productivity, the act of noticing is a dying art. If it's to be restored, it will be found in the priority of rest and the art of slowness that characterizes it. Abraham Heschel, one of the great Jewish philosophers of the twentieth century,

2. Rees, "New Directions in Australian Spirituality," 78.

3. Moltmann, *God in Creation*, 286.

describes the sabbath as a great cathedral, a "palace in time" set apart from all other time. "Six days a week we wrestle with the world, wringing profit from the earth," he writes. "On the Sabbath we care for the seed of eternity planted in the soul."[4] Stepping into the cathedral so as to nurture this eternal seed is a choice: a choice to be still, to breathe deeply and to know that God is God. It is a choice we are invited to make as a matter of course.

The call of Jesus to salvation and the call to sabbath rest are not entirely different things. The invitation of Jesus in Matthew 11 is a call to rest at the deepest level.

> Come to me, all you who are weary and burdened, and I will give you rest. Take my yoke upon you and learn from me, for I am gentle and humble in heart, and you will find rest for your souls. For my yoke is easy and my burden is light. (Matt 11:28–30)

In an ancient Aramaic version of these words, Jesus says, "Come to me and I will rest you, I will Sabbath you and you will find Sabbath for your souls." The salvation we find in Jesus Christ is an all-encompassing rest. It is rest with God, rest with ourselves, and rest with the world. It describes a state of deep contentment, a peace that is beyond understanding. Our salvation means an end to striving, an end to craving and clawing our way into the presence of God. It is the broad invitation of grace reflected in the bidding of the psalmist: "Be still and know that I am God" (Ps 46:10); "Come to me and I will rest you."

Weekends have changed. Those lazy weekends of my childhood are like a different species to the weekends I know today. On Saturday mornings my father worked overtime. With the shops closed for the weekend at noon, most Saturday mornings were spent wandering the main street and helping mum with the groceries. Once Dad was home, Saturday afternoon was a mixture of gardening, an occasional drive in the hills, or visiting relatives on the other side of town. Saturday night we were home, always. Sundays were entirely predictable: Sunday school in the morning followed by the church service; lunch was always at home—usually a Sunday roast shared with a full table of visitors—followed by an afternoon nap before returning to church again at night. What I remember is that there were well-defined edges between work and play, work and worship, work and family. Everything seemed to know its place.

---

4. Heschel, *The Sabbath*, 13.

Today those edges have disappeared. While the idea of the week's end remains deep in the psyche, its reality is radically different. There is not a day of the week when the shopping centers are closed, not a mealtime when the cafes are empty, not an hour when sport is corralled or a moment when access to emails and social media is shut down. Everything is always *on*. There's no *off*. The result is that, whatever shape our weekend takes, it's guaranteed to be full. According to the demographer Bernard Salt, the old slow weekend of "rest and prayer" is long buried and the boundaries that surrounded it dissolved. In its place is a new anxiety-ridden pace that extends from Monday to Sunday: "sprint, run, sprint, run."[5] We have lost the art of stopping, he says. We have lost the art of slowness.

The extent of this loss is underlined by the work of social anthropologist Thomas Hylland Erikson. He describes the impacts of this new age as a time in which opportunities for slowness have been eradicated, and all gaps have been filled. With speed's relentless ascendancy, the possibilities for elements of life to be lived slowly are diminished. The truth is, whenever the values of fast and slow come up against each other, fast wins.

Fast time is the time of the clock. It is measured, relentless, and inflexible. It proceeds in persistent increments and is a rule unto itself. It stands independent of the events of life and proceeds regardless. By contrast, slow time is natural time. It is the time of nature, the seasons, and the body. It is the time it takes to be born, to heal, to grow and flourish, to grieve and to die. Slow time is imprecise and variable. It's connection with the events of life is intrinsic. The writer of Ecclesiastes describes a time for every purpose under heaven. Natural time—time given by God for all the events, encounters, and emotions of life—takes whatever time it takes. It cannot be rushed. The great tragedy of modern life is that we have surrendered control to clock time. We have given in to what appears to be its inevitability. As sociologist Barbara Adam says, "When the invariable time of the clock is superimposed on living systems, it is the living systems that are required to adapt."[6] And so our weekends of slowness are subsumed.

What's more, Erikson says, we live under an avalanche of information, so much so, we are pickled in it. Our lives are dominated by screens

---

5. As quoted in McCulloch, "Death of the Weekend," 20.

6. Adam, "Time," 123.

large and small and we move at speed from one issue to the next, one encounter to another. The result is we live a continuous series of "saturated moments without a 'before' and 'after', a 'here' and 'there' to separate them."[7] The demands of this accelerated and saturated *now* are so persistent we simply have no time to reflect on yesterday or to anticipate tomorrow. In fact, the resource in shortest supply is time to remember, reflect, or renew. Under these circumstances, Moltmann describes the modern person as "homo accelerandus:"

> He has a great many encounters, but does not really experience anything, since although he wants to see everything, he internalizes nothing and reflects upon nothing. He has a great many contacts but no relationships, since he is unable to linger because he is always 'in a hurry'. He devours 'fast food', preferably while standing, because he is no longer able to enjoy anything; after all, a person needs time for enjoyment, and time is precisely what he does not have.[8]

We may not always see ourselves in words like these, but most of us will acknowledge the increasing difficulty it is to internalize: to sit with one image, one story, or one encounter for any length of time. Our daily lives are often like an edition of the evening news. A story comes across the screen detailing the most extraordinary atrocities in some part of the world: images of bodies being dragged from the rubble or news of a family bereft. We are horrified, confronted, challenged, or moved. But before any of those feelings can take root, we have moved to the next story.

When the pace of our lives means rarely slowing down long enough to even know what we feel, think, or hope for, our capacity for a meaningful contribution to life is jeopardized. Theologian Robert Banks describes the tyranny of a world in which so many people "have not heard from themselves for a long, long time." "They who are 'on the run'," he writes, "never meet anyone any more, not even themselves."[9] The impact of this tyranny is most commonly named by the poets, those who take time to see and understand. Indeed, it takes Mr Curly, an imaginary sage from a fanciful place, to name a reality we sense intuitively to be true: "love cannot take root in this sad situation." A less fanciful sage Judith Wright names a similar truth. In the frantic activity that so marks our lives, she

---

7. Erikson, *Tyranny of the Moment*, 2.

8. Moltmann, Wolterstorff, and Charry, *A Passion for God's Reign*, 39.

9. Banks, *The Tyranny of Time*, 66.

says, we fail to remember "the Dream" or find "the Thing"; we fail to have our hearts shaken by our deepest longings for they are unknown.[10] The truth is, if our hearts are ever to be shaken, if we are to remember our "one thing," then the weekend of quiet and slowness needs to become more than an occasional footnote to our lives. It must be a regular part of the text.

I have spent a large part of my working life pastoring churches and a great deal of time with colleagues committed to the same profession. Pastors, vicars, and priests are a competitive bunch, as beset with insecurities as any other professional group. In my first church appointment I recall attending monthly meetings of clergy from the local area. Every time we met, our talk moved to the "unique" pressures of Christian ministry and inevitably to our testimonies of busyness. In a spirit of unspoken competition, I recall one story topping them all. This middle-aged pastor with a furrowed brow told us that he had not been at home with his family for forty-one consecutive nights, all in the name of ministry. A muffled gasp went around the room. It was a response of both shock and admiration. "Now there's a real disciple," we silently agreed; "one prepared to count the cost." In retrospect, I am appalled.

Our relationship to rest speaks eloquently of our understanding of God. If one's need for rest is that thing to be overcome, to be navigated around in our effort to prove our worth, earn our stripes, or compensate for our failings, we may well question our perception of God and what this God is like. Psalm 23, perhaps the most familiar psalm in the Bible, speaks of God as a loving and attentive shepherd leading those in his care to places of rest, tranquility, and peace: "He leads me beside quiet waters; he restores my soul." But that was certainly not the God of my earliest years in ministry. The words of an enthusiastic preacher from my youth still rang in my ears: "Better to burn out for Jesus than rust out for the devil!" The urgency of the call, the enormity of need and the example of my peers were coupled with an understanding of God as an inspiring but demanding taskmaster.

"The Lord is my supervisor," begins Edward Vasicek's paraphrase of the psalm that resonates too deeply to be comfortable; "He makes me cut down the green pastures; he leads me to jog alongside rapid waters." It concludes with this frank admission: "Surely busyness and pressure shall

---

10. From "The Child" in Wright, *Collected Poems 1942–1970*, 36.

follow me all the days of my life; and I will run to and fro in the house of the Lord forever."[11] There is no doubt, our vocation as disciples is to follow, to labor, to proclaim, to serve, to give of ourselves sacrificially as fellow bearers of the cross; but should this calling drive us into the ground without sustaining moments of delight, without seasons of restoration and renewal, then the God we point to and the gospel we embody will be good news to no one. Eugene Peterson's version of Psalm 23 tells of a God who beds us down "in lush meadows" and provides "quiet pools" to drink from.[12] This is the God of quiet intervals, the one who provides spaces of healing and peace—periods of stillness and renewal—from which we can move out into the world as followers of Jesus.

Sleep as a Spiritual Practice

Despite Shakespeare lauding sleep as the "chief nourisher in life's feast,"[13] the proposition that sleep can be a spiritual discipline is often a hard sell. If spiritual practices are acts of intention and choice, the cynic will say, then surely in falling asleep we surrender intention and enter a zone of neutrality where nothing of spiritual consequence happens. That said, the proposal that up to one third of our lives—perhaps twenty-five years in all—is spiritually empty is an even harder case to support.

Think first of what life is like without sleep. Those who have been parents to newborn babies recall this with anguish. Prolonged sleep deprivation can result in a depth of despair difficult to fathom from the outside. I have sat with numerous parents whose sleep patterns have been thrown into chaos by the presence of an infant and for whom desperation is palpable. I have seen similar impacts in those who battle medical conditions that limit prolonged and deep sleep. One's entire sense of wellbeing is threatened. The prevalence of sleep deprivation is a serious issue in society with evident impacts upon health and wellbeing. A recent national survey here in Australia found 25 percent of Australians reporting frequent sleep difficulties with up to 10 percent suffering diagnosable sleep disorders.[14] Similar results have been found in the US where 28 percent of respondents report insufficient sleep as an almost

11. Vasicek, "The Workaholic's 23rd Psalm."

12. Peterson, *The Message: Psalms*, 33.

13. From Macbeth, Act 2, Scene 2. Quoted by Martin, *Counting Sheep*, 4.

14. Hillman and Lack, "Public Health Implications of Sleep Loss," S8.

daily event.[15] One of the most prominent sleep researchers of the past century concludes we live in a sleep-sick society.[16] A leading specialist in general respiratory and sleep medicine at Melbourne's Alfred Hospital was recently reported as saying, "Ever since the lightbulb was invented, the mobile phone and the internet, sleep disorders are skyrocketing. It's as much a problem as obesity or alcohol abuse but because it's happening at night it's often ignored."[17]

Such is the problem, there are huge pharmacological industries set up to provide us medicated pathways to sleep. The sleepless become desperate, and it's no wonder they do. Sleep deprived people suffer high rates of depression, depleted psychological stamina, poorer decision-making capacities, loss of concentration and focus, poorer thinking skills, strained relationships with those they love, and diminished capacity to cope with the smallest challenges of life. Indeed, humans can survive longer without food than they can without sleep.

With all this in mind, we begin to appreciate the gift that a good night's sleep is and what an extraordinary impact it has upon the receptivity of our hearts and minds. If we begin with the assertion that sleep is a gift of God, we are at the beginning of a view of sleep that is more central to our spirituality than we may have thought.

1. Sleep as an Act of Faith

As a father to young children, I carried a high degree of anxiety around the depth at which I sleep. While my beloved sleeps like a cat, alert to the slightest noise or movement in the house, I sleep deeply and am rarely disturbed. It has always been that way. My anxiety related to the presence of these little people in my life and their need to be attended to no matter what the hour, especially if my beloved was away from home. What if I simply slept through their distress? With responsibility entirely in my hands, my uncertainty often kept me from going to sleep in the first place. As it turned out, I had nothing to worry about. Some sort of

15. Centers for Disease Control and Prevention, "Perceived Insufficient Rest or Sleep among Adults."

16. Dement, *Some Must Watch While Some Must Sleep.*

17. Quoting Professor Matthew Naughton, in Stark, "Australians Need Quality Shut-Eye," 6.

paternal instinct kicked in and all was well, but I did learn something about the act of sleep I have never forgotten. Sleep is an act of faith.

With or without children, sleep is a tangible act of surrender. By giving our body and mind over to sleep, we relinquish control. For an extended period each day we drop our guard and let go. From a spiritual perspective, this is not unrelated to our trust in God. The psalmist says, "You, O Lord, are a shield around me . . . I lie down and sleep; I wake again for the Lord sustains me" (Ps 3:3–5). Why this level of trust? Because "he who keeps Israel will neither slumber nor sleep" (Ps 121:4). Rest easy for God is awake.

I remember clearly my introduction to the child's prayer, "Now I lay me down to sleep, I pray thee Lord my soul to keep, and if I die before I wake, I pray thee Lord my soul to take." It was in my early years of Sunday school. We met in the church kitchen for lack of other space and sat on the tiniest of chairs. My teacher was a warm and motherly woman with whom I felt safe, but I didn't like her prayer. I lay in bed at night imagining the possibility of God snatching away my soul while my eyes were closed. Though still not a prayer I use, I have sat with enough dying people to appreciate it more than I did in Sunday school. The labored breathing of a person as they edge closer to the end has had me praying on more than one occasion that their ultimate sleep would come, that God would take their soul and let them rest. Kept or taken, our souls are in the hands of God and when we sleep that surrender of our souls is tangible.

Sleep is the gift of a loving God, a shepherd leading us daily to a quiet place of rest and solitude. By surrendering to it, we acknowledge our dependence and the limitations of our powers and responsibilities in the world: this world is yours, God, not mine.

> Unless the LORD builds the house,
> those who build it labor in vain.
> Unless the LORD guards the city,
> the guard keeps watch in vain.
> It is in vain that you rise up early
> and go late to rest,
> eating the bread of anxious toil;
> for he gives sleep to those he loves. (Ps 127:1–2)

2. Sleep as Space for God to Speak

In an ancient Scottish prayer, God is described as the "Weaver of Dreams." The prayer bids this God to "weave well in you as you sleep."[18] In the stories of the Bible, it is in dreams that God often speaks, reveals, commissions, or directs. There's the story of Joseph and the dreams that so riled his brothers, but would lead him into positions of influence and power (Gen 37). There's Solomon's dreams in which God came to him, conversed with him and gifted him (1 Kgs 3). There's Daniel and his ability to interpret dreams that identified him as a man of God (Dan 2). In the birth stories of Jesus, an angel visits an unsuspecting Joseph in his dreams and reveals God's plan for him and his family (Matt 1). After the child's birth, the angel returns to Joseph's dreams, warning him of the dangers ahead and directing him and his family to a place of safety (Matt 2). It was in a dream that the Apostle Peter received wisdom from God that would affect the development of the early church (Acts 10), as did Paul for the direction of his mission (Acts 16).

Acknowledging all of these, I confess I have no dramatic dream stories of my own. Frankly, I rarely remember my dreams, and if I do they are mostly odd; certainly nothing I could pin on God. That said, there have been dreams that are telling in the anxieties they name and the concerns they highlight. And there have been moments when I have woken from a night's sleep with a clearer sense of something or release from a particular concern.

When my beloved and I were living in California, I attended a lecture by a psychologist who nudged his audience to pay greater attention to their dreams. His take-home challenge was that we keep a small notebook and pen by our beds and make a habit of writing down something about our dreams immediately after having them. I went to him after the lecture. "But I hardly remember them," I said. He replied, "The trick is to make yourself wake up immediately after a dream and note it down. You'll remember them!" I looked at him quizzically. Clearly he had never slept with me. "Try it!" he smiled as though he knew something I didn't.

So that night I began. I placed a small notebook by my bed and a pen. "I will wake up," I said with more skepticism than confidence. Wonder of wonders, I did. In fact, over a three-month period I filled my notebook with mostly incoherent scribbles. Even more, as I looked back through them I could see particular themes, anxieties, images, and

18. From the *Garmina Gadelica*, quoted in Simpson, ed., *Celtic Blessings*, 97.

people crop up repeatedly. Compost for my usual practice of journaling had never been so rich. In this simple exercise I learnt more about my unconscious world of concern than I could have imagined in my waking hours. While I would not tag God on all of the things that surfaced, I did learn that there is wisdom to be had and God's presence to be discerned, even in my dreams.

Michael Leunig, the muse for my small companions from Curly Flat, is also the writer of prayers, gentle prayers that name the elements of life in simple ways. One of those is a prayer for our dreams. "We give thanks for the darkness of the night where lies the world of dreams," he writes, and bids God to gift us with good dreams and memory of them, "that we may carry their poetry and their mystery into our daily lives."[19]

3. Sleep as a Form of Sabbath Rest

Just as the principle of Sabbath rest is kept and maintained in the weekly formula of one in seven, so daily hours of sleep are part of a God-ordained rhythm that marks our days. As God's rest is celebrated and honored on the final day of the creation week, so that celebration marks the end of each day: "and God saw that it was good."

Sleep is a conclusion, a benediction on the day now gone. It is our daily declaration of completion. In the morning we wake; we wash, dress, and nourish our bodies for the day ahead. From there we travel and work and learn, we trade and serve, we organize and provide. We eat and relate. We converse, reflect, and work some more. We eat again. We play. We talk. And then, when all is done, we lay our bodies down in the same place as we began. We sleep. It is good. Within this rhythm of life, sleep is more than a physiological necessity. It is a God-ordained act, an act of virtue and character. Indeed, it is a spiritual act.

While staying in a monastery in central England in my early twenties, I found in the otherwise empty bottom drawer of my bedside table a prayer printed onto a piece of moth-eaten card. Clearly it had sat there for some time, unseen and unused. I had to brush away a pair of earwigs and good covering of dust to read it. As I did, it struck a chord and I copied the words into my journal. Since then, I have seen it in more credible places than a dusty drawer. It comes from the Celtic traditions of Northern England. What struck me at the time, and does still, is that it

---

19. Leunig, *A Common Prayer*, 7–8.

is a corporate prayer rather than one that is purely personal. Whenever I use it, I do so imagining that I pray this prayer with countless others, both present and past. Together, as the great congregation of faith, we lay our heads down in the darkness of the night and claim the stillness of our God.

> May we rest this night in the stillness of your being.
> O Radiant Dawn, splendor of eternal life,
> come and shine on us
> that we may sleep in the warmth of your radiance.
> O Emmanuel, God with us, we will lie down with you
> and you will lie down with us.
> And the dawn will come and so will your appearing
> And we shall know as we are known
> And in pleasure you will receive us.
> Call forth this night bearers of your presence.
> Call forth this night believers in your truth.[20]

---

20. One version of this prayer is quoted by Simpson, ed., *Celtic Blessings*, 102.

PART 3

Nurturing a Different Way in the Church

12

Resourcing the People of God

Through the chapters of this book we've traversed significant territory. In search of the presence of God and a way of seeing that acknowledges God at the center of life, we've looked in many places. We have moved from the home to the neighborhood; from the kitchen and laundry to the local café; from the supermarket to the running track; from the sporting arena to time with friends; from the workplace to weekends of rest; and from family meals to the nightly routine of sleep. What's important to the journey is this: while the territory we've traveled is diverse, it's all right under our noses. There are no seas to cross in search of God, no pilgrimages to faraway, holy places. The invitation of the book has been not to come away to some other place, but to press more deeply into the places in front of us. Why? Because Christian faith teaches us that God is as present here as God is anywhere.

My hope is that this book is an encouragement to people of faith of all traditions and stages. Whether you're mature in faith or just starting out, a serious student of the Bible or still finding your way around it, it is my prayer that you are inspired along the way. Even more, I hope that you leave this book with a greater awareness of God's calling in your life, no matter how ordinary it seems. If that is the case, then my time has been well spent.

In this final chapter I move from addressing all readers to a particular audience. As a pastor, I want to speak directly to other pastors: those whose task it is to encourage, nurture, and strengthen the faith of God's people. Just as all callings are holy and obligating, so is ours; and it is one we are bound to take seriously.

Regardless of tradition, size, or location, our churches are home to people who need us. They need us to cheer them on in their journey. They need us to inspire, resource, and equip them for a spirituality that makes a difference to their lives. They need us to curate worshipping opportunities that connect them more deeply with the presence of God in the world. Some even need our permission and blessing to pursue God in more immediate ways than they have traditionally done. Our role as pastors, coaches, and guides is important.

The truth is, pastors' lives are drenched in God, or at least in the language of God. We spend the vast majority of our time engaged in the community and ministry of the church. We preach God; we talk God; we work for God. Everything we do has connections with the rituals and symbols of spirituality. Granted, we may not always feel that way, but for those who look on from the outside, the connections between us and God could not be clearer.

It is easy for us to forget that this is not the case for the majority of those who gather in our churches week by week. What is explicit and taken for granted for us is often tenuous and fragile for others. While they may sing of the sustaining peace of God on Sunday, they show up to the office on Monday morning under an avalanche of deadlines, tensions, disgruntled coworkers, and budget lines under pressure. While the pastor's sermon may have been a masterful exegesis of Romans 6 or a rousing defense of egalitarianism in the church, connections with the challenges they face with fractious neighbors next door or the rebellious children they return home to after the service are hard to find.

I write this chapter in the middle of January. The celebrations of Advent and Christmas are packed away along with our welcome of the new year. Life picks up speed again and the weekly routines of ministry kick back in. As I have sat down to prepare my first sermon for the year, I have done so in the midst of a steady stream of pastoral appointments.

I have sat with a much-loved older member of our church who now spends her days and months confined to a room in an aged-care home. As illness and age take their course, she has lost all ability to communicate. What she recognizes or hears from those who come and go is a mystery. Every day, her husband of fifty-eight years sits with her and holds her hand. Without fail, he arrives in the early afternoon and stays beside her through the evening meal. This dear man is as regular at Sunday worship as one can be. He sings and prays and listens with grace; but little do those who sit around him understand what he carries each day and what it costs.

I have shared coffee with a young woman beginning her second year as a receptionist at one of the city's five-star hotels. Originally from southeast Asia, her choice to study in Australia has turned into a longer stay than she imagined. She is here without the close support of family and with constant challenges of language and culture to meet. As I often remind her, she is very brave. Though she is now working in the industry she aspired to be part of for so long, it has turned out to be a more demanding world than she imagined, especially challenging to her values as a Christian. "Sometimes it feels like more than I can cope with," she confides.

At breakfast today I had my routine appointment with a man who retired from his life's work in the education sector one year ago. It was a fulfilling career that affirmed his identity and worth in myriad ways. The last twelve months have brought a mixture of relief and loss, freedom and anxiety, rest and restlessness. He describes it as one of the most challenging transitions he has faced. "There is no end of things to keep me busy," he often says, "but I struggle to know who I am or who I am meant to be."

While each of these encounters is unique, conversations like these are the bread and butter of pastoral ministry. These are the people who need us. They need us to do two things. Firstly, they need us to provide time, space, and community in which they can express and deepen their faith, claim God's hope and grace for their lives, and be reminded of life's purpose and calling. Secondly, they need us to be aware of and take seriously the worlds they inhabit during the week, the challenges they face, and the questions that press in upon their lives. If we are to affirm the people who sit in our pews as the priesthood of the church, our obligation is to ensure we are nurturing and equipping them for the calling and duties of priesthood; but to do so amidst the complexities of the lives they live, not the lives we imagine for them.

Back in 1961, philosopher Elton Trueblood published a little book entitled *The Company of the Committed*. At the time it was a radical manifesto for the church, one based on a strident critique of church leadership that rendered the people of God servants to the programs of the institution while failing to release them as the priesthood of God in the world. Sadly, Trueblood's call was largely ignored by the church of his time and his voice marginalized by its white-collared gatekeepers. Regardless, and despite its dated language, the book remains an inspiring read and its thesis critical to the flourishing of the church's mission.

As a Quaker, Trueblood had little time for religious faith that was segmented from what he called "the common life" of the people. Especially puerile, in his view, were the disconnections of *place* (confining religious expression to church buildings), *time* (keeping religious fervor to Sunday mornings) and *personnel* (surrendering the idea of a religious calling to the clergy) that dogged the church of his day.[1] He warned that such disconnects rendered "the company of the committed" impotent as agents of a life-changing gospel. In doing so, he wrote, "we make religion relatively trivial, concerned with only part of experience when it ought to be concerned with the whole of life."[2]

In light of this conviction, Trueblood argued for a radical reframing of ministry and spirituality. He called for an end to the division between secular and Christian responsibilities—between the work of the marketplace and the work of the church. He described this division as "damaging and vicious," leaving the promotion of the gospel to a select few.[3] For Trueblood, the so-called "ministry of the laity"—the work of the congregation in contrast to the work of the pastor—needed recasting as the main game rather than an aside to true ministry. Trueblood argued that "the only kind of lay ministry worth encouraging is that which makes a radical difference to the entire Christian enterprise."[4] In other words, lay ministry is not some second-rate auxiliary to the real thing. It *is* the real thing—men and women engaged at the forefront of everyday life as ministers of liberation and redemption. When it comes to ministry, the old idea may have been that the lay people of the church were the pastor's helpers, he wrote, but "the new and vital idea is that the pastor is the helper of the ordinary lay members in the performance of their daily ministry in the midst of secular life."[5]

To all of this I can say a resounding "amen," as can many of you. My sense is, the theological resistance Trueblood met among church leaders in his day has dissipated. Affirmation of the ministry of the people of God—all the people of God—is shared by many more pastors today than

1. Trueblood, *The Company of the Committed*, 9.
2. Ibid., 10.
3. Ibid., 39.
4. Ibid., 62.
5. Ibid., 63.

it might have been fifty years ago. That said, our practice lags behind. To a large degree, we continue to function in churches built on a model of ministry that is strongly church-focused and program-centered. Furthermore, the extraordinary energy and resources we continue to pour into the Sunday gathering, dwarfing our investments elsewhere, communicates a premium on God's presence as a *temple reality* more than it is a *world reality*.

In over thirty years of church ministry, I have seen the complexities and demands of the church—as a community, an organization, and a provider of programs—ask a great deal of church members. The expectations of pastors, denominational leaders, and congregations themselves are that a successful church is a busy church—one with an array of services, programs, committees, and ministries that demand substantial levels of voluntary labor and investment. We may well affirm the ministry of the people of God on the front lines of our society, but our demands on those who sign up as serious disciples to keep the church and its programs ticking along say otherwise. What's more, our most persistent models of spirituality continue to preference withdrawal from Trueblood's "common life" so as to nurture the soul. The language of our prayers, liturgies, and music reinforces this truth every Sunday.

The definition of spirituality I proposed in the early chapters is this:

> Spirituality had to do with discerning and responding to the presence and purposes of God through Christ in every place, every task, and every encounter of every day.

If we accept such an inclusive definition of spirituality, then our role as pastors is both clarified and challenged. Firstly, it clarifies the shape of spirituality we are responsible for nurturing. Our first duty is to ensure our people have the tools to discern God's presence in their lives, as well as the understanding and courage necessary to participate in God's work in the world. Secondly, it challenges us to ensure the church's investment in the *places, tasks,* and *encounters* of everyday life are prioritized in our approach to mission and our equipping for ministry.

I return to the two things our people need from us: (i) to provide a time, space, and community in which they can express and deepen their faith, bringing the challenges, questions, and longings of their lives into God's presence; and (ii) to be aware of and take seriously the worlds they inhabit during the week, encouraging and resourcing their growth as the priesthood of God in the world. It is these two needs that have significantly shaped my ministry for many years now. With varying degrees of success and some notable failures, with moments of great reward and some of struggle, I have worked to make these two needs central to my priorities and focus as a pastor. While I have few impressive stories to tell, I am constantly surprised by the people of God as they travel ever more deeply with Christ in their lives, and as they engage as ministers of the gospel in their homes, neighborhoods, workplaces, and communities with courage and faith.

In the remainder of this chapter, I want to suggest ways we can prioritize these two needs in our ministry, first, in the way we *gather* on a Sunday and the form our worship takes, and second, in the way we encourage and resource the people of God once they *scatter* throughout the community the rest of the week

The Church Gathered

Years ago, I came across a book in a second-hand shop that had been mysteriously misshelved. It stood between two volumes, one on urban planning and the other on the peculiar mating rituals of bees. The book in between was *The Everyday God* by the English theologian J. G. Davies. Careful to avoid the bees, I pulled Davies off the shelf and began reading.

This chance find was a formative one for me. As a young pastor I was struggling to understand the purpose of worship. As pastor of a small community—a fledgling church in a new housing estate—I knew these people were doing it tough. The dysfunctionality of their families was exacerbated by the economic struggles of their working-class community. So much of the worship practice I saw modeled elsewhere felt like an awkward fit here. On one hand, I saw worship that was grand and triumphalist in language and theology, rendering God an enthroned monarch or an armed commander-in-chief. Amidst the realities of low-cost housing, youth unemployment, and high rates of domestic violence, worship like this felt out of place. On the other hand, I saw forms of worship that were so intimate as to be almost romantic in form. With their "hold me, love me, touch me" songs and "please daddy" prayers, God sounded more like a boyfriend, or perhaps a benevolent, if slightly eccentric uncle you could hit up for a loan.

My conundrum at the time was this: if worship is the response of God's people to the wonder of God's holiness in the world, that world needs to be taken seriously. This was not the case in what I saw around me. In the first form, the realities of the world were commonly ignored in favor of a dogged affirmation that God is enthroned on high. In the second, the inference was that in face of life's challenges all we really needed was another hug from Jesus. The trouble is, if I am not into hugs or if the challenges of my world only deepen, the sentiments of eternal devotion are hollow.

What I found in Davies's book was an opportunity to think again about the purpose of worship—to consider afresh the nature of God's holiness and its connection to the life of a worshipping community. According to Davies, the holiness of God—that extraordinary confluence of the transcendence and imminence of the divine—is not something to be comprehended apart from the world we live in. Indeed, we encounter it most profoundly in the midst of life, not in a time, place, or state of mind set apart from it. "The holy is not an *a priori* category," he argues; "it is not something that can be apprehended apart from other experiences." He continues by affirming the holiness of God as a reality encountered "in, with and under ordinary human experience." Indeed, he says, "it is the depth of that experience."[6]

With this in mind, Davies helpfully describes the worship of the gathered church as a "disclosure situation." That is, it's a practice that gets us ready to recognize and respond to God's holiness in the world. It fine-tunes our antenna for the divine in every aspect of our lives. This means that worship is not a practice set apart for and contained by the church service. "Worship is an activity that springs out of life in the world," Davies concludes.[7] Our worship flows from that life, celebrates and bears that life before God, and leads us back into that life with a renewed awareness and commitment. Worship in the church and worship in life are part of one continuous response to God's presence in the world.

This broad and world-connected sense of worship has implications for the way we structure and lead worship for the gathered church. Here are some that have become important to me.

1. Language in Worship

As leaders of worship, we should watch our language. For better or worse, it is our voices that get heard most consistently in the gathering. Because

6. Davies, *The Everyday God*, 87.

7. Ibid., 307.

of this, we hold a high degree of responsibility in setting the tone and emphases in worship. The language we use and the routine focus of our words shape the theology of our people in significant ways. In our calls to worship, prayers, sermons, and benedictions, we proclaim theological priorities over and over again. Too often we do so without thinking.

I have a long-standing practice of writing out calls to worship and benedictions in full. There are upsides to this practice, and downsides too. Words on a page stored in files are both a resource we can draw on and evidence we might prefer to forget. In a recent review of my files, I was not prepared for the degree to which I favor certain names and titles for God over others. Words like *father, lord, creator, redeemer,* and *almighty* appear routinely. None of these are wrong, of course, but God is revealed to us in so many others ways: as *mother, midwife, designer, architect, builder, gardener, nurse, advocate, provider, confidant, comforter, healer, keeper, nurturer, suffering one, hiding place, host, chef, teacher, judge, neighbor, friend* . . . and so it continues. While terms like *lord, almighty,* and *redeemer* in relation to God are rich in meaning and important to maintain, they are not common language beyond the doors of the church. Many of the alternatives are. It is not about surrendering some words in favor of others, but being sure our language is appropriately broad and inclusive of life. God certainly is!

So, too, with the community information we highlight in the context of worship. If the only personal references I make are to those who are ill or traveling—both code for reasons why these people are not present in worship—it creates an unspoken perception that the focus of our community is *here* not *there*. If, however, we are able to routinely celebrate achievements and milestones in the workplace or on the sports field, identify neighbors and friends outside of the church in need, highlight local schools, community groups, and political leaders who deserve our prayers, we move from the language of *huddle* to the language of *reach*. The point is, if we are about making clear connections between the worship of Sunday and the life of our people, our language is important.

2. Prayers in Worship

I grew up in a church that valued extemporaneous prayers over those written down. We had a strong suspicion of "empty" and "repetitious" words parroted by rote. We preferred prayer as evidence of God's Spirit present in the moment. I still love a good extemporaneous prayer spoken from the heart. It can be the most moving evidence of a person steeped in God's presence and convicted by faith; I feel my own spirit carried along. Then again, I have heard more than a few off-the-cuff public prayers that are nothing but empty waffle struggling for gravity, purpose, or conclusion. "Don't you know who you're speaking to?" I want to ask.

The language of our public prayer says a great deal about our theology. What we understand to be of concern to God; what emphases we give to praise or thanksgiving over confession, asking over listening, personal need over public concerns; and especially, the style of language we revert to in prayer. For me, one of the benefits of written prayers—whether our own or those from our tradition—is that we can see these things more clearly in our preparation. Most especially, though, preparing written prayers allows us to be sure we are taking the neighborhoods we inhabit and the paths we traverse each day into the presence of God with intention and forethought.

One of the things I have done with members of my community is to lead prayer-writing workshops in which we write prayers together that reflect the places and challenges of our lives. What comes out of these workshops are some of the most creative, heartfelt prayers with immediate connections to life within and beyond the church doors. The use of them brings an attention to our praying that is life-giving.

The church I pastor sits at the heart of a thriving city. It's a busy neighborhood surrounded by the sounds of commerce, trade, and constant movement. Though old city churches are often described as refuges of peace amidst the city's chaos, we are also part of the chaos and glad to be so. The world beyond our front door is not *another* world but *our* world. This is a prayer and a call to worship written specifically for our community. There is nothing generic about it. Like many of the prayers we choose to use, it couldn't be prayed anywhere else but in our church. And therein lies its worth.

> We gather today in the presence of God;
> not a God far off and far away,
> distant and removed.
> No, this God, this Emmanuel,
> is the One who chooses to be near,
> right here,
> right now.

Come now, Emmanuel,
God of our neighborhood,
Lord of our lives.

This is the God of Collins Street,
the God of history, beauty, art and commerce;
the God whose love for those in suits
with black umbrellas knows no end;
the God whose grace is the same yesterday, today and tomorrow.

Come now, Emmanuel,
God of our neighborhood,
Lord of our lives.

This is the God of Swanston Street and of six-o'clock traffic,
the God who is as present in the rush hour as in the stillness;
the One who sits on the Flinders Street steps with the lonely,
offers love to the distracted,
peace to the confused
and grace to the lost and the angry.

Come now, Emmanuel,
God of our neighborhood,
Lord of our lives.

This is the God of Baptist Place,
the God of laneways and hidden corners—
the places where pain and struggle are hidden from view,
where graffiti and artwork hint at stories untold
and where the refuse gathers as routinely as our failure.

Come now, Emmanuel,
God of our neighborhood,
Lord of our lives.

This is the God of Russell Street,
the God of office towers and corner pubs,
the places where people work, create, scheme, and trade;

the sidewalk tables where they drink and eat and forget;
the places where weariness overwhelms
and simple pleasures restore.

Come now, Emmanuel,
God of our neighborhood,
Lord of our lives.

This is the God of Little Collins and little vistas,
of bookshops and trendy boutiques,
of coffee grinders and small distractions;
the God who is always "just there" and around every corner.

Come now, Emmanuel,
God of our neighborhood, Lord of our lives;
it is with you that we meet today,
the One who chooses to be near,
right here,
right now.
Amen.

3. Storytelling in Worship

Everyone loves a good testimony. In churches they are usually stories of conversion. I remember as a young boy receiving a little booklet to help me prepare my testimony. I was about to be baptized (in the Baptist way) and telling my story of conversion was essential to the ritual. The booklet suggested I prepare the story in three parts: (i) my life before I met Jesus; (ii) how I met Jesus; and (iii) my life since I met Jesus. To be honest, I had to be creative. Having been born into the church and raised in its shadow, I felt as though my meeting Jesus was more like having a church friend arrive for Sunday lunch than a life-altering encounter. For me, conversion has been more a process—a journey that's still going—than a moment to recall. Still, I did my best and found some pre-adolescent failings to confess on my way to redemption. Most importantly, that gracious community loved and welcomed me into faith regardless.

The limitation of testimonies is that the form can render our life in the world either a roadblock to faith or an aside to the real agenda of God's work. In my experience, the possibilities of storytelling in worship are so much more than this. The practices of storytelling allow us to bring into the gathering of God's people the encounters, discoveries, struggles, successes, failings, and questions of our lives, and to do so in the context of the faith that shapes us.

This past year, two gifted members of our church offered a series of workshops to the congregation called "the stories of our lives." These women are seasoned storytellers who blend together stories of mythology, stories real and fictional from across the world, and stories from their own experience into the most engaging presentations. What they offered participants was a forum in which they would work alongside each person to identify, nurture, and develop a story from their own lives for telling to others. If, once the process of development was complete, the participants were ready to share that story with the congregation, they could do so. What flowed from this was the most wonderful sequence of stories shared over a string of Sundays.

In the first week, I introduced this series to the congregation as "stories of faith," a phrase I used repeatedly. Several of the participants winced at this, feeling as though their stories had no clear connections to faith. "But I don't mention God in my story," one said in panic. "This story has nothing to do with my coming to faith," said another. In light of the extraordinary stories these people told, including themes of loss, forgiveness, failure, reconciliation, redemption, and vocation, and arising out of the contexts of work, school, home, and family struggle, I was reminded just how deeply we are enculturated by divisions between faith and life, between what constitutes a story of faith and what is just a story. True, there were no traditional tales of conversion in the mix, yet each one testified powerfully to the presence of God's Spirit and to the sacredness of life. Frankly, if our gathering for worship requires that we leave such stories at the door as unsuitable to our purpose, then we have seriously misjudged the purpose of worship itself.

4. Preaching in Worship

There is an occasional debate among pastors about what role preaching plays in worship. More significantly, the questions relate to what forms or styles of preaching are most important to the church's growth. Depending on who is asking, the questions are diverse: Are we preaching the Bible? Are we proclaiming the gospel? Are we speaking prophetically on issues of justice? Is our preaching relevant to the culture we are in? Are we speaking to the pastoral needs of our people? All of these are good and important questions. We like to imagine we can say yes to all of them. Of course, that's rarely true, but at least many of us are trying.

In the midst of all that, one of the tasks of preaching increasingly important to me is *demonstration*. While proclamation of truth, exegesis of the Scriptures, teaching of good theology, and addressing the challenges of life and culture are all important, what the people of God need from me in the pulpit is a demonstration of how we can think, reflect, and act in the world as people of faith. To put it crudely, it's not so much about telling the people what to think, as how to think. Part of my task as a preacher is to demonstrate how to discern our way through the complexities and issues of life, and how to set upon actions that embody our faith and make a difference in the world.

The fact is, the people who gather in churches on Sunday face situations and challenges unique to their lives, communities, professions, and circumstances. What's more, they likely know much more about these than their pastors ever will. No matter how fine our peaching, how biblically literate or culturally informed we are, there is so much of life that sits outside of our experience and expertise. What's more, there is a sea of wisdom and insight sitting before us each week. It seems to me that we need to find ways in our preaching to nurture that wisdom, allowing it the freedom and space to flourish before God. We may well be proclaimers of truth, but perhaps a role that is equally important is that we are facilitators for the discovery and living of truth. There are two practical things I have been involved in that illustrate this.

In a series of sermons titled *The Monday Connection* I gave as a visiting speaker for a congregation, I met a very articulate woman, a CFO for a large real estate company, who cornered me after the first service with insightful questions about her work. She faced numerous challenges as a Christian within a commercially competitive business. I suggested to her that we meet during the week, flesh out a particular case study together and, in place of my next sermon, have a conversation before the congregation. In it we would draw on her experience and the realities of the commercial landscape she was part of, and bring these into dialogue with biblical and theological insights. In a sense, it was a public wrestling match with the application of Christian ethics to a very particular work-place experience. What followed was one of the more engaging conversations I've been part of and, according to the congregation, one of the more intriguing and challenging sermons they had heard. Most important, perhaps, was that the woman involved was able to bring her professional life into the heart of the church's worship. Our task was to do theology together. My role was to ask the right questions and point the way to resources—biblical, theological, and pastoral—that were applicable.

Once a year, as a complement to the Melbourne International Film Festival, Collins Street hosts its own festival of films on a series of Sundays, complete with cinema screen and high-quality projection. In truth, we ask the congregation to watch a particular film in the week prior to the service and then in the gathering we provide a reflection on the story around a sequence of scenes selected from the film. Whatever the film and whatever the words we share from the front, our real purpose is to demonstrate a form of theological reflection. What we are saying is, here is how we can listen to a story of our culture, engage intelligently and critically with it, then address questions of faith and life it raises for us. Over the years we've ranged widely: from Roberto Benigni's Italian love story *Life is Beautiful*, to Paul Thomas Anderson's confronting American drama *Magnolia*; from the cinematic poetry of Terrence Malick's *The Tree of Life* to the delightful Disney Pixar animation *Up!* Every film we have watched has provided ample connections with the great themes of Christian theology and the depths of human experience. Our hope is that the instincts of our congregation for discernment and engagement are strengthened as a result.

5. Rituals of Sending in Worship

On a warm November evening in 2016, I joined a gathering of Baptist pastors in a small city restaurant. We met to celebrate twenty-five years since our ordination to the Baptist ministry. It had been a quarter of a century since the nine of us knelt before a state assembly of the denomination to be publically set apart for "the ministry of word and sacrament" in the churches of Victoria. Despite my ambivalence about this rite of ordination—an ambivalence that still nudges at me twenty-five years later—this was a significant experience for me. It was as though the people of God had gathered from far and wide and, in response to the question of my gifting and calling for ministry in God's church, said in unison a loud and resounding "Yes!" To a large degree, it is this "Yes!" from God's people that has held, prodded, and sustained me in all the years since.

My commitment to the priesthood of all God's people colors much of my work and teaching. So much so, I am occasionally questioned as to why I hold onto ordination. "Doesn't such a rite only add to the disempowerment of those who don't have it?" they ask. "Why not give it up?" "I can't do it!" I say. The truth is, surrendering my ordination would be like handing back God's call upon my life with a "thanks, but no thanks." I can't do that, and I won't. What I want, however, is that every person in the church would experience that affirmation; that every person of faith would hear that "Yes!" from God and God's people. That possibility remains a significant motivation in my work.

There are numerous ways I have sought to do this. Some have been a success while others, frankly, have fallen flat. Regardless, it is a story one of my students told me that reminds me just how valuable it is to keep at it. This student pastors a small rural church in the far northwest of our state. Around 50 percent of his congregation are farmers, many of them producing wine and olives, growing fruit, or harvesting vegetables. At the time of his story, it had been a difficult few years in the region and many of the farmers were doing it tough. In conversation with his leadership, he decided it was time to be more explicit in addressing the issues the community was facing. Part of this plan was to include a series of sermons in which he gathered all of the biblical references to God as farmer, gardener, orchardist, and vine grower, and all the imagery of produce—things like olives, fruit, oils, grain, leeks, and onions. He then drew on these references to paint pictures of God's interest and investment in their lives and livelihood. What's more, he asked the farmers to tell their stories of struggle and success and to recall past experiences of God on the land.

While many of the farmers were reluctant starters, week by week the process and the stories gathered steam. On the final Sunday of the series, he invited the farmers and their families to bring symbols of their work and produce to the church. What they showed up with was a colorful array of fruits and vegetables, farming implements, photographs, hats, working boots, and even a fencing post. At the beginning of the service he asked that these symbols be placed on the communion table, then, following some carefully worded prayers and affirmations, he invited the congregation to stand. With the farmers gathered in a circle around the table, the young pastor prayed for them, reminding them of their calling and gifts, and asking God's Spirit to fill them and empower them for the work ahead. He said that afterwards there were hugs all around the congregation, more than a few tears in tired eyes, and, most importantly, a new awareness of God for this small community.

The Church Scattered

No doubt, the Sunday gathering—or the routine gathering of a faith community whenever it happens—is important, most especially in the preparation we give to it. What's obvious, however, is that the time our community members spend *gathered* pales in volume compared to the time they spend *scattered* in all corners of our towns, neighborhoods, and cities. If Trueblood is right—that it's into these places of life the people of faith are called as ministers of liberation and redemption—the question of how we support and cheer them on is critical. There are some things about our practice that are worth considering.

1. Taking Pastoral Care on the Road

One of the most effective means of caring for the people of God and demonstrating the priority we give to their lives is to take our ministry of care to them: to the neighborhoods where they live, the communities in which they serve, and the places in which they work or study. Granted, it is a time-consuming business, but there is a case to be made for its priority.

There was a time—back when churches had "parishes" and pastors rode bicycles from vicarage to homes to local pub—when pastoral care "on the road" was standard. As time has passed the landscape has changed. The old idea of the parish has almost disappeared. Many of our people travel significant distances to gather on a Sunday. What's more, for good and ill, a pastor's work is now more office-centered: people with particular needs are more likely to come your way than you go theirs. While resurrecting the vicar's bicycle may be a step too far, there's certainly value in recapturing the best of past practice if it benefits the ministry of those we care for.

My experience of visiting people in their homes, neighborhoods, and workplaces is one of the most enriching of my ministry. First and foremost, it is enriching for me. I may look out on my congregation on a Sunday and value the diversity and stories of those who gather. I may hear snippets of news and catch a glimpse of the challenges they face as we talk in the church's portico, but really, my Sunday vision is narrow. It is when I go to these people, sit at their kitchen tables, walk their neighborhoods with them, or meet them at their workplaces, that my vision is extended and my awareness deepened immeasurably. The enrichment for them comes most often in the validation my presence brings to their world, and in the more focused listening I can do when the realities of their lives are tangible.

2. Taking the Rites and Rituals of the Church to the Marketplace

Some of the most memorable moments of affirmation for members of congregations I've led have come when it's not just me that enters their world, but a group of us. Some years back, in the context of a home church, we decided together to take our weekly mid-week gatherings to the neighborhoods and workplaces of those attending.

We sat after hours in the classroom of a first-grade teacher in the smallest of chairs, heard her tell us about each of the children in the class and the home and learning challenges they faced. We heard of the school politics and the disengaged leadership that she struggled with. Most significantly, we broke bread together on her desk and prayed God's blessing on her ministry and on those she ministered to.

We visited a scientist's laboratory, heard the most baffling explanations of his research and of the bureaucratic processes to secure funding for his work. We looked through his microscopes and peered into refrigerator units at odd-looking specimens and samples. We then wandered over the road to a fast-food outlet, opened the Bible together and read passages about our vocation as people of faith.

We met together on the front porch of an elderly woman's house, her home for more than thirty years. From there we walked her neighborhood together as she told us stories about her suburb, her neighbors, and of the recent influx of migrants from places like Vietnam and China. Back in her living room, and over glasses of wine and a plate of scones with jam and cream, we devised a psalm together in which we captured some of the thoughts, feelings, and questions we had heard our host name in her walk.

There are things we commonly do in the gathering—rituals and sacraments that have a very 'church' feel to them—that, when transplanted into the neighborhoods and workplaces of our people, can become the most empowering symbols of God's interest and presence in our lives.

3. Resourcing the People for Ministry

For all our talk of the priesthood of believers, our sermons on the ministry of daily life, our pep talks about living the way of Jesus, and our promotion of spiritual practices in ordinary places, people can leave our services really none the wiser about how it all works. They may be inspired but they are not resourced. If the focus of the church's priestly ministry is on the front lines of daily life, we need to think carefully and creatively about how we resource and equip people for the task.

The first and continuing step in this is to ensure that our church programs are not so consuming that they leave our people with no discretionary time for anything else. The second step is to provide resources and opportunities that help people embrace their everyday lives as spiritually significant.

In my experience, this resourcing is not so much about handing them six steps to neighborhood evangelism, a set of Bible studies to do with work colleagues, or a ten-point plan for ethical shopping. It's more to do with providing forums and conversations for people to tell their everyday stories, name their challenges, and, in conversation together, open new windows on their situations or determine pathways forward that are constructive and within reach.

When we bring a group of people together who inhabit a particular locale, their reflection on where they live and how they think about God's presence there is no longer thinking in isolation. They may be able to determine small steps they can take together to support each other, initiate neighborhood events together, or pray more specifically for each other in their neighborhood relationships.

When we have someone in our community who is passionate about ethical consumption and finding ways to live more simply and more locally, there is opportunity for their story to be told and the invitation for others to a more serious study of the issues at stake and the biblical resources that relate.

When members of our community are struggling to understand what it means to live their faith in their work, or when they are facing particular challenges in and through their work, these are ideal times for "the body of Christ" to do its thing. While not every person struggling with workplace issues wants more than the reassurance of our prayers, there are others who value the interest and companionship of those who can come alongside. I have seen senior educators in a congregation make time to meet with first-year teachers to listen to their stories and to pray for them. I have witnessed the impact of a small-group Bible study putting aside its prepared plan for the evening in favor of helping a group member think through their decision to remain in or leave a workplace. This is "the body" at work.

When the pace of life is wearing and we see evidence of life's pressures bearing down upon members of our congregations, there is opportunity for our communities to intervene. It is not so much about telling individuals what they should and shouldn't do. It has more to do with developing community practices and forging covenants of sabbath and renewal together that provide a level of support one person or household cannot lay hold of alone.

In all of these ways, we are resourcing the people of God and treating their everyday lives as the priority they are.

What I have offered in these last few pages is, I hope, not a new list of pastoral obligations; rather, a sharing of experience, perspective, and conviction from one pastor to others. You will have more wisdom to bring to the table, stories of success and struggle that only you can tell, and correctives to my thinking where it's needed. Regardless, I urge you to look again at the lives of those you minister to and with—to see each one as an embodiment of God's presence in the world, a conduit of the love of Jesus, and a vessel of God's Spirit called to fill and renew the world in every place, every task, and every encounter of every day.

Bibliography

Adam, Barbara. "Time." *Theory, Culture and Society* 23, no. 2–3 (2006) 119–26.

Aelred of Rievaulx. *Spiritual Friendship*. Translated by Mary Eugenia Laker. Edited by Douglas Roby, Cistercian Fathers series. Kalamazoo, MI: Cistercian, 1977.

Allison, Dale C., Jr. *The Silence of Angels*. Valley Forge, PA: Trinity, 1995.

Allon, Fiona. *Renovation Nation: Our Obsession with Home*. Sydney: University of New South Wales Press, 2008.

Alomes, Stephen. "Australian Football as Secular Religion." In *Australian Popular Culture*, edited by Ian Craven, Martin Gray, and Geraldine Stoneham, 46–65. Cambridge: Cambridge University Press, 1994.

Augustine, Saint. *Confessions*. Translated by R. S. Pine Coffin. London: Penguin, 1961.

Austin, Michael W. "Sports as Exercises in Spiritual Formation." *Journal of Spiritual Formation and Soul Care* 3, no. 1 (Spring 2010) 66–78.

Bainton, Roland H. *Here I Stand: A Life of Martin Luther*. New York: New American Library, 1953.

Banks, Robert J. *God the Worker: Journeys into the Mind, Heart and Imagination of God*. Sutherland: Albatross, 1992.

———. *The Tyranny of Time*. Homebush: Lancer, 1983.

Barrowclough, Nikki. "Out of the Frying Pan and into the Wok." *Good Weekend: The Age Magazine*, June 22, 2002, 16–21.

Baum, L. Frank. *The Wizard of Oz*. Reissued ed. London: Puffin, 2012.

Bauman, Zygmunt. *Consuming Life*. Cambridge: Polity, 2007.

Benjamin, Walter. *Charles Baudelaire: A Lyric Poet in the Era of High Capitalism*. Translated by Harry Zohn. London: Verso, 1973.

Bevan, Judi. *Trolley Wars: The Battle of the Supermarkets*. London: Profile, 2005.

Bilotta, Vincent M., III. "Originality, Ordinary Intimacy, and the Spiritual Life: Welcome! Make Yourself at Home." *Studies in Formative Spirituality* 1, no. 1 (1980) 83–91.

Blythman, Joanna. *Shopped: The Shocking Power of British Supermarkets*. London: Fourth Estate, 2004.

Boff, Leonardo. *Sacraments of Life, Life of the Sacraments: Story of Theology*. Translated by John Drury. Washington, DC: Pastoral, 1987.

Bonhoeffer, Dietrich. *Letters and Papers from Prison*. London: SCM, 1953.

———. *Life Together*. Translated by J. W. Doberstein. 1st British ed. London: SCM, 1954.

———. *Sanctorum Communio: A Dogmatic Inquiry into the Sociology of the Church*. Translated by Ronald Gregor Smith. London: Collins, 1963.

Boyer, Ernest, Jr. *Finding God at Home: Family Life as a Spiritual Discipline.* San Francisco: HarperSanFrancisco, 1991.

Brasher-Cunningham, Milton. *Keeping the Feast: Metaphors for the Meal.* Harrisburg, PA: Morehouse, 2012.

Brown, Peter. "The Rise and Function of the Holy Man in Late Antiquity." In *Society and the Holy in Late Antiquity*, edited by Peter Brown, 103–52. New York: Faber & Faber, 1982.

Buber, Martin. *Between Man and Man.* Translated by Ronald Gregor-Smith. Rev. ed. New York: Routledge, 2002.

Buford, Bill. *Heat: An Amateur's Adventures as Kitchen Slave, Line Cook, Pasta-Maker, and Apprentice to a Butcher in Tuscany.* London: Jonathan Cape, 2006.

Busch, Akiko. *Geography of Home: Writings on Where We Live.* New York: Princeton Architectural Press, 1999.

Caillois, Roger. *Man, Play, and Games.* Translated by Meyer Barash. Urbana, IL: University of Illinois Press, 1961.

Cavanaugh, William T. "When Enough Is Enough: Why God's Abundant Life Won't Fit in a Shopping Cart, and Other Mysteries of Consumerism." *Sojourners* 34, no. 5 (May 2005) 8–14.

Centers for Disease Control and Prevention. "Perceived Insufficient Rest or Sleep among Adults—United States, 2005–2008." *Morbidity and Mortality Weekly Report* 60 (2011) 239–42.

Channon, Jim. "Creating Esprit de Corps." In *New Traditions in Business: Spirit and Leadership in the 21st Century*, edited by J. Renesch, 53–66. Oakland, CA: Berrett-Koehler, 1992.

Chittister, J. D. *Wisdom Distilled from the Daily: Living the Rule of Saint Benedict Today.* New York: HarperCollins, 1991.

Cody, Gemima. "Two Square Metres of Civilisation." In *Kitchen Table Memoirs: Shared Stories from Australian Writers*, edited by Nick Richardson, 180–90. Sydney: HarperCollins, 2013.

Coe, John. "Resisting the Temptation of Moral Formation: Opening to Spiritual Formation in the Cross and the Spirit." *Journal of Spiritual Formation and Soul Care* 1, no. 1 (2008) 54–78.

Cornford, Jonathan. *Coming Back to Earth: Essays on Church, Climate Change, Cities, Agriculture and Eating.* Northcote: Morning Star, 2016.

Cossell, Howard, and Peter Bonventre. *I Never Played the Game.* New York: Morrow, 1985.

Cowan, James. *Journey to the Inner Mountain: In the Desert with St Antony.* London: Hodder & Stoughton, 2002.

Curry, Rick. *The Secrets of Jesuit Breadmaking: Recipes and Traditions from Jesuit Bakers Around the World.* New York: HarperCollins, 1995.

Davies, J. G. *The Everyday God: Encountering the Holy in World and Worship.* London: SCM, 1973.

de Botton, Alain. *The Pleasures and Sorrows of Work.* Hamish Hamilton: Camberwell, 2009.

Dement, William C. *Some Must Watch While Some Must Sleep.* San Francisco: W. H. Freeman, 1972.

Dewey, John. *Art as Experience.* Reprint ed. New York: Perigee, 2005.

Diehl, William E. *The Monday Connection: On Being an Authentic Christian in the Weekday World*. San Francisco: HarperSanFrancisco, 1991.

Dillard, Annie. *Pilgrim at Tinker Creek*. London: Jonathan Cape, 1974.

Dreyer, Elizabeth. "Traditions of Lay Spirituality: Problems and Possibilities." *Spirituality Today* 39, no. 3 (1987) 196–210.

Droel, William L., and Gregory F. Augustine Pierce. *Confident and Competent: A Challenge for the Lay Church*. Notre Dame, IN: Ave Maria, 1987.

Dunn, James D. G. *Word Biblical Commentary: Romans 9–16*. Word Biblical Commentary, vol. 38B. Edited by David A. Hubbard and Glenn W. Barker. Dallas: Word, 1988.

Dupleix, Jill. "Ghosts of Kitchens Past." *The Age*, March 17, 1998, Epicure 3.

Enticott, David. "God and Football: A Personal Reflection." An unpublished lecture for *Spirituality of Everyday Life*, Whitley College, University of Divinity, 2009.

Erdozain, Dominic. "In Praise of Folly: Sport as Play." *Anvil* 28, no. 1 (2012) 20–34.

Erikson, Thomas Hylland. *Tyranny of the Moment: Fast and Slow Time in the Information Age*. London: Pluto, 2001.

Evans, Kathy. "The Buddy System." *Sunday Life,* April 28, 2002, 16–20.

Feucht, Oscar E. *Everyone a Minister: A Guide to Churchmanship for Laity and Clergy*. St Louis: Concordia, 1974.

Food Marketing Institute. "Supermarket Facts 2015." https://www.fmi.org/our-research/supermarket-facts.

Foster, Richard J. *Celebration of Discipline: The Path to Spiritual Growth*. London: Hodder and Stoughton, 1978.

Frost, Michael. *Eyes Wide Open: Seeing God in the Ordinary*. Sutherland: Albatross, 1998.

Galli, Mark. "The Prodigal Sports Fan." *Christianity Today* 49 (April 8 2005). Online only: http://www.christianitytoday.com/ct/2005/114/53.0.html.

Gannon, Thomas M., and George W. Traub. *The Desert and the City: An Interpretation of the History of Christian Spirituality*. New York: Macmillan, 1969.

Goodman, David. "Comparative Urban and Suburban History: An Interview with Kenneth Jackson." *Australasian Journal of American Studies* 12, no. 1 (1993) 65–72.

Gopnik, Adam. *The Table Comes First: Family, France, and the Meaning of Food*. London: Quercus, 2001.

Grayling, A. C. *Friendship*. Vices and Virtues. Edited by Richard G. Newhauser and John Jeffries Martin. New Haven, CT: Yale University Press, 2013.

Gros, Frédéric. *A Philosophy of Walking*. Translated by John Howe. London: Verso, 2014.

Guttmann, Allen. *From Ritual to Record: The Nature of Modern Sports*. Updated ed. New York: Columbia University Press, 2004.

———. *Sports: The First Five Millennia*. Boston: University of Massachusetts Press, 2004.

Harvey, Lincoln. *A Brief Theology of Sport*. London: SCM, 2014.

Heschel, Abraham Joshua. *The Sabbath: Its Meaning for Modern Man*. New York: Farrar, Straus & Giroux, 1975.

Hillman, David R., and Leon C. Lack. "Public Health Implications of Sleep Loss: The Community Burden." *Medical Journal of Australia* 199, no. 8 (October 21, 2013) S7–S10.

Hoffman, Shirl James. *Good Game: Christianity and the Culture of Sports.* Waco, TX: Baylor University Press, 2010.

———. "Whatever Happened to Play?" *Christianity Today*, February 2010, 21–25.

Holt, Simon Carey. *God Next Door: Spirituality and Mission in the Neighbourhood.* Brunswick East: Acorn, 2007.

———. "A Mortgage, a Motor-Mower and a Mission: Following Jesus into Suburbia." In *Speaking of Mission: Volume 2*, edited by Michael Frost, 49–64. Macquarie Park: Morling, 2013.

Howard, Thomas. *Hallowed Be This House.* San Francisco: Ignatius, 1979.

Huizinga, Johan. *Homo Ludens: A Study of the Play Element in Culture.* London: Paladin, 1970.

Humphrey, Kim. *Shelf Life: Supermarkets and the Changing Cultures of Consumption.* Oakleigh: Cambridge University Press, 1998.

Jensen, David H. *Responsive Labor: A Theology of Work.* Louisville: Westminster John Knox, 2006.

Jones, W. Paul. *Trumpet at Full Moon: An Introduction to Christian Spirituality as Diverse Practice.* Louisville: Westminster John Knox, 1992.

Jurgensen, Manfred. "Highpoint Carlton." In *The Greatest Game*, edited by Ross Fitzgerald and Ken Spillman, 128–33. Richmond: William Heinemann Australia, 1988.

Keen, Sam. *Apology for Wonder.* New York: Harper & Row, 1969.

———. *To a Dancing God.* New York: Fontana, 1971.

Kingston, Beverley. *Basket, Bag and Trolley: A History of Shopping in Australia.* Australian Retrospectives. Melbourne: Oxford University Press, 1994.

Kitson, Jean. "The Table." In *Kitchen Table Memoirs: Shared Stories from Australian Writers*, edited by Nick Richardson, 118–34. Sydney: HarperCollins, 2013.

Klein, Naomi. *No Logo.* London: Flamingo, 2000.

Klugman, Matthew. "Emotional Devotees: Approaching the Inner World of Australian Rules Football Fans." In *Football Fever: Moving the Goalposts*, edited by Matthew Nicholson, Bob Stewart, and Rob Hess, 207–21. Hawthorn: Maribynong, 2006.

Knight, David M. "A Practical Plan for Lay Spiritual Formation." *Studies in Formative Spirituality* 9, no. 1 (1988) 7–16.

Knox, Malcolm. *Supermarket Monsters: The Price of Coles and Woolworths' Dominance.* Carlton: Black Inc., 2015.

Langley, Sophie, and Andrea Hogan. "Research Survey Reveals More Australian Grocery Shopping Habits." *Australian Food News*, May 18 2015.

Leunig, Michael. *A Common Prayer.* Burwood: Collins Dove, 1990.

———. *The Curly Pyjama Letters.* Ringwood: Viking, 2001.

Levine, Judith. *Not Buying It: My Year without Shopping.* London: Simon & Schuster, 2006.

Lewis, C. S. *The Four Loves.* London: Collins, 1960.

Lichtenstein, Nelson. "Wal-Mart: A Template for Twenty-First Century Capitalism." In *Wal-Mart: The Face of Twenty-First Century Capitalism*, edited by Nelson Lichtenstein, 3–30. New York: The New Press, 2006.

Little, Graham. *Friendship: Being Ourselves with Others.* East Melbourne: Text, 1993.

Mackay, Hugh. *The Art of Belonging.* Sydney: Pan Macmillan, 2014.

———. *Turning Points: Australians Choosing Their Future.* Sydney: Pan Macmillan, 1999.

Martin, Paul. *Counting Sheep: The Science and Pleasures of Sleep and Dreams*. London: Flamingo, 2003.

Maunder, Patricia. "Worth the Walk." *The Age*, June 7, 2007, 15.

McCulloch, Janelle. "Death of the Weekend." *Sunday Life: The Sunday Age Magazine*, March 19, 2006, 18–22.

McFague, Sallie. *Blessed Are the Consumers: Climate Change and the Practice of Restraint*. Minneapolis: Fortress, 2013.

McGinn, Bernard. "Withdrawal and Return: Reflections on Monastic Retreat from the World." *Spiritus* 6 (2006) 149–72.

McGovern, Charles. *Sold American: Consumption and Citizenship, 1890–1945*. Chapel Hill, NC: University of North Carolina Press, 2006.

Miller, Daniel. *The Theory of Shopping*. Ithaca, NY: Cornell University Press, 1998.

Moltmann, Jürgen, Nicholas Wolterstorff, and Ellen T. Charry. *A Passion for God's Reign: Theology, Christian Learning and the Christian Self*. Edited by Miroslav Volf. Grand Rapids: Eerdmans, 1998.

Moltmann, Jürgen. *God in Creation: An Ecological Doctrine of Creation: The Gifford Lectures 1984–1985*. London: SCM, 1985.

———. *The Source of Life: The Holy Spirit and the Theology of Life*. London: SCM, 1997.

Moriarty, Micheline Wyn. "Sport and Children's Spirituality: An Australian Perspective." *International Journal of Children's Spirituality* 18, no. 1 (2013) 103–17.

Murphy, Michael, and Rhea A. White. *In the Zone: Transcendent Experiences in Sports*. Rev. ed. New York: Penguin, 1995.

Murphy, Wendy Wiedenhoft. *Consumer Culture and Society*. Thousand Oaks, CA: Sage, 2017.

Nagaratman, Vaishali. "Supermarkets Sweep: Aldi's Share of the Aussie Market Still Rising." Roy Morgan Report. Melbourne: Roy Morgan Research, 2016.

Norris, Gunilla. *Being Home: A Book of Meditations*. New York: Bell Tower, 1991.

Norris, Kathleen. *Dakota: A Spiritual Geography*. New York: Houghton Mifflin, 1993.

———. *The Quotidian Mysteries: Laundry, Liturgy and "Women's Work."* New York: Paulist, 1998.

O'Donovan, Oliver. "The Loss of a Sense of Place." *Irish Theological Quarterly* 55, no. 1 (1989) 39–58.

Ohler, Frank. *Better than Nice and Other Unconventional Prayers*. Louisville: Westminster John Knox, 1989.

Oliver, Mary. *New and Selected Poems, Volume 1*. Boston: Beacon, 2004.

Pahl, Ray. *On Friendship*. Themes for the 21st Century. Cambridge: Polity, 2000.

Palmer, Parker J. *The Active Life: Wisdom for Work, Creativity, and Caring*. San Francisco: HarperSanFrancisco, 1990.

Pannenberg, Wolfhart. *Christian Spirituality*. Philadelphia: Westminster, 1983.

Paulsell, Stephanie. *Honoring the Body: Meditations on a Christian Practice*. The Practices of Faith Series. Edited by Dorothy C. Bass. San Francisco: Jossey-Bass, 2002.

Peterson, Eugene H. *Leap over a Wall: Earthly Spirituality for Everyday Christians*. New York: HarperSanFrancisco, 1997.

———. *The Contemplative Pastor: Returning to the Art of Spiritual Direction*. Grand Rapids: Eerdmans, 1993.

———. *The Message: Psalms*. Colorado Springs: NavPress, 1994.

Plunkett Analytics. *Supermarkets, Grocery Stores, Food Stores and Convenience Stores Industry (U.S.)*. Houston: Plunkett Research Ltd, 2016.

Pocock, Barbara, Natalie Skinner, and Philippa Williams. *Time Bomb: Work, Rest and Play in Australia Today*. Sydney: NewSouth, 2012.

Pollan, Michael. *The Omnivore's Dilemma: A Natural History of Four Meals*. New York: Penguin, 2006.

Preece, Gordon. "'When I Run I Feel God's Pleasure': Towards a Protestant Play Ethic." In *Sport and Spirituality: An Exercise in Everyday Theology*, edited by Gordon Preece and Rob Hess, 25–48. Hindmarsh: ATF, 2009.

Rahner, Hugo. *Man at Play or Did You Ever Practice Eutrapelia?* Translated by Brian Battershaw and Edward Quinn. London: Burns & Oates, 1963.

Rees, Frank. "New Directions in Australian Spirituality: Sabbath Beyond the Church." *Colloquium: The Australian and New Zealand Theological Review* 47, no. 1 (May 2015) 75–88.

Richardson, Alan. *The Biblical Doctrine of Work*. Ecumenical Biblical Studies. London: SCM, 1952.

Rittenhouse, Bruce P. *Shopping for Meaningful Lives: The Religious Motive of Consumerism*. Eugene, OR: Cascade, 2013.

Roxburgh, Alan J. *Missional: Joining God in the Neighborhood*. Grand Rapids: Baker, 2011.

Ryan, Thomas. "Discipline and the Spiritual Life." *Spiritual Life* 40, no. 3 (1994) 162–68.

Sayers, Dorothy L. "Why Work?" In *Creed or Chaos*, edited by Dorothy L. Sayers, 47–64. London: Methven, 1947.

Schmemann, Alexander. *For the Life of the World: Sacraments and Orthodoxy*. Crestwood, NY: St. Vladimir's Seminary Press, 1973.

Schneiders, Sandra M. "Spirituality in the Academy." In *Modern Christian Spirituality: Methodological and Historical Essays*, edited by Bradley C Hanson, and *American Academy of Religion Studies in Religion* no. 62, 15–37. Atlanta: Scholars, 1990.

Seth, Andrew, and Geoffrey Randall. *The Grocers: The Rise and Rise of the Supermarket Chains*. 3rd ed. London: Kogan Page, 2011.

Sexton, Reid. "Are You Being Served? Not How You Used to Be." *The Sunday Age*, October 7, 2007, 8.

Sheldrake, Philip. *Spirituality: A Brief History*. 2nd ed. Chichester: Wiley-Blackwell, 2013.

Simpson, Ray, ed. *Celtic Blessings: Prayers for Everyday Life*. Chicago: Loyola, 1999.

Smith, Amanda, and Tim Stoney. "The Name of the Game." *Eureka Street* 11, no. 6 (2001) 26–29.

Solnit, Rebecca. *Wanderlust: A History of Walking*. New York: Penguin, 2000.

Solomon, Jack. *Signs of Our Time: Semiotics, the Hidden Messages of Environments, Objects, and Cultural Images*. Los Angeles: Jeremy P. Tarcher, 1988.

Stark, Jill. "Australians Need Quality Shut-Eye: $10bn Wake-up Call on Health Policy." *The Age*, March 1, 2008, 6.

Stevens, R. Paul. "Friendship." In *The Complete Book of Everyday Christianity: An A-to-Z Guide to Following Christ in Every Aspect of Life*, edited by Robert J. Banks and R. Paul Stevens, 435–42. Downers Grove, IL: InterVarsity, 1997.

Stretton, Hugh. *Capitalism, Socialism and the Environment*. Cambridge: Cambridge University Press, 1976.

Symons, Michael. *The Pudding That Took a Thousand Cooks: The Story of Cooking in Civilization and Daily Life*. Ringwood: Viking, 1998.

Taylor, Barbara Brown. *An Altar in the World: Finding the Sacred Beneath Our Feet.* Norwich: Canterbury, 2009.

Taylor, John V. *The Go-between God: The Holy Spirit and the Christian Mission.* London: SCM, 1972.

Teilhard de Chardin, Pierre. *Le Milieu Divin: An Essay on the Interior Life.* Translated by Bernard Wall. London: Collins, 1957.

Torre, Stephen, and Peter Kirkpatrick, eds. *The Macquarie Dictionary of Australian Quotations.* Sydney: Macquarie Library, 1990.

Trueblood, D. Elton. *The Company of the Committed.* New York: Harper and Row, 1961.

Vander Hart, Mark D. "Resurrecting the House." *Mid-America Journal of Theology,* no. 25 (January 2014) 83–100.

Vasicek, Edward. "The Workaholic's 23rd Psalm." Printed in the *Christian Counselors Newsletter,* Melbourne, October 1992.

Veblen, Thorstein. *The Theory of the Leisure Class.* New York: Penguin, 1994.

Wadell, Paul J. "Shared Lives." *Christian Century,* September 20, 2011, 11–13.

Weber, Max. *The Protestant Ethic and the Spirit of Capitalism.* London: Routledge, 1992.

Wendt, Jana. *Nice Work.* Carlton: Melbourne University Press, 2010.

Willard, Dallas. *The Spirit of the Disciplines: Understanding How God Changes Lives.* New York: HarperCollins, 1988.

Williams, Rowan. *The Wound of Knowledge: Christian Spirituality from the New Testament to St. John of the Cross.* London: Darton, Longman and Todd, 1979.

Winton, Tim. *Island Home: A Landscape Memoir.* Melbourne: Penguin, 2015.

Wirzba, Norman. *Food and Faith: A Theology of Eating.* New York: Cambridge University Press, 2011.

Witherington III, Ben. *Work: A Kingdom Perspective on Labor.* Grand Rapids: Eerdmans, 2011.

Workman, Herbert Brook. *The Evolution of the Monastic Ideal: From the Earliest Times Down to the Coming of the Friars.* London: Charles H. Kelly, 1913.

Wright, Judith. *Collected Poems 1942–1970.* Sydney: Angus and Robertson, 1975.

Wright, Wendy M. *Sacred Dwelling: A Spirituality of Family Life.* New York: Crossroad, 1989.

Zeldin, Theodore. *Conversation: Talk Can Change Our Lives.* Mahwah: Hidden Spring, 1998.

Printed in Australia
AUOW01n1813220318
295971AU00002B/3

9 781498 278850